T0301993

Critical Event Studies

Within events management, events are commonly categorized within two axes – size and content. Along the size axis events range from the small scale and local, through major events, which garner greater media interest, to internationally significant hallmark and mega events such as the Edinburgh Festival and the Tour de France. Content is frequently divided into three forms – culture, sport and business. However, such frameworks overlook and depoliticize a significant variety of events – those more accurately construed as protest.

This book brings together new research and theories from around the world and across sociology, leisure studies, politics and cultural studies to develop a new critical pedagogy and critical theory of events. It is the first research monograph that deals explicitly with the concept of critical event studies (CES) – the idea that it is impossible to explore and understand events without understanding the wider social, cultural and political contexts. It addresses questions such as: can the occupation and reclamation of specific spaces by activists be understood as events within its framework? And does the activity of such activists in these spaces constitute a *leisure* activity? If those and similar activities can be read as events and leisure, what does admitting them into the scope of events management and leisure studies mean for our understanding of them and how the study of events management is to be conceptualized?

This book will be of interest to undergraduate and postgraduate students on events management and related courses, and scholars interested in understanding the ways in which events are constructed by the social, the cultural and the political.

Karl Spracklen is Professor of Leisure Studies at Leeds Beckett University. He has been Chair of the Leisure Studies Association and is currently Vice-President of Research Committee 13 (Sociology of Leisure) of the International Sociological Association. He has researched and published widely on leisure theory and leisure studies, with particular interests in music, tourism, sport, sub-cultures and the idea of communicative and instrumental leisure.

Ian R. Lamond is Senior Lecturer in Events at Leeds Beckett University. He is a member of the Political Studies Association, Media Communications and Cultural Studies Association and Leisure Studies Association. His research interests are wide ranging and include: critical event studies; protest as event; events in contested spaces; event theory; and the sociology of political institutions.

Routledge Advances in Event Research Series

Edited by Warwick Frost and Jennifer Laing
Department of Marketing, Tourism and Hospitality, La Trobe University, Australia

Critical Event Studies

Karl Spracklen and Ian R. Lamond

Routledge
Taylor & Francis Group

LONDON AND NEW YORK

First published 2016
by Routledge
2 Park Square, Milton Park, Abingdon, Oxon, OX14 4RN

and by Routledge
605 Third Avenue, New York, NY 10017

First issued in paperback 2021

Routledge is an imprint of the Taylor & Francis Group, an informa business

© 2016 Karl Spracklen and Ian R. Lamond

Publisher's Note
The publisher has gone to great lengths to ensure the quality of this reprint but points out that some imperfections in the original copies may be apparent.

British Library Cataloguing in Publication Data
A catalogue record for this book is available from the British Library

Library of Congress Cataloging in Publication Data
Names: Spracklen, Karl, author. | Lamond, Ian R., author.
Title: Critical event studies: a guide for critical thinkers/Karl Spracklen and Ian R. Lamond.
Description: New York, NY: Routledge, 2016. |
Series: Routledge advances in event research series | Includes bibliographical references and index.
Identifiers: LCCN 2015050893 | ISBN 9781138915145 (hardback) | ISBN 9781315690414 (ebook)
Subjects: LCSH: Special events—Management. | Special events—Social aspects. | Protest movements. | Leisure—Political aspects.
Classification: LCC GT3405 .S69 2016 | DDC 394.2—dc23
LC record available at http://lccn.loc.gov/2015050893

ISBN 13: 978-1-03-224247-7 (pbk)
ISBN 13: 978-1-138-91514-5 (hbk)

DOI: 10.4324/9781315690414

Typeset in Times New Roman
by Keystroke, Station Road, Codsall, Wolverhampton

Contents

Introduction

Rationale, definitions and aims

This book is the result of the happy coincidences that bring frustrated academics together. We both teach at the same university, but in different schools within the same faculty. Karl is in the School of Sport, but in the social sciences of sport and leisure, and a strong defender of critical thinking and the interdisciplinary traditions of leisure studies at a time when leisure courses and modules are being replaced by such subjects as sports management and sports marketing. He does not wear a tracksuit, but is surrounded by colleagues who do. Ian is in the School of Events, Tourism and Hospitality, teaching events management and despairing of the lack of criticality anywhere in the subject field. Both of us consider ourselves to be active researchers, critical social scientists and politically radical. This book is our attempt to introduce to events management the same kind of interdisciplinary, socio-cultural critical thinking that has transformed leisure studies.

This is a polemical research monograph for critical thinkers, whether they are undergraduate and postgraduate students on events management and related courses, or scholars interested in understanding the ways in which events are constructed by the social, the cultural and the political. It is the first research monograph that deals explicitly with the concept of what we call critical event studies (CES) – the idea that it is impossible to explore and understand events without understanding the wider social, cultural and political contexts of those events. *Critical Event Studies* is the title of this book, but it also refers to our ultimate goal of radically reshaping both the teaching and the academic study of events. We know there are critical researchers in leisure studies and events management who will welcome this book, and this turn.

There is a need for this book and this call for action because events management is still stuck in its operational management paradigm. The textbooks that currently dominate events management teaching focus on operational and logistical aspects of how events are delivered, managed and evaluated. The main text for most courses is Bowdin *et al.*'s *Events Management* (2012). Now in its third edition, this text focuses on the EMBOK (Events Management Body Of Knowledge) model that was pioneered by the authors nearly ten years ago. As a toolkit approach for training people in the core skills required for delivering events in an events industry, it is an excellent volume. The framework at the book's core, however, has developed little since its first articulation. Its approach is one that focuses on events as a neo-liberal economic driver and construes events as depoliticized. Therefore, it does not address any of the issues at the heart of this book.

The framework of an operational handbook for the delivery of events is central to most books that are currently used in the teaching of the field and – though completely unlike our monograph – represent the principal competition for our book. This is particularly true of Conway (2009), Raj *et al.* (both 2009 and 2013), Bladen and Kennell (2012), and Shone and Parry (2010), as well as one that is currently being written by two colleagues at Leeds Beckett. All those texts focus on operational considerations, the nuts and bolts of piecing an event together. Consequently, they focus on a similar set of concerns – event concept development; event planning; event law (including human resources management); risk management; finance and budgetary control; crowd and traffic management; marketing and promotion; environmental sustainability and organizer social responsibility; managing media coverage; evaluation; impact; and legacy. All those elements either explicitly or implicitly derive from Bowdin *et al.*'s EMBOK model, as set out in their events management training framework. There is limited space for a critique of events within those works; if such were admitted, it would undermine the apolitical construal of events that is at the heart of their work. Our book inverts the presuppositions of those texts.

Two works that do at least nod towards the importance of considering the political context in which events take place are Ferdinand and Kitchin (2012) and Getz (2012). However, both of those books still firmly adopt a politically neutral perspective on events, with the dominant frame being that of neo-liberal economic frames of reference. Over half of Getz's book – part three of his text – is devoted to the operational aspects of event delivery. The second part substantively suggests a widening of the areas on which the study of events rests, though these are treated in quick succession: over the 114 pages of that part he covers 29 areas. An average of fewer than four pages per field is hardly an in-depth study of the connections between event studies and those wider disciplinary areas. Getz's opening and closing chapters offer developments of the typologies common to the competitors already considered, but they do not mark too radical a break from them.

Ferdinand and Kitchin's book is slightly different, in that it is more of an edited collection, yet here again the dominant frame of reference is one that harks back to the EMBOK model, with its focus on operational considerations. Part three of their volume does diverge from this – a little – by considering contemporary issues. However, given the edited-collection nature of the work, this is not continued in the other parts of the text, leaving the reader wondering how the parts are meant to fit together. It does not, therefore, hold together particularly well as a textbook.

The closest companion to the book you are reading is Andrews and Leopold (2013). This text is a cursory introduction to socio-cultural explorations of events, and while obviously close in many ways to our monograph, it is only a first step towards what we call CES. Our monograph, with our critical lens, extends, deepens and complements their textbook. While this volume is not a textbook, we hope it will be used and read by those who want to bring criticality and theory to teaching and learning.

This book is the second step in our attempt to overhaul events management. The first was the convening of a symposium on 'Protests as Events, and Events as Protests', in June 2013. We were curious to see who was doing research in this interdisciplinary political space. We were excited by the radical possibilities of redefining events as inherently political. We wanted to explore the possibility of seeing activism also as leisure. We were pleasantly surprised to attract approximately seventy people – artists and activists as well as academics. A virtual network and an edited collection (Lamond and Spracklen, 2015) have emerged from that symposium. The response to the latter indicates that there is a groundswell of interest in destabilizing the old events management.

We trust that this volume will satisfy the growing interest in CES, and hope that it will lead the subject field. It does not tell you how to make money or run an event. It does not tell you how to use a fire extinguisher. Events management is already transforming to become more critical, so this textbook is of the *zeitgeist*, while also influencing and shaping that *zeitgeist*. It brings together new research from ourselves and others, and theories from around the world and across sociology, leisure studies, politics and cultural studies to develop a new critical pedagogy and critical theory of events. It is this theoretical synthesis that constitutes the global significance of our work. This is why we wish to develop a subject field related to events management called critical event studies. This book is the latest step, but not the final step, in that journey.

Detailed synopsis and chapter headings

There are twelve main chapters and a short conclusion. Each chapter will introduce a theme, develop a critical discussion by looking at actual events or other spaces, and use case studies from the academic literature. As this is a polemical research monograph that we hope will shape the field, the conclusion will rehearse the key critical themes that have emerged from the previous chapters and sketch out a way forward for radical reform in the teaching of events, and research about events.

Chapter 1: Critical event studies: theories and practices

In this chapter we introduce the key theories and practices that need to be understood by students who engage in studying events critically. We assume that students are unfamiliar with any social or cultural theory, so the chapter is written in a way that makes the ideas clear and accessible. As well as exploring theories, each section sketches out the kinds of practices that are implied in the theoretical frameworks that are developed. The first section focuses on Jürgen Habermas's work on communicative rationality and instrumentality, as adapted by Spracklen to understand leisure. The second section discusses Pierre Bourdieu's ideas of social and cultural capital alongside Antonio Gramsci's notion of hegemony. The third section discusses the ideas of Michel Foucault on governmentality and Guy Debord on spectacle. The final section introduces the work of Zygmunt Bauman and Slavoj Žižek and explains how they point to a postmodern understanding of events. This chapter is necessary as an underpinning to the rest of the book, so each section will be interlaced with real-world examples and problems, helping readers to move between the theory and the practice.

Chapter 2: Events and contested space (real and virtual)

In this chapter we explore the idea of space and spatiality. Events take place in spaces, and they are also spaces in their own right. In the first section we introduce readers to ideas from cultural geography about the construction and contestation of social and cultural spaces. We use the work of Henri Lefebvre and others to show that spaces are always the subject of negotiation and struggle between different individuals and social groups. In the second section we explore how events are shaped by – and, in turn, shape – social and cultural spaces in the real world. In the third section, we explore how digital technology and the internet are changing the ways in which events interact with spaces through the emergence of virtual space. In the final section, we introduce the idea of eventization – the ways in which public spaces are becoming private, privatized spaces. We return to some of the critical lenses outlined in the first chapter to make sense of the ways in which individuals move through event spaces and other spaces, and the opportunities and limitations such movement creates.

Chapter 3: Event mediatization

In this chapter we look at the relationship between events and the mediatization of society. Events shape the news and wider popular cultural spaces. But they also shape the way in which we think about what is newsworthy. And events normalize the mediatized practices and ideologies of modern, global capitalism. In the first section we explore theories of mediatization and the cultural industry from Adorno to Žižek, to see how they might apply to modern events. In the second section we focus on mega-events to explore how events are mediatized, and how they mediatize wider society. In the third section we look at the ways in which counter-hegemonic struggles might use the relationship between events and mediatization in their favour. In the final section we briefly debate the consequences of increasing mediatization and globalization on the role of events.

Chapter 4: Events and power

In this chapter we look at the crucial role events play in sustaining and challenging power. Mega-events might be activities in which hegemonic power is protected and in which power is removed from spectators. Such events, which have truly global audiences, are strictly controlled and subject to security and surveillance, limiting the power of those in attendance. But events may also be spaces and activities in which power is redistributed from centres to margins. In the first section we expand the discussion from Chapter 1 about hegemony and governmentality to explore how such power is normalized in actual examples of events from around the world. The second section reintroduces the idea of communicative rationality and applies it to the leisure practice of choosing to get involved in various events. Here we show that power is challenged and decentred wherever such rationality operates.

Chapter 5: Events and memory

This chapter explores the ways in which events might be sites for the construction of cultural and/or collective memory. The first section focuses on theories and practice relating to the notion of remembering and remembrance. We explore the notion that national holidays and ceremonies are events/festivals where particular kinds of memory are preserved at the expense of others. In the second section we investigate the ways in which events have their own collective memories, providing powerful ways of belonging and powerful, communicative leisure spaces for people who can share the memories. In the final section we look at the ways in which event spaces transform memories into products, drawing on the Habermasian theory of instrumentality to provide a strong critique of this turn.

Chapter 6: Commodification of events

In the first five chapters the arrow of time has pointed to an increasing commodification of events as we enter the present and the near future. In Chapter 6 we focus more closely on the processes in which events become commodities, and event participants become consumers. In the first section we return to the key theories of Gramsci, Adorno and Habermas relating to the rise of capitalism and the power of capitalism and other instrumental rationalities in the period of modernity, using mega-events such as the Olympics and the FIFA World Cup as our case studies. In the second section we discuss the shift to postmodernity, the supposed decline of nation-states' power, and how this has increased commodification. The final section explores the ways in which commodification might be resisted though events.

Chapter 7: Protests as events

This chapter develops our framework (Lamond and Spracklen, 2015) of understanding protests as events, events as protest, and activism as leisure. We introduce readers to various forms of protests as events, including organized 'chaos', non-violent direct action, and protests that are tangential to other events. We draw on new case studies on these practices and situate them in our deeper theoretical framework. The first section acquaints readers with our own framework and situates it in broader studies of new social movements. The second section focuses on activism and protest as communicative and serious leisure, drawing on the work of Spracklen and Stebbins. The final section uses the work of Žižek and Bauman to explore the ways in which protest events might be understood as interdictory spaces.

Chapter 8: The colonization of event discourse

In this chapter we look at the ways in which the norms, assumptions, practices and discourses of events management have been extended into two separate but related fields: leisure and popular cultural spaces; and the pedagogy and curricula of undergraduate degree courses around the world. The first section returns to the idea of eventization, introduced in Chapter 2. We show that this is not only progressing at the level of public spaces but proceeding in a hegemonic fashion to shape all manner of spaces and activities that are only loosely connected to events management. In the second section we concentrate on how leisure and cultural spaces are being eventized through a process of colonization. In the final section we focus on the ways in which the academic study of leisure has become eventized.

Chapter 9: Resilience and events

This chapter explores how events might be spaces and activities where individual and social resilience might be created. In the first section we theorize the idea of resilience, drawing on social psychological definitions before providing a post-structural critique of resilience that draws on the work of Foucault and Žižek. In the second section we examine and critique events managers' and practitioners' claims about the kinds of resilience that might be built into an event. In the third section we explore how resilience in events might best be understood in a social, cultural and political context. In the final section we probe the limits of the concept of resilience when applied to events.

Chapter 10: Events and misrule

Mikhail Bakhtin famously wrote about the carnivalesque, the riotous, counter-hegemonic, transgressive mood that overturns normal life in the liminal spaces of festivals. Historically, events were spaces for the maintenance of social order through the release of energy and the playfulness of the carnival; but carnivals were also spaces where villains could be kings for a day, and the ruling classes abandoned their rigid control, albeit temporarily. In this chapter we develop a critical account of the idea that events may be spaces for misrule and transgression. In the first section we introduce theories of transgression and apply them to events. In the second section we develop Bakhtin's idea of the carnivalesque through a discussion of the meaning of liminality in modern events. The final section returns to Debord and examines how events might be seen as spaces for subversion and communicative forms of spectacle.

Chapter 11: Can there be an emancipatory event studies?

In this chapter we propose that there can be an emancipatory 'event studies', but such a thing demands the lens of critical theory: that is, event studies as an academic discipline needs to engage with theories and research from radical feminism, critical race theory, queer theory and others to develop an under-standing of both oppression and emancipation at work in events. In the first section we begin to map out the theories and research that might help us develop such studies. Then we attempt to make sense of a number of examples of events using this critical lens. In the final section we sketch out what events practitioners might do to make their events more emancipatory.

Chapter 12: Events histories and narratives

In our final main chapter we are interested in what we call the 'hidden history' of events: that is, events as oppression; events that solidify relationships of power and domination; and events as propaganda. In the first section we explore theories from history and political studies that shed light on the forms and structures that hide the narrative purpose of cultural activities such as events. In the second section we explore specific events, such as food and drink festivals, to show how such histories and narratives are hidden by the normalization of the everyday and the mundane. In the final section we look at how such hidden histories and narratives might be brought to light and played with by subversive, counter-hegemonic appropriations of such event spaces.

1 Critical event studies
Theories and practices

Introduction

In order to begin studying events critically we need to address two central concerns, neither of which has, to date, been given much detailed thought within the events management literature. They are as follows: to what does 'event' refer to; and what constitutes the context in which the event, under such a construal, occurs? These questions are not separate concerns: the second rests very definitely on how you understand the first. While these two concerns may seem relatively simplistic, a thorough reflection on them, on the theories that support them and on the practices such theories enable us to articulate opens up the study of events beyond the boundaries in which it currently operates. Of the two, the first is somewhat easier to handle: it is principally a definitional issue, and one to which we will now attend.

Etymologically the word 'event' derives from the Latin *eventus*, which directly translates as 'to happen' or 'the occurrence of an incident' (Cunliffe, n.d.). Within the events management sector Getz's definition is commonly assumed: 'An organised occasion such as a meeting, convention, exhibition, special event, gala dinner, etc. . . . often composed of several different yet related functions' (Getz, 2005: 16). As is frequently the case, the devil in the detail here is the well-trodden villain '*et cetera*'. In *Event Studies: Theory, Research and Policy for Planned Events* (Getz, 2012), he develops the idea further, refining it to refer to, using his terminology, 'planned events'. However, the transition from event to planned event is significant as it fills in some of the assumptions behind the initial 'etc.'. Where event as organized happening only touches context lightly, a planned event is something much more robustly associated with a context. It suggests it is a response to a perceived situation while carrying with it a set of objectives as identifiable outcomes. Getz seems to locate the study of events as first at the heart of, and wholly within, events management, which itself is a key field within tourism management. This locates the construction of event, and the concomitant construal of events management, as predominantly driven by a commercial frame of reference. Such a frame of reference is found throughout the events literature, the vast majority of which focuses on factors that locate events in a paradigm that is either directly connected to, or influenced by, contemporary capitalism, particularly the variant that is more commonly referred to as neo-liberalism.

A critical approach to the study of event needs to begin by problematizing this frame of reference. At its most basic level we define event as 'that which intervenes the mundane'. We understand that such interventions will be contested by some of those impacted by them, and that they are never simple, surgical-like incisions; if anything, they are more like ragged lacerations with consequences far beyond those of the location of the wound. Being clear on context and its relationship to event is thus central to a richer understanding of what CES is. The remainder of this chapter concerns our second issue. It will consider the theories and practices relevant to understanding the context within which our construal of event occurs. In order to do that we need to begin by considering the current frame of reference that dominates the study and analysis of events.

To begin, let us give some consideration to the context that lies behind the prevailing view of event within the events management/event studies literature. Neo-liberalism, it could be argued, is a rather overused term that is not always thought through as a set of ideas. It is often paraded before the reader, who is expected to nod sagely, without establishing if he or she has really grasped what it means. The sense of it that is used in this chapter is close to Jim McGuigan's (2006, 2009a) notion of 'cool capitalism'. This is the capacity for the current incarnation of capitalism to absorb disaffection with it into itself. A central aspect of this is its ability to frame identity and human relationships (even those ostensibly reacting against it) through the reification of identity as consumer and brand, normalizing relationships within and between those two elements through a discourse of the market place.

Events have become almost the archetypical cool capitalist product. They are now one of the major currencies through which nations and global businesses seek a competitive advantage by attempting to distinguish themselves from one another (Kavaratzis *et al.*, 2014). Events have become the lingua franca through which an enormous range of people and organizations, from politicians to corporate CEOs, the 'creative class' (Florida, 2012) to the current darlings of the mass media, as well as provincial dignitaries and lowly local hopefuls, attempt (with varying degrees of success), through the production of and participation in events, to communicate, shape and frame the world around them.

In order to get to grips with the context in which such an interpretation of event can be articulated we need to have a thorough grasp of some key concepts in social and cultural theory, using those ideas as a foundation upon which to review the different kinds of practice that are implied by them. As such, this chapter acts as a point of return for much of the discussion you will find throughout the book. Theories and concepts sketched here will be echoed in the subsequent chapters, where they will be developed and interrogated further, applied to various examples and case studies, enabling you to understand better what it means to adopt a critical attitude to the study and analysis of events.

The remainder of this chapter will be divided into four sections. In the first Habermas's work will be assessed, in particular his conception of the public sphere and the lifeworld (*lebenswelt*). A reflection on those notions, and their associated ideas, will enable us to understand better how events can be used to distort communication. The idea that events can be understood as a form of social and cultural capital that has the potential to distort human relationships leads us to consider the role of dominating hegemonic forces. The second section will thus concentrate on developing Bourdieu's conceptualization of social and cultural capital and Gramsci's formulation of hegemony. Those ideas, however, present us with a challenge as they seem to diminish the liberatory potentialities of events even further. In the third section that concern is interrogated more deeply through a discussion of Foucauldian concepts of discourse, regimes of truth and biopolitics, and Debord's notion of the spectacle. While offering us some insight, those theories are found to provide an ambiguous response to the concerns raised in our deliberation on Gramsci and Bourdieu. Nevertheless, they lead us on to the final section. There we ask if some route through those issues can be found in Žižek's construal of 'event' and Bauman's formulation of liquid modernity. In so doing we are drawn to a refreshed perspective on the public sphere and communicative rationality.

In the conclusion, we argue that, despite its twists and turns, our odyssey has been important in itself, and not just for its eventual homecoming. The path we have followed reinforces our commitment to the view that a critical approach to the study of events is not only important for those engaged in event studies and events management research, but of real value to the social sciences as a whole.

The public sphere and the lifeworld

At its core, the work of Jürgen Habermas is an attempt to theorize, and robustly ground, what is required to establish a good society (Habermas, 1987). In *The Structural Transformation of the Public Sphere* (Habermas, 1992a), Habermas lays the groundwork for much of his later work. In it he suggests that the public sphere was a space where individuals met to discuss, challenge and develop alternatives as a response to the societal problems they perceived around them. It was the forum and space through which power could be held accountable and political authority could be confronted. In that regard it was very much an Enlightenment-like project, where the acts of reason could be victorious, and Habermas alludes to the historical role of the coffee shops and intellectual life of earlier times (Habermas, 1992b). However, the past tense is significant – as will become clear.

Habermas suggests that there needs to be a level of communicative rationality if the public sphere is to exert such an authority (ibid.). This differs from the more common construal of rationality, which locates reason in a rigorous system of deduction, rooted in an objective world of facts (Wittgenstein, 1973), independent of human norms, actions and values. Habermas suggests that rationality is intrinsically normative. It is not a process that leads to successful communication; rather, it is, to a significant extent, constituted through those self-same human norms, actions and values that establish what it is to communicate successfully

(Habermas, 1997). In order to achieve that, there must be a universal pragmatics of meaning. If we are unable to share meaning at a real and practical level, so that any discussion involves participants having a common expectation of what fits and what does not fit with the issue being addressed, then the topic cannot be substantively considered. Consequently, no body, individual or group can be held accountable, and communication breaks down. Successful communication becomes impossible. Communicative rationality is possible within the public sphere only if we can be assured of a universal pragmatics of meaning.

However, such a universal pragmatics is not, itself, without foundation. In order for meaning to have the capacity of being shared, there must be a substantial and coherent level of shared experience. Drawing on the concept of the lifeworld, developed by the founder of phenomenology – Edmund Husserl (1999) – Habermas proposes that the *lebenswelt* exists as that background environment of practices, competences and capabilities that constitutes our daily life. As we will discuss later, that background forms key elements of what Bourdieu (1984) describes as the social and cultural capital we carry with us.

To take stock, then: it is through shared experience (*lebenswelt*) that we are able to communicate through a universal pragmatics. That universal pragmatics secures the possibility of communicative rationality, which in turn means that discussion within the public sphere can successfully articulate bodies (individual and group) as accountable for their actions. Thereby, those bodies can be challenged, alternatives can be generated, political power can be exerted, and we have a good society. There is, however, a problem. For Habermas, the public sphere has been undermined through the growth of mass media; particularly a mass media dominated by advertising and public relations. He believes those forces have distorted communication to such an extent that we have become passive consumers rather than a critical public.

The mass circulation of narratives has resulted in a fragmentation of the *lebenswelt*, undermining universal pragmatics, which, in turn, has distorted (or, in Habermas's terminology, 'colonized') communicative rationality. In its place we are now in a world of instrumentality, where meaning is meaning for a pre-prescribed purpose and those purposes are multiple. In order to manage the complexity emergent from such a diverse instrumentality the former communicative rationality has been replaced with a technical one. This rationality brings with it regimes of authority and power, reframing the horizon of the background competencies and practices that form the fabric of the *lebenswelt* itself. Capitalism is one such technical rationality; it mediates communication through its own system of rules, legitimizing certain forms of reason over others, formulating modes of interaction to such an extent that it becomes naturalized to the point of becoming mundane.

How does this relate to the study of events? At one level, events can be seen as sites where the *lebenswelt* is fragmented, forming their own pragmatics of meaning appropriate to the event itself. This fragmentation produces its own public sphere, generating communicative relationships, criteria of rationality, norms of behaviour, rules of interaction and so forth. This is most clearly discernible in sports events and other areas where fandom is a key component of the event. The phenomenon of *cosplay*, where fans dress as characters from their favourite films, TV series, comics or video games, which is common to many fan-based events, is just one of the many ways in which these communicative relationships may be observed in their articulation. Of course, cosplay is also prevalent at sports events, where supporters of a team wear replica strips of their favourite players. Such fragmentation has an impact by distracting meaningful debate away from wider societal issues through the generation of more minor concerns – a bread and circuses (Debord, 1977) argument. Moreover, the management of a fragment, through the management of the events associated with it, has the potential to steer those communicative relationships. Such manipulation reverses the role the public sphere once had in challenging power, developing alternatives and showing how others are accountable for their actions. Those managing the event now establish the rules of rationality, setting the horizon within which communication becomes possible.

Nation-states' battles to host large, global-audience events, together with the lesser conflicts between global brands and businesses to secure sponsor/partnership relationships with the organizing bodies of such events, indicates the significance they now possess. The impact of coordinating such relationships – as it were, the technical rationality of the event – can have significant repercussions for those doing the coordination (witness the allegations of corruption in FIFA; see, for example, Jennings, 2015), other associated organizations (as, for example, in the case of the International Olympic Committee awarding the Discovery Channel global rights to broadcast the Olympic Games from 2022 onwards; see Gibson, 2015), and individual participants/supporters.

Events are social and cultural capital; they have become a key component of how the *lebenswelt* is colonized and steered. In order to progress we need to have a clear understanding of what is meant by 'cultural and social capital' and why, particularly (though not exclusively) in capitalist societies, it is steered in the way it is. To do that, we need to consider some of the ideas of the sociologist Pierre Bourdieu and the political theorist Antonio Gramsci.

Habitus and hegemony

Whereas Habermas places communicative relationships at the centre of the social world, Bourdieu (1984) sees the body and practices in the social world in which it engages. As such, Bourdieu's theory acts as a counter to theories that suggest human behaviour and interaction are products of rational choices made by actors. In place of such rational choice approaches, Bourdieu argues that the social world is split into different, socially structured spaces that support (although not always consciously) their own means of production and reproduction through systems of domination. He calls such spaces 'fields' (Bourdieu, 2011 [1986])). Actors within those fields do not engage in an ongoing process of calculation to determine the most rational course of action; instead, they exhibit a set of cognitive and bodily dispositions (or, using his terminology, a *habitus*) that present their orientation to the field in which they participate. The *habitus* of an actor, or group of actors, is an implicit, practical logic that encompasses modes of legitimation, schemes of perception, ways of thinking and acting (Bourdieu, 1992). It blurs the boundary between subjective and objective by focusing on the body and its practices. An actor's location within a field becomes embodied in a deep and pre-reflexive way: it is a 'feel' for the game in which the actor is acting, to the extent that it assumes the place of the mundane, the unquestioned natural order. To some extent, the idea of field is consistent with that of *lebenswelt*, as the background environment of competencies and practices (Habermas, 1987); the field also resonates with the ideas of form of life and language game found in Wittgenstein's (1951) later work. However, Bourdieu moves beyond the limits of those concepts to an analysis of the forces at work within the field.

For Bourdieu, the dynamics of the field are manifestations of the struggle of the actors within it to occupy a dominant position. That struggle concentrates on the control of capital within the field (Bourdieu and Wacquant, 1992). With his collaborator Wacquant, Bourdieu identified three forms of capital which, they argue, are the centres of the competition for dominance within and between fields. They refer to those forms as: economic capital; cultural capital; and social capital. Before we proceed, it is worth outlining how Bourdieu and Wacquant use those terms.

Economic capital is used in a sense that is consistent with much mainstream economic theory; it is that in which an investment is made in order to generate an income. In classical economics it was principally used to suggest the equipment a business would purchase in order to produce its goods or services. In more recent economic thinking, particularly that of Gary Becker (1964) and the Chicago School – which Foucault (2008) calls *ordoliberalist* – the concept has been extended to encompass other classical factors of production, specifically land (material resources) and labour.

For Bourdieu and Wacquant (2002), *cultural capital* refers to any asset that can be used to mobilize cultural authority. As such, it can encompass skill sets, recognized competencies and capacities, as well as less tangible indicators of authority and responsibility within a field or set of interactions. How social actors actively engage and deploy their cultural capital, through the symbolic systems of their practices, becomes an essential element in the sustainability and reproduction of a field's structures of domination and the articulation of its own legitimacy.

Social capital covers those additional resources that accrue from the existence of a stable network of actors. These are held together by a more or less conscious awareness of internally institutionalized relationships of acquaintance, while also embracing a recognition of the actor's location and role within the network (ibid.).

The interplay between those three forms of capital forms the symbolic systems of the actors within a field. Symbolic violence is the means by which one group of actors can, consciously or not, impose their symbolic system as that which is dominant within a field (Bourdieu, 1992). In so doing the actual arbitrary nature of the social order is overlooked, ignored or assumed as having a deeper connection, one that is construed as the natural order – and thus mundane. This is very similar to Gramsci's conceptualization of hegemony.

Gramsci was arrested for anti-state activity in Mussolini's Italy on 8 November 1926 (Fiori, 1990). While in prison he extended and developed his thinking about how capitalism sustains itself in a series of notebooks. In these, the concept of hegemony emerges as the means by which capitalism is able establish and maintain control. Gramsci argues that, unlike the systems of the past, which sought dominance through the application of violence and coercive intimidation, the bourgeoisie sustains its position of power through its dominance over the language of culture. In so doing its world view becomes embedded and proliferates. Its normative frame of reference ceases to be simply its own to become embraced as common sense, and as such the values of the middle classes assume the role of the values of everyone. In so doing capitalism becomes incontestable and reproducible, and the status quo is maintained (Gramsci, 1973). This seems a rather bleak concept: in a dominant hegemony the oppressed are fatalistically trapped in a world where their actions serve only to perpetuate their own oppression. We seem to have returned to the bread and circuses we encountered when discussing the colonization of the *lebenswelt* in Habermas's theories.

Gramsci, however, suggests a possible escape. If capitalism has become hegemonically dominant by controlling the language of culture, then the working class should develop its own counter-culture. In an argument that was later echoed in the pedagogic ideas of Paulo Freire (1970) and Augusto Boal (1998), Gramsci argued that the oppressed needed to develop their own means of education that would result in the emergence of class-connected intellectuals. Those intellectuals would then be able to articulate a language of culture that gave voice to the position of the oppressed, which could, in turn, lead to the ultimate overthrow of the dominant hegemony.

The idea that an oppressed class can acquire its own language of culture and use that to challenge its own oppression can be seen as resonating particularly well within Western capitalist music cultures. Jazz, rock and roll, flower power with its attendant festivals, punk, house and its associated illegal raves are all examples of oppressed groups developing their own language of culture to challenge the prevailing hierarchy and status quo. However, they did not overthrow capitalism or even remove oppression. Instead, as suggested earlier in this chapter, capitalism in its current iteration (McGuigan, 2009a) has absorbed those forms of dissent and their events into itself. The dominant hegemony has effectively colonized the dissenters: the sixties hippy is now the CEO or president of a global enterprise; the punk, once feared, has become a photo-opportunity for more tamely dressed visitors to resorts that host big-business-sponsored seventies festivals; the rave organizer hosts million-dollar club events with huge corporate support at beach destinations around the world. To get a better understanding of how this has happened, we need to consider the thinking of Michel Foucault and Guy Debord.

Governmentality and the spectacle

For Foucault, governmentality is the art of governing, sometimes referred to as 'governmental rationality', which has the dual objectives of producing citizens who are best suited to fulfil a government's policies and bringing to bear organized practices through which those citizens can be controlled through processes of self-correction and self-regulation (Foucault, 2008, 2014). As such, it encompasses much more than the public practices that overtly operate through the administration of state politics.

While not always presented as such, the interrogation of governmentality as the production of systems of auto-surveillance and concomitant self-adjustment formed the foundation of much of Foucault's most widely known work. Throughout his work on madness (2005), prisons (1991) and sexuality (1976), power and knowledge are conflated to the point where meaning, practice and authority fuse. Discourse, understood as the operation on meaning beyond the level of the sentence, formulates the framework through which the world and the subject's location within it become recognizable, knowable and self-regulatable. To use the Foucauldian terminology, through discourses of expertise, regimes of truth are established that facilitate a technology of the self and the other (Foucault, 2002).

Expertise, Foucault suggests, has three connected characteristics. First, it is grounded in its own claims to objectivity, to which it gives the status of a de-politicized rationality: that is, it identifies itself as neutral and scientific. This self-articulation as fact, with associated specialists who know and exclude others through declaring them unknowing, enables expertise to be mobilized as a foundation for rational discussion. Thus the second characteristic is the forming of new relationships of power and knowledge (ibid.). Those relationships form the means by which the subject can be discussed, evaluated, treated and educated. Through such expertise, the discourse creates the social reality in which the subject emerges and, as such, becomes the third characteristic: that is, the subject recognizes and maintains its self, and its association with the other, through the internalization of the discourse. It thereby becomes self-correcting, operating in such a way as to be consistent with the prevailing governmental rationality.

For Foucault, the rhetoric of neo-liberal governmentality as a *retreat* of the state was an obfuscation. The actuality was a *decentring* of power, restructuring the relations of power within society so as to facilitate the possibility of government at a distance, where society's members played an active role in keeping themselves in line (Foucault, 1991). This idea of self-surveillance – which appears increasingly in his later thinking, superseding his concept of the panopticon (the maintenance of order through the potential observation of a hypothesized other) – forms the basis of his bio-politics (Foucault, 2008), where political power can be exercised effectively in every aspect of human life.

Arguably it is the internalization that is the hallmark of the governmental which suggests that the Gramscian idea of the oppressed mobilizing their own counter-culture in order to overthrow their oppressors is unlikely to succeed. In order to attain its own language of culture through which to overthrow the dominant hegemony, the oppressed must recognize themselves as subjects who are distinct from that hegemony. However, if the self is a construction of that hegemonic power, it is difficult to see how they could distinguish themselves from it. The problematizing of the distinguishability of the self and the governmental rationality (which constrains the self's construction) makes the formulation of a counter-culture to that rationality unthinkable.

Through his critique of modernity, Guy Debord, one of the founding members of the Situationist International, suggests that mid-twentieth-century capitalism emerged from the increased significance of the spectacle. His conceptualization of the spectacle, which some equate with the mass media (Debord, 1977), draws heavily Marx's ideas of commodity fetishism and alienation (see, for example, Marx, 1973). According to Marx, capitalism separates labour – factor in the pro-duction of goods that actually does the work of producing the output – from the object of its production (ibid.). There are many ways in which such a separation is achieved, including the deskilling of the worker through the division of labour and replacing the value of generating the output with that of the wage accruing from the work. However it is achieved, the separation creates a disconnection between the producer and what is produced (alienation). Nevertheless, capitalism is sustainable only if the product becomes realized as profit through its con-sumption. The product, therefore, needs to become a desired object (fetishism); a commodity's sole purpose is to be sought and consumed. The commodity and its consumption become the object of desire for the labour involved in its production.

In Debord's society of the spectacle, capitalism, through the operation of a mass media, advertising and public relations, offers the subject an imaginary of the commodity that no amount of consumption could ever satisfy. Through those channels, what is produced and how it is encountered are framed by the forces of domination. The commodity, the desire for it and the insatiable desire to consume it thus rule the worker, instead of the worker ruling the commodity. Debord (1977) argues that capitalist culture is little more than a rigged game, where subversive ideas are permitted in public discourse only once they have been trivialized and sterilized of any corrupting influence. In this process voices counter to the main-stream are exploited and reabsorbed back into it as a means of adding a touch of spice to refresh older ideas.

This conceptualization resonates strongly with McGuigan's 'cool capitalism' – neutralizing dissent through the commodification of dissatisfaction and selling back to the dissenter as a depoliticized product. The current situation of event studies and events management fits neatly into this framework. One example in the English-speaking West could be the rise of the Pride Festival. At one time a declaration of radical otherness, an articulation of solidarity against a domina-ting culture that often violently attacked its members, Pride events have now mostly become spaces of conspicuous consumption. Many are ticketed, with large-scale corporate sponsors declaring their sexuality blindness. The power of the pink pound constructs individuals not as social and political agents, but as economic actors who support a dominant hegemony that is still intrinsically LGBTQ-phobic.

With the ideas of Foucault and Debord we seem to have painted ourselves even further into a corner than when we were considering Bourdieu and Gramsci. In the next section we will consider how Zygmunt Bauman's concept of liquid modernity and Slavoj Žižek's construal of the Event can begin to lead us out of this predicament. By supplementing their thought with Stuart Hall's development of the ideas of Gramsci, the later lectures of Foucault and Spracklen's interpretation of Habermas, we will be able to see how a truly critical approach to the study of events becomes a real possibility.

Liquid modernity, the Event and beyond

Unlike most of our preceding theorists, Bauman's initial concern is not to offer a critical assessment of capitalism per se; instead, he turns his attention to the associated idea of modernity. For him, the essence of the modernist project was the removal of uncertainties in order to establish a degree of order over the natural and social world (Bauman, 2000). Solid structure, he suggests, lay at its heart. That solidity was articulated, both normatively and administratively, through the formulation of substantial bodies of rules that regulated behaviour and interaction. Acquiescence to implicit and explicit hierarchies, controls and categories helped human life appear familiar, ordered and secure, rather than chaotic and threatening. Key here is the suggestion that this security was only *perceived*, rather than real. Bauman argues that no matter how well meaning the modernist project to remove uncertainty was, it could never be sustained; the management of the chaotic nature of human life could never be complete.

He goes on to claim, in a move reminiscent of Debord, that the latter half of the twentieth century saw a shift in society. The focus was no longer on humanity as producers; instead, we were more accurately portrayed as consumers. But the freedom to consume, to have the capacity to purchase and use such purchases to explore and develop new identities, is possible only through diminishing modernity's previous promise of security. In Bauman's terms, we replaced the former 'solid' modernity with one that is better understood as 'liquid' (Bauman, 2007).

Liquid modernity is much more focused on individual feelings of uncertainty, as we synchronously try to hold together conflicting reactions and beliefs towards the objects of our attention. We may proudly declare our environmental consciousness by attending a festival that promotes sustainable lifestyles, with its robustly 'green' agenda evident in its production and maintenance values, while concerning ourselves only minimally with the vast carbon footprint we have generated in order to reach the event. Where dissonance is felt we quickly seek arguments that sublimate the contradiction. The replacement of earlier perceived established structure with self-chosen patterns, which exclude the individual from the previous traditional networks of stability, adds a burden of responsibility that was not formerly recognized in society. Humanity becomes nomadic, with life exhibiting the normative mindset of the visitor; everything is shifting, provisional, and we are just briefly passing through. But such a bleak view of our contemporary situation is only one possibility. It hinges on the assumption that human beings, from the mid-twentieth century onwards, have been characterized purely as consumers.

In developing Gramsci's ideas, Stuart Hall (1993) argues that people should not be seen simply as producers or consumers but rather, when it comes to the culture of which our lives are part, as both simultaneously. For Hall, culture is a critical site of social intervention where relationships of power are both formed and disrupted. His theory of reception claims that all forms of communication, interaction and interrelationship require modes of encoding and decoding. While institutions, such as the media, may seek to encode communication, framing it in such a way as to contain a particular range of desired messages, we are all active in the process of decoding those messages. We are therefore also *producers* of meaning.

Hall developed his reception theory framework by identifying what he called its four codes (ibid.). First, there is the dominant, or hegemonic, code. Here, the encoder expects the decoder to recognize the code as the dominant code and decode it in the manner the encoder wishes. In so doing the message becomes perfectly reproduced, and the prevailing hegemonic order is maintained. The second code – the professional code – works alongside the dominant code to reproduce the intended meaning. However, it masks the hegemonic quality of the code by placing a layer of professionalization over it. This is reminiscent of our earlier discussion of expertise in Foucault's work. Meaning becoming mediated through a lens of specialist language, role and categorization. Negotiated coding, the third code, acknowledges the overarching hegemony within the encoded message. However, it carries a recognition that some form of interpretation is required at a local – point of application – level. The dominant code might not be explicitly recognized by the recipient. Implementation is thus not the dominant code but a distorted variant of it that better suits the context in which the decoder is operating. Finally, the oppositional code recognizes the explicit and implicit inflections of the dominant code in the message. Despite that recognition, the decoder is determined to decode the message in a globally contrary way. In so doing the message is not simply distorted but twisted in on itself and frequently used against itself in acts of cultural dissent.

While encoders seek – through repetition of the hegemonic narrative they transmit – to establish a culturally specific interpretation as a globalized common sense, the potential for creating new/alternative meaning through the productive act of decoding means other interpretations are always possible. But where are these other interpretations coming from? To answer this question, we need to understand what Žižek terms 'the Event'.

Žižek's (1989) starting point is a critique of the classical Marxian position that the reality of human relationships is hidden by the dominance of ideology which overlays it. Rather than masking reality, Žižek suggests (in a position that resonates with Foucault's thinking on discourse as knowledge and power) that ideology constructs reality. Ideology is the ontological fabric of a dominant hegemonic system that shapes and frames the world in which social relations and interactions take place. Our current context, he argues, is one where political decisions have become depoliticized because the overarching system is considered mundane – simply part of the natural order of things. However, this is not the same corner in which we seemed to be trapped after our previous discussions. Just as Hall suggests that all systems contain distortions because of the productive act of decoding, Žižek argues that the ontological fabric of a hegemonic system will contain ruptures. These ruptures cannot be fitted into the reality constructed by the ideology, so Žižek refers to each of them as 'the Event'.

The idea of Event as rupture harks back at least to the work of Derrida (2001), whose construal of it placed it in opposition to structuralist conceptions of reality. For Žižek (2014), the Event exposes 'the Real', understood as that which can never be symbolized, something which no set of signifiers could ever fully integrate into the horizon of a subject's experience. It is not an exposure of a deeper reality, hidden by the ideological mask of a system of domination, but a profound phenomenological encounter. Together with Badiou (2003), Žižek argues that the Event has profound implications for the emergence of the politically aware subject.

Towards the end of his life, in his lectures at the Collège de France, Foucault, through a series of reflections on classical Greek literature and philosophy, discussed ideas relating to the speaking of truth to power, to which he gave the term 'parrhesia' (2011a, 2011b). According to Foucault's description, the parrhesic act, the utterance of truth to power, while requiring some degree of institutionalized context, opens up the utterer to unspecifiable risk, as the impact of what is produced cannot be codified through that context; it stands defiant against the categorization that precedes it. To this extent, parrhesia is illustrative of Event; and a central element of Event must be parrhesial.

A solitary voice against a hurricane has, in and of itself, little impact. Similarly, it does not work as a ground for establishing a working context in which our initial understanding of event, presented earlier, can occur. However, a community of parrhesial voices could. Such a community of voices, with its own pragmatics of meaning, would be able to contest a dominant hegemonic system. It would carry greater potential for speaking truth to power, for orchestrating a parrhesial Event. Here we return to the point from which we began our exploration of the theories and practices that inform a critical event studies: Habermas.

Spracklen's (2011a, 2011b, 2013) work on reframing the project of leisure studies, through his application of Habermasian concepts (and particularly the tension between communicative and instrumental rationality) enables him to reconceptualize leisure. Not only can leisure be constructed instrumentally through consumption; it can also be understood as communicative action. As such, it carries the subversive potential for generating counter-discourses to the dominant hegemony. While protest and protest events would seem be the archetypical examples of this (della Porta, 2015; Lamond and Spracklen, 2015) the emergence, growth and articulations of such Event-full communities (in the sense of Event derived from Žižek), their communicative rationality and their pragmatics of meaning become the context to which a CES is drawn.

Conclusion

In the earlier part of this chapter we described the journey to establish the theory and practices associated with contextualizing event within CES as an odyssey. Just as Odysseus had to undertake many trials and detours in order to return home to Penelope, we have had to undertake a journey through a range of theories of the social world, the individual agent and the relationships between them in order to return to a point resembling that of our departure. So what are we to make of adopting a critical approach to the study of events?

We established, early on, that our starting point was the problematization of the common construal of event that is found within much of the event studies and events management literature. That particular issue was resolved in a relatively straightforward manner by setting out a working understanding of event as 'that which intervenes a context'. The issue then became understanding context in such a way as to be meaningful for a critical approach to the study of events. That inquiry led us from Habermas, through Bourdieu and Gramsci, Foucault and Debord, to Bauman, Hall and Žižek, only then to return to the later work of Foucault and, ultimately, back to Habermas.

What has become clear is that the theories and practices required to progress a CES are complex and nuanced. Where the study of events management is predominantly operational, and the primary focus of event studies is the relationship between the event and its context (most commonly interpreted through the prism of 'cool capitalism'), a critical event studies is interested in the context's relationship to the event – specially, though not exclusively, when that context stands (in part at least) in contestation to the event. A truly critical event studies is thus not only a matter of interest for researchers and students who are interested in events, but one that can form an analytic lens throughout the social sciences and humanities.

We shall explore these ideas further, within different frames of reference, over the coming chapters. However, fundamentally, we are asking a similar question: how does our understanding of an event change when we consider the context's relationship to it?

2 Events and contested space (real and virtual)

Introduction

When we think about an event, whatever its scale, whether it has a global audience, such as the FIFA World Cup, or a local one, like a village fête, we imagine it taking place in a space. The relationship between the space in which an event takes place and the event itself can range from the multiple and complex to the relatively simple and mundane. A mega-event could take place in a state-of-the-art, conceptually intricate stadium designed by a world-renowned architect. Meanwhile, the local fête might require only a few people pitching up their budget gazebos while Maud, from the village nursery, gives the green a once-over with a hover-mower. Yet events can also be spaces in their own right. When we think of Glastonbury, for example, the distinction between the space and the event seems to evaporate. And what about Woodstock for those who profess not to remember it and those who get tired of hearing other people tell them that they can't remember it, because they were there? Additionally, developments in information and communication technology, and the growth of web-based and digitally connected events have meant the identification of a location with an event can, in some instances, be highly problematic. Reflecting on event and space in such ways leads us to think about the way the two are interlinked, and what that might mean for a critical approach to the study of events.

In this chapter we discuss what informs how space can be construed within CES. We begin by considering how space has been commonly discussed within much of the events management and event studies literature. In so doing we also explore why such a construction of space is problematic when adopting a critical approach to investigating events, while acknowledging that some of these issues have, in recent years, become increasingly recognized and considered by researchers who are active within mainstream approaches. The next section then draws on ideas from cultural geography, phenomenology, poststructuralist thought and critiques of late capitalism to ask: in what ways might space be understood within CES? We reflect on some of the key developments made by such theorists as Gaston Bachelard (1964), Henri Lefebvre (1992) and Michel de Certeau (1988) to outline a position that construes space as fundamentally contested. Our third section investigates that idea further by considering the linkages and interconnections between event, territoriality and discourse, and the material and virtual space they traverse. Finally, the discussions that have run through the chapter are drawn together to show how, within CES, the relationship between event and space offers an alternative way of undertaking event studies, one that widens its reach and enables the development of new research questions and novel methodological approaches.

Space from the perspective of mainstream events management/event studies

Within mainstream events management, space is understood, primarily, as location. Such a location may be purpose built for the hosting of events (for example, a conference centre, exhibition arena or sports stadium) or it may be a space for either alternative uses or multiple uses (that is, for activities in addition to hosting events), such as the aforementioned village green, a community hall or a club house. Clearly, when it comes to planning, the appropriate selection of the space in which to locate an event is of real importance.

So, quite rightly, there is substantial discussion about how to select a venue/ location in many of the manuals that focus on the operational aspects of events (see, for example, Bowdin *et al.*, 2012). Crucial for the successful delivery of a planned event is also how the space, at the selected location, will be managed. Even the village fête will need some form of site plan if the space on the green is to be used effectively, without actively working to undermine anyone's enjoyment of the day's proceedings. A consideration of where to locate the different elements and facilities of the event will have a profound impact on how people attending will navigate, experience and encounter both the individual elements of what is going on and the event as a whole (Morgan, 2008). Let's face it, a food stand next to the portable toilets is never going to feel right. The effective planning of how people are likely to navigate space when arriving at and participating in whatever is happening at a large multi-activity site, if conducted in a manner to be most effective and to enhance the attendees' experience, is a highly detailed, statistically driven, complex task. When done correctly, large numbers of people can be guided and steered through the various sub-events within something like a music festival while barely noticing that the layout and coordination of the space are having a significant impact on their transit (Berridge, 2012).

Through careful management, congestion can be minimized; locating key resources (such as the toilets, the stages and the beer tent . . . though not necessarily in that order) becomes almost intuitive; emergencies are managed efficiently; and the focus therefore becomes having a good time. We do not advocate a critical approach to the study of events in order to challenge or undermine the hands-on, need-to-know pragmatics of how such 'happenings' are realized operationally. However, such an approach leads us to ask an important question: how is space to be understood within this arena of activity? Following Lewin (1966), such spaces can be conceptualized as hodological: that is, understanding space in a manner that is 'unlike the Euclidean continuum of points . . . [rather,] it is constituted of regions with boundaries between them' in a manner that 'permits [a] use of the concept of direction . . . which will correspond essentially with the meaning that direction has' (Rainio, n.d.). In this instance the meaning of 'direction' is interlaced with facilitating the realization of a 'successful' event. The hodological character of managed event space establishes its construal within the discourse of events management; it combines the marketization of that space with a concomitant construction of it as an area where risk needs to be mitigated.

Space marketization is a substantial area for discussion in its own right. (We deal with it more substantially in Chapter 6, where it is considered from the perspective of the more theoretically grounded concept of commodification.) The consequence of such marketization is to frame participation (even in many events that claim to be anti-capitalist) as some form of consumption. Important here is that marketization's many forms within an event space are all associated with risk. Some examples will help to illustrate this. Risks that are linked to some of the larger elements of an event are quite clear and commonly relate to personal injury. Health-and-safety issues around use and location of equipment, staging, hazardous substances, drug use and so on are all relatively predictable risks. In that such risks have a direct connection to costs, they have a significant impact on the viability of an event. However, some mundane practicalities in the initial planning – such as which food and beverage concessions are most suitable, and how much external providers should be charged – also carry risks that must be addressed and mitigated. This encompasses a broad range of perceived threats to the operation of an event, such as a poor attendee experience resulting in a negative reputation. Artists have been known to withdraw from events because of this. There is also the possibility of performer walkout, such as when Morrissey terminated his performance at the 2009 Coachella Festival in California because he could 'smell burning flesh' (BBC, 2009). A major concern, particularly in events management, is *brand association* when considering which products or suppliers should be chosen as headline sponsors or principal providers (see, for example, BBC, 2015c; Ferdinand and Kitchin, 2013; Karhus, 2012). Even at a small scale, viability risks may occur if the price elasticity of the concession is such that income generated falls below that required to support its presence and thus, in the medium term, the ongoing viability of the event. There are also risks associated with licensing, the potential for antisocial behaviour, medical emergencies and so forth. To a significant extent, then, the sub-text to the construction of space within the standard events management/event studies discourse is the control of risk.

Arguably the greatest risk relates to people, because attendees are the most unpredictable element within any planned event. Managing participation is an exercise in directing, channelling, and placing limits on the degree of euphoria and misrule (Brown and Hutton, 2015; Matheson and Tinsley, 2016). This is where the presence and character of surveillance are drawn into the discourse. Marshals on the ground, CCTV units, drone cameras and video units are now common elements at most large-scale events. At the level of events with global audiences, the complexity of security and surveillance is comparable to what one would find in a military dictatorship (Samatas, 2011; Sugden, 2012). During the London 2012 Olympics, for example, the security personnel included ground-to-air missile operatives on the roofs of surrounding buildings to protect the Olympic Park from aerial 'terror' attack (Boykoff and Fussey, 2014; Graham, 2012). Such measures contribute to extending the physical space of the event beyond what is experienced by the attendee. But as the physical world has become increasing enmeshed in its connectivity to the world of digital information and communication technology, so, because of the linkage between space and risk within its discourse, the understanding of space within mainstream event studies has had to change. What is less well developed is how that revision also impacts 'event'. It is difficult to see how the militarization and high-tech surveillance of material and digital spaces around planned events can maintain a position of political neutrality.

On 26 January 2011, in an attempt to restrict the Egyptian people's utilization of social media as a means of mobilization, President Hosni Mubarak blocked direct access to Facebook, Google, Hotmail, Twitter, YouTube, Chinese search engine Baidu and some proxy services (*Guardian*, 2011). The ineffectuality of that measure is a matter of historical record. While several researchers have contributed to the debate on the role of social media in information sharing and mobilization (Bennett, 2012; Castells, 2012; Lim 2012), others (Gerbaudo, 2012; Hill, 2013) have contended that its significance in 2011's 'Arab Spring', while important, has been overplayed. That said, the discussion centres on the role and significance of social media in those events; there is no suggestion that communications technology played *no part whatsoever*. Even if it could be argued that the use of social media was largely irrelevant in the uprisings in Egypt and elsewhere, at that time there was a perception that the digital 'public sphere' (Boeder, 2005) *was* relevant to the events that were unfolding on the streets. Mubarak's regime surely would not have tried to block the digital public realm if he had not perceived it as a threat.

Rioting erupted on streets around the UK between 6 and 11 August 2011. Associated with those events was a substantial amount of damage to property and looting from shops in the affected localities. Since then there has been much speculation concerning the role mobile phone messaging services – in particular Research in Motion's (RIM) BlackBerry Messenger (BBM) – played in coordination and information sharing among the groups that engaged in the civil unrest. Such was the extent of the claimed use of such services that *The Economist* referred to the turmoil as 'The BlackBerry Riots' (*Economist*, 2011), while the MP for Tottenham, David Lammy, called for BBM to be suspended – at least temporarily.

These two examples illuminate how hybrid spaces, where events take place materially and the associated digital networking and interaction of actors extend the construal of space, contribute to an argument, articulated through a discourse of securitization around the management and study of events, for progressing developments in surveillance. On 21 June 2013 the US federal government charged a former US National Security Agency employee, Edward Snowden, with espionage (*Washington Post*, 2013). Snowden claims that various security agencies, not just in the United States, have been monitoring email and social media communications across millions of users – every day – for years. The purpose of the monitoring is ostensibly to ascertain and evaluate potential risks to 'national security': that is, the risk of 'terrorist attack' on the activities (events) of the state.

In this section we have shown how a base-level interpretation of space common to all scales of event, as it is understood in mainstream events management and event studies, is associated with attempts to control and manage risk. However, if we look at how the relationship between risk and space has had to adapt to developments in information and communication technology, we begin to see that its conceptualization undermines the construal of event within most standard events management and event studies literature. The next section will explore alternative approaches to understanding space in order to lay the groundwork for understanding its significance when adopting a critical approach to the study and analysis of events.

Theorizing space

A completist will never be satisfied with any selection of thinkers who have pondered the question of how we are to understand the idea of space. Some boundaries need to be set if the task of considering alternatives that embrace the prevailing construal of space in events management and event studies discourses while also extending and deepening it is to be achievable within the limitations of this chapter. So we make no claim to cover everything here; instead, we draw on ideas that emerged from the mid-twentieth century onwards and are now considered exemplary across several fields in the humanities and social sciences. To begin, we consider space from a phenomenological perspective, before moving on to see how that was articulated in the work of Gilles Deleuze. Then we reflect on some key ideas within cultural geography concerning the social production of space. Understandings of space as a potential place of resistance, derived from the work of de Certeau and Foucault, form the next section. Then we briefly consider the connections between space, territoriality and discourse. In conclusion, we pull some of the threads of these ideas together to suggest an alternative to the construal of space within mainstream events management and event studies. This embraces aspects of its conceptualization in those areas while extending and deepening it into one that is better equipped to work within a critical approach to the study and analysis of events.

Space and phenomenology

Although other philosophers used the term 'phenomenology' before Edmund Husserl (1859–1938), he is commonly associated with its emergence as a distinct approach and influence during the twentieth century (Moran, 2000). Grounded in a tradition that combined the thinking of Kant and Hume, Husserl embarked on a radical project that bracketed metaphysical speculation as to the existence of the thing in itself, independent of experience, to focus on the thing as an object of experience. The technique of bracketing concentrates attention on the noumenally given rather than the noetically posited. The philosopher Gaston Bachelard and the geographer Yi-Fu Tuan have been instrumental in developing these ideas into a phenomenological interpretation of space.

In *The Poetics of Space* Bachelard (1964) applied his own particular phenomenological attitude to architecture. He undertook this project in a bid to ascertain the impact architectural space has on the lived experience of those occupying that space. In this he differed from the conventional architectural thinking of his contemporaries, which tended to privilege the perspective of the architect in constructing meaningful space by placing it on a higher plane than the experiences of the occupants. In his reflections on the house, as a prototypical example for understanding the phenomenology of space, Bachelard argues for a number of spatial types. Such types include basements and attics, hallways, doorways and drawers. He describes a number of different spatial types with a degree of poetic flourish; in so doing he tries to show the phenomenological significance of such spaces to those who encounter them, use them and live within them. Space is construed in its affective impact on the viewer/inhabitant; as such, Bachelard advocates an architectural understanding of space that values an imaginative engagement with the meaning of space, above that of some prescribed code or aesthetic.

Bachelard's object of attention, when it comes to understanding space, is very much a domestic context. Yi-Fu Tuan, by contrast, is more interested in trying to understand our relationship to space on a much broader scale. In *Topophilia* (Tuan, 1974) – a term that also occurs in Bachelard's *The Poetics of Space* – Tuan seeks to understand our human relationship to space by offering an approach for addressing issues of how we perceive it, structure it and evaluate it. Unlike his precursor, whose focus was on the static space of buildings, Tuan views the movement *through* space, from one place to another, as central to our experience. Space and place become co-dependent, with space more closely associated with temporality, while place is more closely connected to the immediate physicality of the world around us. Movement through space marks the transitions from place to place, with the meanings associated with the physicality of those places shifting as we make those transitions (Tuan, 1977).

There seems to be, at least on the surface, a definite link between the phenomenological interpretation of space in Bachelard and Tuan and the economic ideas of James Gilmore and Joseph Pine. In *The Experience Economy* (Pine and Gilmore, 1999) they argue that, partly due to the growth of information technologies and changing consumer expectations, the economies of highly developed nations are no longer dominated by classical economics, which concentrates on the distribution of scarce resources. Instead, they are based on the production of memorable events, while the marketization of memory itself is becoming a product. (We shall discuss the linkages between event and memory, including its neo-liberal commodification, in Chapter 5.) Central to the difference between the two approaches is an atomistic phenomenalism that reduces experience to data derived from the organic senses of sight, smell, taste, touch and hearing. By reducing experience to these five discernible and commodifiable sources, experience economics is able to produce tangible outputs for production and sale. However, that reduction abstracts out a crucial affectivity around space that fundamentally lies at the heart of Bachelard's and Tuan's phenomenological project. What is important here is the question: what constitutes space within our experience? Phenomenology is, in its essential form, a descriptive discipline. The early work of Deleuze developed this into one that approached an understanding of the formation of identity and the subject (Deleuze, 2014 [1968]).

Whereas Husserl had bracketed off all metaphysical speculation of the thing in itself, Deleuze poked at it with a sharp stick. What is it that constitutes the identity of things as entities within the world? In *Difference and Repetition* (ibid.) and *The Logic of Sense* (Deleuze, 2015 [1969]) Deleuze offers an alternative to the classical construction of the relationship between identity and difference. Traditionally, difference was understood as an effect of identity – that is, the objects we encounter were taken to have relatively stable identities and difference would emerge when they were compared to one another. So, for example, in the Platonic theory of forms, it could be argued that an object's identity was anchored in its ideal realization, and differences distinguished one ideal form from another. It is the object's independent stability that makes it noetic (accessible through some form of metaphysical revelation), rather than noumenal (given in experience); that, in turn, results in the ultimate inaccessibility of the thing in itself, which Husserl tried to address through his development of phenomenology. Deleuze flips that relationship around and argues that we do not derive difference from identity; rather, all identity is an effect of difference. What we take as the object in itself is actually an endless series of differences that we categorize into varying degrees of stability, thereby enabling the production of identity. This leads to what seems to be a paradoxical position – that space itself is not spatial (we will discuss this in more detail when we consider Lefebvre below). It becomes a unifying principle that acts as a condition for experience. Space is not an abstraction deduced from the existence of things, but an intrinsic element in a system of differentials that produces our experience of the spatial, the temporal and our sensation.

The social production of space

Lefebvre's interest in space and the reproduction of the social relations of production emerged in his work just before and in the years following the student unrest in France during May 1968. *Writings on Cities* (1996), *The Survival of Capitalism* (1976 [1973]) and *The Production of Space* (1992) form the theoretical foundations of his exploration of urban space and our actions and interactions within it. His central argument is that space is a product of social relationships. More than a simple assemblage of people and things, it is a complex construction, arising from the values we hold and socially produced meanings, which frame our perception and affect how we understand our actions and interactions.

Lefebvre suggests the modes by which space is produced (modes of spatialization) range from physical space – understood cosmologically, which can be apprehended mathematically – to more complex social spatialities where meaning and signification are socially produced. That social mode of spatialization, he goes on to suggest, can be analysed through a tripartite dialectic. *Le perçu* is space as perceived, with all its contradictions, understood in this mode as common sense – which, as one of Lefebvre's commentators, Rob Shields, says, is 'ignored one minute and over-fetishized the next' (Shields, 1999: 160). The second element is *le conçu*, or space as it is discursively constructed within the theories and practices of those professing expert knowledge, such as city planners, architects and so forth (pretty much those professionals whom Bachelard's work was to critique). The final part of his dialectic, *le vécu*, refers to the spatial imaginary prevailing at the time. Lefebvre's use of 'imaginary' derives from Lacan and, to some degree, Gramsci: it can be interpreted as similar to Gramsci's idea of hegemony, as discussed in Chapter 1.

Through the dialectical interplay of those three analytic frames, Lefebvre (1976 [1973]) argues, dominance is reproduced, and the dominant hegemonic orientation of capitalism is sustained. Irrespective of one's own position on the Marxism that lies at the heart of much of Lefebvre's analysis, his consideration of space does suggest an important shift in how we are to understand it with respect to CES. His work moves the question on from a consideration of what space is to a more critical one of the purpose of space; pragmatically, this criticality is of greater value as an analytic tool. What are the processes by which space is produced and spatial relationships are reproduced? In that regard his work has been developed by the cultural geographer Edward Soja and the post-colonial theorist Homi Bhabha.

In *Postmodern Geographies* Soja (2011 [1989]) suggests human life constructs its own particular mode of critical spatial awareness. He combines Lefebvre's tripartite dialectic with his own 'trialectic', which merges real and imagined spaces with the hybrid spaces that emerge between them, to conceptualize what he calls 'Thirdspace'. Soja (1996: 56–7) suggests:

> Everything comes together in Thirdspace: subjectivity and objectivity, the abstract and the concrete, the real and the imagined, the knowable and the imaginable, the repetitive and the differential, structure and agency . . . Anything which fragments Thirdspace into separate specialized knowledges or exclusive domains – even on the pretext of handling its infinite complexity – destroys its meaning and openness.

This, however, feels like it is trying to be everything to everyone; consequently, it is very little to anyone in particular. By apparently absorbing all differentials into its construal, Thirdspace risks removing any opportunity to critique and challenge domination; it therefore undermines any sense of event as that which intervenes or disrupts, as we identified in Chapter 1. If it is to be useful as a concept that helps us understand space within CES, it needs to have something more substantial.

By drawing together ideas around enunciation as an act of cultural utterance – that is the articulation of a cultural presence – and (somewhat confusingly, for us) Thirdspace (which, for Bhabha, is an ambiguous area where two or more cultures interact), Bhabha (1994) opens the door for such a development. Space becomes an ambivalent area of discourse, one that challenges the perceived stability of the dominant hegemony through the temporally disruptive character of the enunciation of difference. It is through enunciation that dominating systems of reference are exposed as politically present, revealed as practices of oppression and suppression. In so doing they become open to contestation, amenable to resistance, and the signs they employ are appropriable – translatable and readable in new ways. This leads us on to a consideration of what it means for space to be understood as contested and an arena of resistance.

Space and resistance

For the most part, thus far this chapter has focused on the experience of space. When we discussed Bachelard and Tuan, we considered the phenomenological description of space; with Deleuze, Lefebvre, Soja and Bhabha, we looked at the different ways in which space is constructed. Michel de Certeau's (1988) critique of the practices of everyday life and Foucault's (1986a) call for the development of a systematic heterotopology, which was not published until after his death, are of interest because they both approach an understanding of space through an inquiry into the social practices that take place within it.

The Practice of Everyday Life (de Certeau, 1988) is arguably de Certeau's most influential work, and not simply when we try to understand the role of space from the perspective of CES. In it he develops a critique of how we are directed through the environments in which we live while engaging in practices that undermine, subvert and seek to alter the clutter of the mass culture that surrounds us. Two concepts, in particular, stand out here as important: strategy and tactics.

Strategy refers to the means by which institutions, governments and other structures of domination construct space, with the specific end of managing how we navigate and interact with it. Though de Certeau's focus is the physical world around us, it does not require a significant leap of the imagination to see how this idea can also connect to virtual spaces, and to the hybrid environments emerging through developments in augmented reality systems. The growing ubiquity of game theory in fields interested in developing models that try to map human behaviour as a strategic activity and the correlative use of gamification (the application of game design elements in non-game contexts) across multiple disciplinary areas strongly indicate the influence of subtler ways of managing and manipulating both our passage through and our interactions within space.

As the development of a systematic approach to the production of rules, strategy shapes the territory within which we act. The layout of streets, the arrangement of buildings, the presence (or absence) of open spaces and so forth all construct environments that attempt to direct our behaviour. The augmented reality systems appearing on the mobile devices many of us carry with us offer price comparisons on products across different retail outlets as we walk by, and tell us if they are cheaper online. They let us know how the school we are passing scored in the latest national survey, as well as the educational attainment levels and employability profiles of past pupils. And they provide details of and directions to the nearest food outlet for our preferred cuisine. All of this impacts on how space is being formed around us, articulating us as *Homo Consumericus* (Saad, 2011). But, for de Certeau (1988), strategy is never fully successful: there will be cracks, fissures, into which the wanderer can articulate the space in ways not considered by its strategy. By using tactics, not necessarily consciously, we are able to subvert the strategy that the powers of domination try to impose. *La perruque* (literally 'the wig'), a way of conducting our lives during those periods when we have sold our labour to an organization, subverts the relationships of organizational power; the way we walk through the city is never fully determined by any of the maps and plans that form the way it is inscribed. The activity of our daily lives is a process of poaching the territory of others. Such acts – small, performative revolutions – overlay space with alternatives and potentialities.

The idea that the environments through which we travel and interact have multiple layers of meanings – comprising an urban palimpsest upon which we, through our actions, inscribe, erase and re-inscribe ourselves – is what Foucault (1986a) refers to as a heterotopia. Space ceases to be an absolute that provides the conditions that make experience possible, instead becoming a condition that opens up possibilities and potentialities. Spaces interlink; they carry multiple and complex associations simultaneously; they can whisper the future while containing histories that can, with work, be returned to the foreground. The homogeneity, or commodified difference, imposed by late capitalism fails fully to grasp a fundamental liquidity of space (Bauman, 2007) that is simultaneously simple and complex, fixed and transient, stable and contested. It becomes the ground upon which resistance is a possible. Pala (2015: 14) argues that Foucault's call for a heterotopoly of space – in a lecture he delivered in 1967 – is a motif that runs through all of his thought, forming a 'microphysics of power'. How this heterotopic microphysics of power can be understood is significant, and one to which we now turn.

Space, the microphysics of power, and discourse

An understanding of discourse is of central importance to any analysis of power (see, for example, Bourdieu, 1992; Foucault, 2002). However, in order to make that claim, we do need some clarification as to what we mean by 'discourse'. As a term, it is notoriously slippery, emerging from a relatively straightforward interpretation as language in interaction through an analysis of meaning beyond the level of the sentence to something much messier – an entanglement of language, practice, ritual behaviour, and relationships of power and domination. It is at that messier end of the spectrum of 'discourse' that we find the microphysics of power.

In his *Philosophical Investigations* Wittgenstein (1951) introduces two new ideas of some relevance here: language games and form of life. Of the two, language games are the simpler, in a formative sense. Illustrated through the example of two builders exchanging instruction and action in realizing a construction, Wittgenstein develops a nuanced view of language that interlaces word, action, interaction and, significantly, a relationship between the two actors. Block, pillar, slab and beam do not merely name objects; they are objects with functions, they are instructions, they form the means by which an action can be understood as correct; they suggest positions of authority and subservience; and so on. They are forming what Foucault (2002) would later call a discourse.

Even at this level we can begin to see how these overly simplistic interactions both constitute space and display an important connection between space and power. Form of life is less well developed in what we have of Wittgenstein's writings. What it does seem to exhibit is a complex multi-layering of more elaborate language games, building up even more elaborate forms of interactional/negotiated meaning/action connections. It is the form of life that sits implicitly in even the simple language game that imbues one speaker with authority, enabling the articulation of the word 'block' to refer to a complex set of relations and actions that result in the correct item being passed to the caller and the caller receiving that item in a manner that is intelligible to the giver. From a Foucauldian perspective, if we translated the builders' language into that of a clinician and patient (Foucault, 1973), and changed the context from a building site to a clinic, we would immediately see form of life taking on characteristics of the micro-manipulations of power in a discourse.

How does this connect to the earlier idea of heterotopology? Here, we need to refer back to the flip Deleuze made in his consideration of the relationship between identity and difference. Just as he suggested we do not begin with identity and then discern difference – rather difference produces identity – so it is that there is no such thing as space in which discourse takes place; instead, discourse produces space. A farmer's field may be a place of work, a festival site, a fracking opportunity, the place where two lovers consummate their mutual desire, a battlefield where Roundhead and Cavalier fought to the death, the site of a future petrol station on a proposed bypass, a sacred ground for the Druidic community and so forth. None of these spaces has an ontological priority over any of the others; some will be complementary, others will be confrontational; all have meaning and imply a range of relationships, modes of communication and rationality, forms of acceptable interaction and so on. Understanding the discourse helps us unpack the different ways that space is being constructed as territory within a discourse (Foucault, 2009). We use the word 'territory' here to suggest that the occupation of space is a key symbolic indicator of power. As we shall discuss shortly, it is in the contestation of territory that we begin to formulate a notion of space that is workable within CES.

Summing up

Over the last few pages we have considered a wide range of theoretical approaches to space that could help us develop an alternative to the standard, operationalized and commodified model of space in mainstream events management and event studies. We have moved from the phenomenologically descriptive, through social constructions of space and cultural geography, to a conceptualization that interprets space as a palimpsest with multiple overlayered and interlaced meanings constituted through social interaction and discursive relationships. We have moved away substantially from a formulation that focuses on location and its marketization to one where hegemonic domination and power form the basis of contested, symbolically rich territory. In the next section we will give more consideration to the idea of event and territory.

Event and territory

Foucault (2009), in his lectures at the Collège de France, suggests a closer discursive connection between space and domination and power. His analysis relocates the analysis of territory away from the material limits of location to one that has a greater concern with the boundaries of power in its relationship to the constitution of the subject. As such, the physical connection between territory and land is broken, to be replaced by physical and digital/material and conceptual domains, socially and discursively constructed, over which power exerts itself. Any discussion of territoriality will, for example, bring with it concerns about how its borders are identified and how they are protected and by whom; what constitutes an object within its frame of reference; who carries responsibilities and how those responsibilities are executed; who has rights of occupancy and how those rights differ with the different agents within its reach.

The land used for a festival can easily be construed as territory. However, within that there are sub-territories. The lighting technician will have specific responsibilities; they will have locations where only they, or an appointed representative, can legitimately go; there will be criteria of rationality that impact on the decisions they can and are called upon to make; they will sit within a chain of authority that makes them answerable to some while in a position of authority over others; there will be multiple and overlapping language games that constitute their form of life; and so forth. But also a discussion forum marks a territory. What can be discussed? How is it to be moderated? Are there any potential contributors or forms of online interaction that are to be blocked? How is the site to be policed and protected from viral attacks, data theft, internet trolls and so on? Despite this concern for security, the break between territory and land, when combined with the concept of heterotopia (Foucault, 1986a) and the liquidity of space (Bauman, 2000) in late capitalism suggests that territory itself is layered. The same space becomes open to multiple interpretations, erasures and revisions, constructing different entities within its frame of reference, as well as differing axiological and affective understandings of those entities. Space as power and territory becomes contested, challenged, problematized, and its occupation becomes an important concern.

Though far from a new thing, the occupation of material space has gained attention in recent years through the events of such groups as the Indignados in Spain and various Occupy communities that emerged around the world between 2011 and 2012. This recent iteration has highlighted the linkages between space, territory, occupation and contestation. As Sitrin and Azzellini (2012: 94) have argued in an 'open conversation' about the language of Occupy, 'the growing commodification of territories by capitalism has raised the need to claim territories for the construction of spaces with alternative values and practices'. The act of occupation is a 'moment of rupture ... that provide[s] an opening to new possibilities' (Halvorsen, 2015: 401), acting as 'catalysts for identity creation, expression, political contention and incubators for social change' (Frenzel *et al.*, 2014: 458). There are suggestions here that the reach of territory is greater than materially identifiable borders, often framed by forces of domination and a need to subvert them by those who are being dominated. Contestation articulates, sometimes generates, new territories, understood discursively as products of the socio-cultural and socio-technical political practices (Painter, 2010). This is one way of understanding the territorial ramifications of activists and whistle-blowers linked to Anonymous and WikiLeaks: that is, the occupation and subversion of power by redefining the space marked as territory by the powerful, and taking eventful protest (della Porta, 2015) to those borders on which one cannot march.

Conclusion

We have covered a substantial amount of material in this chapter. To begin with, we discussed the depoliticized and commodified construal of space that currently dominates mainstream events management and event studies. Here we found that this conceptualization actually masks a deep politicization, through the growth of securitization, that is only rarely discussed in the field. The presentation of space as marketized location was seen as a useful device within a frame of reference that concentrated on operational aspects of the event, but not one that made the study of events amenable to one that adopts a more critical approach. From there, we began to look at alternative ways of understanding space, drawing on ideas from phenomenology, philosophy, cultural theory, cultural geography and social movement studies. In so doing we found space to be multi-layered and complex. Location has given way to territory, which was to be understood as multiple and contested, becoming apparent through a discursive understanding of relationships of power. Even the spaces of everyday life, as considered by Henri Lefebvre and Michel de Certeau, are to be interpreted as a palimpsest where complex meanings – through inscription, erasure and re-scription – layer, become challenged and are problematized. Space, within a critical approach to the study of events, therefore cannot preference one spatial/territorial context over another. It should, rather, highlight contestation and, where possible, indicate how power is being used to exploit and dominate.

3   Event mediatization

Introduction

At the end of May each year, the Eurovision Song Contest is broadcast around the world (Baker, 2008; Charron, 2013). It is a musical contest where each member of the European Broadcasting Union sends a representative act with a new song to perform for the audiences watching on television and in the arena of the live event. The contest was made for television by its founders as a way of bringing European nation-states together through a shared love of pop music (Baker, 2008). The choice of pop music as a vehicle to promote belonging has been made possible by the way in which it is a product of the media complex: pop music has been carried by radio, films, television and now the internet across national borders, into different cultures, so that it has become a marker of global popular culture. Eurovision is the product of a belief in the power of culture and events to make bonds, and it is true to say that its audiences share the knowledge that they are sitting down to watch some outrageously bad pop music (Charron, 2013). But Eurovision carries with it cultural divisions that are magnified by the event's mediatized status. So the United Kingdom is routinely ignored by the rest of Europe, while other European nation-states approach voting in a way that is designed to support friends or attack enemies (Baker, 2008; Charron, 2013). If Eurovision were not mediated through television and the internet, the hype about bias in voting, and Eastern conservatives' accusations that Eurovision is imposing a cosmopolitan, gay-friendly culture on them, would not be so well known around the world. As it is, Eurovision is a spectacle around which both participants and audiences can construct discourses of belonging and exclusion, simplifying the tensions around the event that might otherwise have been left unspoken.

In this chapter we look at the relationship between events and the mediatization of society. Events shape the news and wider popular cultural spaces. For example, Eurovision's worldwide audience and the stories associated with its politics and its performers nearly always ensure that the event achieves prominence on news bulletins before and after the show itself. But events also shape the way in which we think about what is newsworthy: that is, events make us think that things like them are the only things worth knowing about. Moreover, events normalize the mediatized practices and ideologies of modern, global capitalism.

In the first section we explore theories of mediatization and the cultural industry from Adorno to Žižek to see how they might apply to modern events. Next, we focus on two mega-events to see how events are mediatized, and how they mediatize wider society. Then we look at ways in which counter-hegemonic struggles might use the relationship between events and mediatization to their advantage. Finally, we briefly debate the consequences of increasing mediatization and globalization on the role of events.

Mediatization

Humans have always used culture to make sense of their surroundings, their interactions with others and the beliefs and stories of their community (Spracklen, 2011a). In the Middle Ages in Western Europe, Catholic Christianity's power and association with the ruling elites ensured that popular culture was mediated through biblical imagery. The rise of Protestant Christianity in the same region continued to place the Bible in this key role, but it also gave individuals opportunities to read the Bible, make sense of it and apply it to their own lives. Out of this bibliocentric culture came the Enlightenment, the rise of science and the rise of capitalism and modernity (Habermas, 1992a). In the crucial early modern period the development of printing industries that published books, pamphlets and magazines made it easier for writers to find readers, and facilitated the development of reading as a cultural habit. But ruling powers quickly imposed controls on what could be published, using their censorship of the media to impose their ways of thinking about the world. Just as the medieval Bible imposed a particular world-view on people, the new media of newspapers and magazines could persuade people to think whatever the elites wanted them to think – from nationalistic pride in Germany, to jingoistic imperialism in Great Britain, to the inviolability of the free market in the United States of America (Hobsbawm, 1988, 1989). In the twentieth century the tension over free media and control of media was exacerbated by technological developments – first radio, then film and television, then the internet (Spracklen, 2015). The media are important spaces for the development of the public sphere (Habermas, 1992a), so long as they are free of instrumental control. But the history of the media in modernity has been a story of hegemonic power and counter-hegemonic struggle (Hall, 1993).

Mediatization is the way in which our experience and understanding of culture and society is mediated by the media's technologies and industries (Hall, 1993; Spracklen, 2013). There is an enormous range of theoretical work on the power of the media and mediation. An important thinker in cultural studies and philosophy on mediatization is Jean Baudrillard (1986, 1988, 1994, 1995, 2002). For Baudrillard, the postmodern world in which we supposedly live is marked by the construction of what he calls 'hyper-reality'. This is the reality that we read about in newspapers and watch on television news broadcasts. It is real because it is in the media, because it is mediated. But its reality is only ever known to us through such mediatization. In simple terms, the news does not tell us about what is really happening in the world out there; rather, it creates an 'out there' that we believe to be true. Influenced by government spin-doctors, advertisers and assumptions based on their status and education, reporters and editors can give us only this mediated reality, this partial account of what is happening (Bauman, 2007). All we ever know is the hyper-reality, which led Baudrillard to assert that the first Gulf War did not take place. Of course, in Iraq, bombs fell and people died. But the Gulf War *as watched by television viewers in the West* was a simulation, a fable, constructed out of what governments allowed to be transmitted and what journalists believed had to be reported.

In this chapter we shall focus on Adorno's and Žižek's work on mediatization. They are the alpha and omega of mediatization, as it were, but they also provide important guideposts on the way to understanding the role of events in mediatization, and the role of mediatization in events. Adorno is a classical theorist on the culture industry who has influenced many others, while Žižek is a new voice of the left.

Theodor Adorno was a product of the Frankfurt School, a critical theorist who attempted, with Horkheimer (Adorno and Horkheimer, 1997), to make sense of modernity, technology and the role of culture. For Adorno, what we might think of as 'high' culture – poetry, theatre, classical music – is valuable to human well-being because, in its most powerful forms, it provides both aesthetic pleasure and insights into the human condition. He believes that it is the communicative and liberatory value of 'high' culture that makes it such a threat to the ruling elites: if working-class people begin to understand the messages in such culture they will reject their place in the social hierarchy, demand rights and freedoms, and ultimately rise up against their rulers (Hall, 1993). Marx predicted that the proletariat would rise up against the ruling classes once they became aware of their status as marginalized subjects of the capitalist system (Marx, 1973; Marx and Engels, 1987). Adorno (2001) believes this has not happened in the West because the elites have used technology to create what he calls the 'culture industry', which has promulgated a narrow form of culture to the masses. This culture industry is the network of interests that constructs popular culture, including both the governments that issue licences and make laws and markets, and the corporations and capitalists who own the media and the means of production of cultural forms, such as pop music, movies and television shows. In reflecting on the culture industry, Adorno (ibid.: 104) writes:

> Culture cannot represent either that which merely exists or the conventional and no longer binding categories of order which the culture industry drapes over the idea of the good life as if existing reality were the good life, and as if those categories were its true measure ... The appeal to order alone, without concrete specificity, is futile; the appeal to the dissemination of norms, without these ever proving themselves in reality or before consciousness, is equally futile ... But this is precisely what no product of the culture industry would engage in. The concepts of order which it hammers into human beings are always those of the status quo.

So, for Adorno, the content and ideology of popular culture are bereft of potentiality, of resistance, and of communicative rationality. Instead, capitalism constructs a product that has no substance, no deeper meaning other than control, commodification and conformity. Even when there are attempts to modify the emptiness of such cultural forms – for instance, by expressing political anger or artistic endeavour through film, television or popular music – these are fruitless. Adorno believes that each and every attempt to make art from popular culture fails because the forms are inherently constrained. So a director may set out to challenge the political status quo in a hard-hitting docudrama, but the forms of popular culture are limiting. Every docudrama has to follow the rules for making a docudrama, which are rules for film or television. These rules might derive, to some extent, from laws about what is allowed on screen, but they are mainly rules of convention and style. So a popular song, for example, is forever constrained by the need to be sufficiently short to be played on a radio show. Meanwhile, reporting on an event follows rules about what it is to be an event based on laws, capitalist logic, and the technological and structural limitations of both the event's format and the reporting format. Adorno (ibid.) continues: 'In contrast to the Kantian, the categorical imperative of the culture industry no longer has anything in common with freedom. It proclaims: you shall conform, without instruction as to what; conform to that which exists anyway.'

Following Adorno, we might identify the categorical imperatives in the mediatization of the events industry. The events industry is one part of the culture industry, and it is mediatized by that culture industry. Events exist in the real world of the social and the cultural, but the mediatization of these events follows the logic of instrumentality and hegemonic control. There are global events through which we are meant to learn our places, either as privileged insiders (if we have bought tickets) or as marginalized audiences who watch the events on various media. The media use these events to tell us what is important and what is not important in our leisure lives. So the coverage of professional sports and corporate music festivals serves to impose gender order, whiteness, nationalism and the privilege of the Global North. We are sold fashions and identities through the mediatization of events, with those identities ranging from simple conformism to thinking we are free when in fact we are not.

We have already discussed Žižek in Chapter 1. His ideas on mediatization are wrapped up in the larger concerns with Lacan, Hegel and Marx we identified earlier. Žižek wants to critique both structuralists (such as Adorno) for basing their accounts of mediatization on ideas of hegemony and constraint, and post-structuralists (such as Baudrillard) for claiming mediatization means meaning becomes meaningless. Žižek accepts the structuralist accounts of popular culture, mediatization and oppression, but takes from the post-structuralists the notion that the world has changed dramatically because of this mediated culture. In *Enjoy Your Symptom!* (2008 [1992]) he attempts to make sense of popular culture through a critical analysis of iconic American movies. He uses Lacan and Freud to develop a psychodynamic account of how movies create fear and ambivalence in their viewers. In one chapter he explores *The Matrix* (1999), which tells the story of an everyday person in the everyday world who suddenly discovers that the world he knows is in fact a simulation, a form of virtual reality. Like the people in Plato's cave, the characters live their lives not knowing that what they see is an illusion. In fact, their lives are created by an artificial intelligence that connects them permanently to computers and keeps them alive by feeding them fluids through tubes. Such a conflation of metaphysics and postmodern relativism is suitable grist for Žižek's analytical mill, and he expends considerable effort in a bid to make sense of the claims made within it. Žižek (2008 [1992]: 252) then says:

> From another standpoint, *The Matrix* also functions as the 'screen' that separates us from the real, that makes the 'desert of the real' bearable. However, it is here that we should not forget the radical ambiguity of the Lacanian real: it is not the ultimate referent to be covered/gentrified/domesticated by the screen of fantasy; the real is also and primarily the screen itself as the obstacle that always distorts our perception of the referent, of the reality 'out there'.

Reality, for Žižek, follows Lacan's notion that the reality of the process of mediatization is the mediatization itself, the thing that shapes our perception. The reality that is supposed to be represented in this mediated cultural product is a chimera, a fake or false idea of the real, something that has been constructed, according to both Žižek and Lacan. The events that are mediated to us through television, film, the press or the internet are real only through the process of mediatization, and that mediatization is reality as we experience it. Even if we participate in an event ourselves, rather than follow it in the media, our perceptions of that real experience are mediated. We think of the event only through the fabric of the mediation, the screen that Žižek uses as a metaphor for more general mediatizations and representations. He (ibid.) continues:

> For Kant the real is the noumenal domain that we perceive 'schematized' through the screen of transcendental categories; for Hegel, on the contrary, if we subtract from the thing the distortion on the screen, we lose the thing itself ... which is why, for Lacan, who here follows Hegel, the thing in itself is ultimately the gaze, not the perceived object.

As we have said, Hegel is crucial to Žižek's entire political and cultural philosophical programme. For his work here on mediatization, Hegel provides the epistemological rigour for Lacan's claim. Hegel's metaphor of the master and the slave shows how the self needs to reconcile its relationship with the other to become free from the falsehoods of myth, and to become free to think rationally (Hegel, 1976; see discussion in Houlgate, 2012). Hegel's psychology of mind – and theory of human development – is of course highly problematic, as it is wrapped up in the notion that there is a natural progression of human society, and a spirit that shapes society in each stage of that progression. But there is a truth that humans are constantly trying to find self-actualization and validation in the social world. We all want to find love; we want to find respect in our workplaces; and we want happiness in our leisure. The idealization of events in the media is evidence of this, as well as evidence that popular culture more generally is a site that is contested asymmetrically by human agents, but one where all of us are constrained more or less by the assumption and habits we inherit. We are all seekers of the ideal event, and we are all sold crude representations of that ideal event. Žižek (2008: 264) continues his analysis of *The Matrix* by writing:

> What the film renders as the scene of our awakening into our true situation is effectively its exact opposition, the very fundamental fantasy that sustains our being. We are not dreaming in VR [virtual reality] that we are free agents in our everyday common reality, while we are actually passive prisoners . . . it is rather that our reality is that of the free agents in the social world we know, but in order to sustain this situation, we have to supplement it with the disavowed, terrible, impending fantasy of being passive prisoners.

Žižek believes that we are free agents who nonetheless need the fantasy of enslavement to sustain us, because in fact, in the real world, our situation is that we are subjects of such enslavement: we are victims of the capitalist system. In mediating this truth, popular culture is a solace, a source of nourishment, as well as a signpost: a solace because we know we are active agents in our own enslavement, but a signpost that points to a way out of the situation. We allow our enslavement to capitalist hegemony to be imposed on us through the media, but we can see through the act of mediatization that our masters depend on our labour, our capital and our compliance in the maintenance of their hegemony. Following Hegel and Marx, Žižek argues that our hegemonic masters are just as dependent on us as we are on them, so we have the agency and the potential to alter the rules. We can choose to mediate the relationship in a way that challenges and breaks the master–slave bond. We can choose to rebel against the hegemony and the order it imposes through combined political action.

If, in the early 1990s, Žižek was pessimistic about our ability to see through the mediated trick of hegemony, in the first two decades of the new century he has become an active voice in the struggle for a more equal world. For the more mature Žižek (2014), critical analyses of the media and popular culture allow us to see the fakery of the mechanics. In *The Wizard of Oz* the Wizard is first shown speaking ponderously from behind a curtain, in a flash of smoke and lightning. But the truth is soon revealed: the Wizard is just an old man. Žižek's later work shows how this trick can be revealed in everyday life, in popular culture and in politics. The mediatization of events, then, becomes even more a case of magic tricks, of smoke and mirrors. We can see this at work in the examples discussed below.

The Olympics

When the 2012 Olympics came to London, politicians and journalists spoke about the event's 'feel-good' effect, with an opening ceremony that told the story of multicultural Great Britain and medal-winners such as the British–Somali Mo Farah. For the government, the *story* of the Olympics was more important than what actually happened at the event itself. The government wanted the nation to feel that the billions of pounds invested in the event was money well spent; it wanted to distract British citizens from the ongoing austerity that had led to riots the previous summer as well as a series of protests and demonstrations (Graham, 2012; Spracklen, 2012; Thornley, 2012). We do not know the details of the discussions that were held between the government, the local organizing committee and the media, but we do know that the International Olympic Committee (IOC) has become a slick media-savvy organization that spends millions of dollars on favoured (official) partners, maintains wider media operations that protect both the brand and the message, and provides thousands of journalists with various perks (Rowe, 2012). So, in 2012, the BBC and other UK broadcasters maintained an ebullient tone in their coverage, reporting with cheers every British success, celebrating other medal winners, and repeatedly declaring how great the event was. Any critical analysis of the IOC was put on hold for a fortnight. Instead, the reporters merely asked: 'Isn't this event wonderful? Doesn't it bring people together in celebration of great sport?'

The mainstream media did not report stories that would have provided some critical evaluation of the neo-liberal system in which the Olympics and other sports mega-events take place. There was no room for analyses such as those that run through this book. In 2012, academics wrote about the demolition of people's homes to make way for the Olympic Park, the security cordons, the banning of logos and symbols associated with sponsors' rivals, the creation of special traffic lanes for IOC officials and their flunkeys, and the questionable ethics of the entire bidding process (Graham, 2012; Rowe, 2012; Thornley, 2012). Such issues were also reported on the fringes of the British media, such as in the important counter-establishment magazine *Private Eye*. But the mainstream coverage of the event itself was deeply respectful of the IOC, the wider Olympics movement, Prime Minister David Cameron, the Queen, and the Olympic philosophy (competition brings people together and sport can make the world a better place). The coverage pretended to abide by the strict rules of objectivity that supposedly lie at the heart of journalism: all reportage should tell readers or viewers the truth of what is happening. But these rules are an example of Adorno's restrictions in the culture industry, or the mythical morality of otherness discussed by Žižek. What journalists actually do is report what they think is the truth, but their assumptions about what that truth is are shaped by their elite status, their elite university educations, their standing as members of the culture industry and their obligations to retain an audience.

The opening ceremony was a classic example of the limitations of the culture industry. It confused myth with reality, mixing things that might be worthy of celebration – such as the National Health Service – with the more objectionable deification of the Queen. Billions of pounds were spent on the Olympics at a time when health and social services budgets were stretched to their limits or cut altogether, so the ceremony's celebration of the welfare state struck many as a sick joke. Likewise, the desire to portray Britain as a peaceful, multicultural, modern nation – which many commentators discussed – seemed to run counter to the reality of institutional racism, the alienation of minority ethnic youth, and the policies and messages of the two main political parties, which at the time were vying with each other to appear most 'tough' on immigration. Following Adorno's conclusion about the culture industry's categorical imperative, we can see that the media coverage of the Olympics, kick-started by the opening ceremony, was designed to impel viewers to conform, to be good subjects of the Queen, to respect the Conservative government, and to sit in admiration of the IOC.

There is more to the mediatization of the Olympics. Historically, the media coverage of the event was limited to short reports sent by telegraph or telephone to newspapers and radio stations. With the advent of television around the middle of the twentieth century, sports mega-events were sold to media corporations as big profit-making enterprises that would attract dedicated fans, who in turn would be targeted by advertising campaigns built around the events – sponsorship in the places where the events were held, as well as television commercials and sponsorship deals to brand coverage (see Roche, 2000; Rowe, 2012). This allowed the IOC to make huge sums of money from television rights and sponsorship deals. But it also resulted in a change in the reporting of the Olympics. From appearing on a few pages at the back of newspapers, the Olympics became a major television event framed by the demands of broadcasters, which do not always correlate with the best interests of the IOC. The broadcasters want to ensure that the big events within the Olympics – such as the men's 100 metres – or events where a national broadcaster might have a special interest – such as ice hockey in Canada – are timed to maximize their audiences, and their advertisers. The IOC want to help broadcasters and host cities to time events to maximize audiences and profits, too, but they also want the public to watch *all* of the events that take place under the umbrella of the Olympics: summer and winter; Olympics and Paralympics; men's and women's events; and every sport from shooting to dressage. This debate about what is shown, and when it is shown, forms part of the contractual negotiations that occur before each Olympics takes place. The final agreement establishes a form of the mega-event that is shaped by the lens of the media for the viewer. Following Žižek, we might argue that the Olympics mega-event watched by viewers can never be the actual mega-event at which someone participates. It will always be mediated, perhaps by showing only that part of a stadium that is full, rather than banks of empty seats, or by the commentator constantly reminding us how brilliant it all is. But the Olympics we watch – this mediated representation, this *fake* – becomes for us viewers the only Olympic reality we know.

Burning Man

In the globally popular American cartoon series *American Dad*, produced by the transnational Fox Corporation, there is an episode in which the characters attend Burning Man. The episode begins with Stoner Jeff – boyfriend of Hayley, the daughter of all-American dad Stan Smith – and Stan's wife Francine travelling to the festival. Stan and Hayley are forced to follow them, and lots of merriment ensues as the characters take drugs, try to find themselves and attempt to tap into the New Age spirit. Burning Man has also been spoofed in *The Simpsons*, another Fox product that has an even bigger global audience than *American Dad*. Hence, everybody who is influenced by US popular culture – which is everybody in the world where Westernization is at work, which is everybody in the world with a television set and/or a smart phone (Spracklen, 2015) – will be aware of the event. As well as the aforementioned cartoons, the festival has featured prominently in a number of magazine photo-shoots (Chen, 2012), and it has become sufficiently high profile to generate a small industry of academics excited by its potential to change the world spiritually, ethically and politically (Chen, 2011; Osto, 2012).

Burning Man has become a global brand for counter-cultural activism and alternative lifestyles. It was initially set up to celebrate the summer solstice, and it has evolved a set of strong ethical values drawn from radical and anarchist politics (Bowditch, 2013; Osto, 2012). These values include the ideas that everybody is an active participant who makes his or her own entertainment through taking part; that no commercial transactions take place in the event space; that people give gifts; and that everybody is welcome in the space. But over time it has become just another music and arts festival, with people paying hundreds of dollars to gain entry and then get drunk, have sex and do everything else that a typical festival-goer wants to do. It costs a lot of money just to participate, but the cultural capital associated with it also needs to be bought by rich parents: the confidence to attend; the confidence to be an artist; the knowledge of culture and politics gained from a university degree course. Most people could never aspire to visit and participate in Burning Man – it remains the preserve of privileged elites. But the process of mediatization allows others to experience it vicariously, albeit partially. The cartoon spoofs are only part of that process. The internet allows browsers to follow the event with all the seriousness of the people who attend it, whether through the videos and material on the official website or via the many unofficial videos on YouTube. Other Burning Man events have been organized around the world, promoting the brand into the elite league of global entertainment franchises.

But what exactly is Burning Man? The carefully curated Wikipedia entry describes the event as follows:

> Burning Man is a week-long annual event that began in San Francisco's Baker Beach in 1986 and migrated to the Black Rock Desert in northern Nevada, in the United States. The event begins on the last Monday in August, and ends on the first Monday in September, which coincides with the American Labor Day holiday. It takes its name from the ritual burning of a large wooden effigy, which is set alight on Saturday evening. The event is described as an experiment in community, art, radical self-expression, and radical self-reliance. Burning Man is organized by Black Rock City, LLC and has been running since 1986. In 2010, 51,515 people attended Burning Man. 2011 attendance was capped at 50,000 participants and the event sold out on July 24; the attendance rose to 65,922 in 2014. In April 2011, Larry Harvey

announced that the organization had begun the process of transitioning management of Burning Man over to a new non-profit organization called the 'Burning Man Project'.

This narrative, which matches the official history on the Burning Man website, promotes the idea that the event grew organically around a small group of radical artists, neo-pagans and activists, before the numbers attending forced the organizers to raise the price of tickets, establish a company to run the festival, and work closely with the local council. As mentioned, the burning man itself is a wooden figure that is ritually burned at the climax of the event. The Wikipedia page notes that founder Larry Harvey 'stated that he did not see the movie *The Wicker Man* until many years later, so it played no part in his inspiration'. No source is provided for this statement, and it is rather surprising. *The Wicker Man* (1973), a favourite of modern pagans, tells the story of an island community in Scotland who sacrifice a Christian police officer in a burning wicker man; and a similar story appears in Frazer's *The Golden Bough* (1922). Yet Harvey and the other founders of Burning Man want us to believe that their first event in 1986 and the Burning Man ethos emerged *ex nihilo* because they want the event to be unfettered by commodification and the culture industry. They want us to believe that their event – unlike every other arts and music festival – is pure, authentic and a place of spiritual rebirth. Admitting that the event was itself mediated by a cult 1970s B-movie might be an admission too far. The Lacanian and Hegelian other, the magician's trick in the mediatization of Burning Man, depends on all of us believing Harvey's version of events.

Counter-hegemonic resistance

We discuss counter-hegemonic resistance elsewhere in this book, so we do not need to define it here, or discuss the extent to which such resistance is possible in this century. But we can begin to see how mediatization might work to favour those who wish to subvert events or resist the ongoing tide of commodified events.

Consider again the Olympics. In every cycle of this mega-event since the end of the Cold War there have been grassroots movements using the tools of the culture industry to resist the presence of Olympic events (Roche, 2000). In the build-up to the 2014 Winter Olympic Games in Sochi, Russia, for example, a small but significant campaign in the region actively questioned breaches of environmental regulations during the construction of ski-runs and infrastructure in the mountains and the city of Sochi itself (Lenskyj, 2015). As local media outlets were – and are – controlled by the Russian government, the campaigners disseminated their concerns through the internet, then through direct contact with the mainstream media in the West. At the same time, the Russian government was becoming increasingly homophobic in its laws and statements, and the Olympics became the subject of a worldwide political debate about whether it should be boycotted for that reason. Using the power of social media such as Facebook and Twitter, human rights activists, Western-supporting people in states threatened or invaded by Russia, and LGBT campaign groups combined to use the Sochi event to publicize the dictatorial and conservative turn in Russia. The IOC scrambled to find a compromise, avert the potential boycott, and keep the bad news out of the world's media, but the events in Sochi were overshadowed by the negative memes and stories that flooded the internet. Although the campaign failed to alter the Russian polity's aggression and homophobia, it did make these issues more widely known and forced Western governments to issue strong statements against Vladimir Putin's administration.

The continuing failure of the IOC to ensure the Olympics are hosted in places where diversity and equality are valued as highly as fast times is something that campaigners will continue to raise in the media. The internet is an extension of the Habermasian public sphere defined by the press and the broadcast media, but it actually offers campaigners and activists a truly free space in which they can work together, free from editorial control, to publish important counter-hegemonic stories. As Castells (2012) suggests, the networks and possibilities created by the internet have profoundly changed social activism in recent years. Nevertheless, there are still important questions to ask about who gets to read these stories, who has access to the internet, and who controls that access (Spracklen, 2015).

The Occupy movement is discussed in more detail in Chapter 7. This movement has been very media-savvy, planning its protests and events carefully through social media, then making spectacles of the protests, which attract media attention. The idea of taking over and occupying public space in the financial or government district of a major city immediately raises the stakes of the event in the media. News broadcasters are marshalled and briefed by the campaigners, who provide instant updates of developments, such as police attacks, via Twitter. While many mainstream media corporations refuse to report on such events in anything other than a negative light ('violent anarchists confront police' is a frequent headline), some dissenting media organizations report them in a more balanced way. The initial success of the Arab Spring protests was directly related to the power of organizers to marshal supporters online and stay one step ahead of the security forces, who were unfamiliar with the new technologies (Castells, 2012; Spracklen, 2015). Then the burgeoning media coverage was fanned by organizers and local journalists sending video clips and press releases through Twitter, Facebook and email to sympathetic Western journalists. As well as the dissenting organizations which provide balanced coverage for Occupy and similar campaigns, there are thousands of online outlets that provide accurate accounts of the progress of their events.

Mediatization, then, lies at the heart of counter-hegemonic struggles against neo-liberalism in events, and the effects of neo-liberalism on events. It is also central to the success of events that are forms of protest against neo-liberalism. This is a consequence of the modern age in which we live. The culture industry still shapes how we all think and act. Our freedoms to think and act are constrained by global capitalism and instrumental rationality. Yet we are all actors on a stage, playing roles that we think give us meaning and purpose, belonging and identity. Just as events are shaped and mediated by the culture industry, so counter-hegemonic struggles are built within the categorical imperatives the culture industry imposes on us. Occupy campaigners have no alternative. They *have* to use the systems, technologies and language of the news media to promote their message, even if such promotion is only a means to an end. Similarly, the campaigners need to engage with the (post)modern world of social media and the internet because it helps them to disseminate their message and gain supporters. It is ironic that the most successful campaigners against neo-liberalism and its effects turn into models of instrumental rationality, selling their brands, simplifying their messages, and turning the means into an end by competing to increase their numbers of supporters online and on the streets, at events (Spracklen, 2014b, 2015).

Conclusion

This century has seen an acceleration of a number of trends that might be understood collectively as a shift from late modernity to a postmodern or post-industrial, global society (Bauman, 2000, 2007; Spracklen, 2011a). Governments and financial organizations have challenged and removed barriers to trade, placing most of the world in an interconnected, global economy. Nation-states have ceded some of their autonomy and power to transnational corporations and global institutions that support neo-liberalism, such as the EU, the IMF and the World Bank. Industrial economies in the Global North have become post-industrial economies, leaving nation-states in the region divided between small elites with vast reserves of money and power, and a majority that works in temporary and/or badly paid employment, or barely exists on benefits. There has been a sharp rise in the mobility of people, ideas and cultures. For the elites, a shared global culture associated with big cities has become commonplace, while for the masses around the world mobility means migration in search of work or escape from violence. Technological developments make it easier to travel safely around the world. They also make it easier for ideas to spread through television, films and the internet. It is now possible to sit in an apartment in New York and watch a live stream of a Sumo tournament in Osaka on a smart phone.

Clearly, mediatization is at work in this acceleration of globalization. The culture industry is constructing a global public sphere, and a global popular culture, to keep the masses satisfied and compliant with the instrumental logic of instrumentality. Hollywood movies shape and limit a shared ideology and ethics of individualism, of finding the girl or boy and finding oneself. Films, computer games and social media teach everybody the same simple messages about what it means to be a mediated, modern, global human: our music is limited to rap, pop or rock; our choice is limited to *Star Wars* or *Star Trek*; our function in life is to be good consumers, replacing our clothes, computers and phones whenever we are told that new versions should now be purchased (Spracklen, 2015). The global popular culture has its sceptics and its rebels, but, as Žižek shows, it is impossible to step off the stage and resist when we are all actors in the play.

What is the role of events in all this? The very idea of an event is a product of mediatization, and the shift to the liquid modern (Bauman, 2000). Now that our working lives are so precarious, now that most of us have lost the social identity and solidarity of the workplace, we are floating subjects. Our leisure lives have become important sites for the construction of our identity and the preservation of our sanity. We find in communicative leisure activities a way of being human, being social, learning how to grow and develop and escape the mediatized conditions of the current century (Spracklen, 2009, 2011a). Events might be leisure spaces defined by their eventfulness and their social fabric – they are leisure spaces where things happen, where we encounter people. At their basic, communicative level, events are as morally good as any other communicative leisure activity. But through the power of the media and its hegemonic control of popular culture, the 'common-sense' understanding of events has shifted. They are no longer spaces for communicative leisure. They are mega-events – corporate events where we pay to take part, and leave feeling unfulfilled. These mega-events, as we show elsewhere in this book, form part of the commodification of leisure, which has seen leisure spaces shaped by instrumental rationality. In other words, governments and corporations are using the importance we place on events to sell us versions of them that they can control and shape in order to keep us in check, and keep us consuming. We are forever caught in this trap of mediated events.

We can see this trap snaring us in the Eurovision Song Contest, in media coverage of the Olympics, and during Burning Man. We might think there is scope for progressive ideologies at Eurovision, for categorical imperatives that run against the instrumentality of the mediatization: the cosmopolitan campness, for example. But Eurovision is a construct of global media, a form of event that tells people it is good to be consumers, and good to allow nationalism and bigotry to prejudice judgement (Spracklen, 2013). It is a virtual reality, a simulation that serves to normalize nation-states and the pop industry. During the Olympics, we see the ideology of the competitor and the winner, the participant and the best, refracted into myths of national supremacy through the looking-glass of television coverage. The Olympics serves to normalize global capitalism and distract people from the billions of pounds that must be spent to host such events.

We might think that Burning Man stands against these trends of accelerated globalization and commodification, and the organizers and festival-goers might themselves believe that they are being communicative. But in fact it is as much a part of the festival-and-tourism industry as Coachella or Glastonbury. People spend money to turn up to suspend their involvement in the mediatization of instrumental leisure, but in spending that money they are taking an active role in perpetuating instrumental leisure.

4 Events and power

Introduction

This chapter, like Chapter 3, focuses on events that are commonly referred to as 'mega-events' in the events management and event studies literature. Now, a sound argument could be made that though CES critically problematizes *event*, a category such as 'mega-event' has no meaning within its field of enquiry. As we shall discuss shortly, to classify an event as a mega-event is to participate in a neo-liberal discourse that CES challenges. That, however, would be to confuse the *critical examination* of the axiology and ontology constructed within a discourse with an *acceptance* of it. After all, one does not need to *buy into* a simplistic binary model of gender to mount a challenge to naive conceptualizations of sexuality. If we are to understand what is construed as a mega-event within mainstream events management and event studies, and expose it to critical examination, then we need to reflect on those factors that are framing an *event* as a mega-event. In Chapter 3 we explored the mediated articulation of events, and how events are mediatizing wider society. We discussed how the relationship between events and mediatization can be used by the hegemon to legitimize its world-view and dominate. However, we also noted that those forces could be used to work in favour of counter-hegemonic struggles, too. In this chapter we proceed further with that discussion by reflecting on the linkages between events and power. While a reflection on power is relevant to all events that are of interest in CES research, it is through those events which attract global audiences and involve international participation that those connections can be most clearly discerned and discussed. It is thus through a critical examination of cases that draw on a mainstream formulation of mega-event that we are able to highlight relevant questions concerning event and power.

In the first section we ask: what is a mega-event? In so doing we examine how the development of typologies of event, in mainstream events discourse, work to create an imaginary of *event*, normalizing, as a *cultural* political economy, an idealized (utopian) global capitalism by sustaining individual and international relationships of significance to its growth and sustainability. The second section then expands on the connection between mega-events and utopianism. It begins with a discussion of two examples – the Olympic Games and the World's Fair (or Expo, as it is commonly known) – outlining their backgrounds and current articulations, then referring back to a number of points made in the first section. By indicating an association between these examples and an early iteration of a utopian polity, from Plato's *Republic*, we argue that mega-events reveal an instrumental rationality – one that has come to be known as *soft* power. In order to increase understanding of the operation of *soft* power we draw on the ideas of Foucault, specifically his consideration of biopolitics and governmentality. In the third section we locate the preceding discussion of governmentality within our earlier enquiries into theorizing *event* and *space*, as presented in Chapters 1 and 2. By that means we open our inquiry into events and power to the possibility of dissent. It is through dissent that the instrumental rationality of the mega-event can be challenged and subverted through counter-hegemonic struggle. That brings us to our fourth section, where we show how such counter-hegemonic struggles can operate through communicative rationality, engaging in communicative action to challenge existing forms of domination through acts of parrhesia (the speaking of truth to power) and thereby decentre power.

What is a mega-event?

Google's n gram[1] viewer searches a corpus of more than 30 million digitized publications that were published between 1800 and 2012. It then plots the incidence of any word (or part of a word) as a percentage of its corpus in any particular year. The resulting chart gives some indication of how commonly an expression appears in print and when it first emerged. A search of Google's English-language corpus suggests the term 'mega-event' did not appear until the mid-1960s. It was rarely used in that period, and soon faded out of usage altogether. However, it reappeared in the late 1970s, and since 1979 its usage has grown enormously, with a period of accelerated expansion from 2000 onwards.[2] Upon further scrutiny, in the 1960s the term was usually used to describe an experience. So, for instance, the Beatles' concert at Shea Stadium in August 1965, with its estimated attendance of 55,600, was described as a mega-event for the band during the narrative of the film that recorded it.

It is only when we turn our attention to the field of events management that we first come across the term being used to describe the scale of an event itself. For instance, Bowdin *et al.* (2012: 21) categorize events into four scales: local, major, hallmark and mega,[3] with the latter 'those events that are so large that they affect whole economies and reverberate in the global media. These events are generally developed following competitive bidding.' This, they claim, is a refinement and simplification of the definition developed by the tourism academic Colin Hall, who argues that mega-events

> are events that are expressly targeted at the international tourism market and may be suitably described as 'mega' by virtue of their size in terms of attendance, target market, level of public financial involvement, political

effects, extent of television coverage, construction of facilities, and impact on economic and social fabric of the host community.

(Hall, 1997: 75)

Hall's definition seems to have greater reach than that suggested in Bowdin *et al.* (2012), in that there is a suggestion that such large-scale events have 'political effects' and impact upon the 'social fabric of the host community', which are not alluded to in the later, shorter, definition. However, it should be noted that both definitions locate *events* within a framework of the market economy: the first (and more recent) in a globalized arena; the second within the slightly more specialized 'international tourism market'. Even in more recent attempts to define mega-events, such as that offered by Muller (2015), economic impact and global media audience play dominant roles in the definition. But scale is just one dimension through which events are classified. As well as their size, Getz (2012) argues for a typology of events that splits them into eight types:

- cultural celebrations;
- art/entertainment;
- business/trade;
- sports competitions;
- educational and science;
- recreational;
- political/state; and
- private events.

Most of these are explicitly driven by commercial interests, some (such as religious events and small-scale rites of passage) are suggestive of a specific world-view, while others hide their ideological orientation. Possibly most telling is how Getz (2012: 58) defines 'political events', which he describes as:

> produced for or by governments and political parties . . . Most political and state events are security nightmares. When leaders assemble or governments meet, or when a VIP tours, the media pay close attention – and so do people who want to protest or disrupt. It now takes a huge effort, at great cost, to mount these kinds of events.

In all of these models events are framed by their scale, their expense, the security measures they invoke, and the level of media interest in them. Not only are 'protest' and 'disruption' conceptually excluded from being classified as events,[4] but the context is not mentioned in any of these definitions. Events in general, and mega-events in particular, are construed as *things in themselves*. Yes, they have impacts, but the focus is on the event itself. To use a metaphor, such an approach is a little like throwing a stone into a pool and seeing the ripples emanating from where it hit the surface. One can investigate the stone and say the ripples represent the impact it had when it hit the water. However, it is also relevant to ask: what is it about the medium that was hit that means the rock striking it has such an impact? Typologies objectify that on which their gaze falls by abstracting out of a complex and multimodal milieu a discernible *it*. As we discussed in Chapter 1, a key aspect of CES research is to focus on the relationship between the context and the event, the stone and the medium, rather than one's effect on the other. Consequently, the development of a classification system that attempts to construct criteria attributing a distinctive epistemological status to an event (that is: I can recognize, and therefore research, this event because it fulfils a specifiable set of identificatory characteristics) – as events management and event studies implicitly try to do – is viewed as axiologically weighted towards the dominant hegemony in which the *event* occurs.

Despite that, the definitional connection between 'mega-event' and the media attention such typologies develop is of interest in that the size and impact of such *events* expose the multimodality of the *event* much more clearly than those taking place on smaller scales, so they serve to highlight the relationships between event and power. The question 'What is the point of a mega-event?' is particularly pertinent here, and we turn to it now. Merkel and Ok (2015) have made a fascinating contribution to this debate in their analysis of identity discourses in North Korean events and festivals. Here, however, we shall briefly consider the role and value mega-events in neo-liberal democracies.

In North America, Europe, Australia and many similar economies events are associated with two connected ideas: place branding and attracting what the urban theorist Richard Florida terms the 'creative class' (2002, 2005). It is important to begin with some definitions of these two ideas, which interconnect and support each other.

Florida (2003: 8) identifies the creative class as those people who

> engage in work whose function is to create 'meaningful new forms' . . . [such as] scientists and engineers, university professors, poets and novelists, artists, entertainers, actors, designers, and architects . . . nonfiction writers, editors, cultural figures, think-tank researchers, analysts, and other opinion makers . . . [as well as] 'creative professionals' who work in a wide range of knowledge based occupations in high-tech sectors, financial services, the legal and health care professions, and business management.

According to the Department of Culture, Media and Sport (DCMS) just over 2.75 million people were employed in the UK's 'creative economy' – 8.8 per cent of the British workforce – in 2014 (DCMS, 2015). Although the ontology behind the production of such statistics has been questioned (Belfiore, 2009, 2012; Garnham, 2005), an imaginary of the creative class has, at the very least, some rhetorical weight within governmental policy discourse. Significantly, Florida claims, this new class is a central commodity for which globalized neo-liberal economies compete, viewing a state's capacity to attract this class as a significant contribution to its perceived identity and locating it as having an economic vision in the global market place.

The messages encoded in a mega-event – that a nation is vibrant, forward looking, diverse and so forth (characteristics that are central to attracting the creative class, according to Florida (2012)) – can be viewed around the planet, live. According to Reuters (2015), the global audience for the FIFA World Cup Final in 2014 was 700 million, while the IOC's (2014) report on the 2014 Winter Olympics in Sochi estimated the audience at around 2.8 billion. Although, as we discussed in Chapter 1, when we discussed the principles of encoding and decoding developed by Stuart Hall, encoders can never be certain how their message will be decoded, the use of mega-events to leverage a national 'brand' internationally has become a central strategic objective in the hosting of such events (Grix and Houlihan, 2014; Grix and Lee, 2013). A rhetoric of redefining a nation's international standing, combined with internal benefits to health, social cohesion and well-being, interlaces the event with utopian expectations (which are rarely met). The rhetoric is, however, commonly deployed and illuminates a connection between mega-events and a state's use of so-called 'soft power' strategies. We will discuss the governmentality of soft power, and its use internally and transnationally in what some refer to as 'public diplomacy' (Nye, 2008; Signitzer and Coombs, 1992) and 'cultural diplomacy' (Ang *et al.*, 2015; Feignbaum, 2001), respectively, later. However, first we consider the connection between mega-events and political utopianism, focusing on two examples: the Olympic Games and the World's Fair.

Mega-events, utopianism and 'soft power'

In this section we begin by looking at the connection between mega-events and power, and how that links to a rhetoric of the utopian state. We then consider how that power is articulated as 'soft power' both internally – through state's population – and externally – by framing itself as an international 'brand'. To do that, we provide overviews of two mega-events that, while distinctive, share a number of characteristics. We have chosen the Olympic Games and the World's Fair to show that mega-events are not always sport based: they can also encompass the arts, science and commerce (although sport mega-events do tend to combine greater spending with potentially higher financial returns, and they generally attract larger global audiences). After outlining some basic statistics for recent iterations of each event, we consider their historical origins in order to show their rootedness in the political economy of their time, and how the utopian rhetoric that is associated with them is a fundamental element in the exertion of 'soft power'.

The Olympic Games, which are held in a different host country every two years (alternating between a winter and a summer games), is a prototypical event for mainstream event studies research. Such mega-sporting occasions attract huge global audiences. As mentioned, the IOC estimated the TV viewing audience for the Sochi Winter Olympics at 2.8 billion, while Statista (2012) suggests that 4.8 billion people watched the London 2012 Summer Olympics and Paralympics. Similarly, London's Olympic 'village' was built on a massive scale: spread over approximately 250 hectares, at its peak it accommodated some 17,000 athletes from 205 countries. The World's Fair – or Expo – which was most recently hosted by Yeosu, South Korea, is modest in comparison. No TV rights associated with this 2012 event were sold, and it had a visitor footfall of just 8.2 million over a three-month period. In total, 115 countries participated, 98 of which had their own stands, and there were 80 viewing halls on the 25-hectare site. The South Korean government claimed that a total of 79,000 people were employed in the construction, maintenance and delivery of the event.[5]

Both events require substantial infrastructural investment, and both aim to attract large global audiences and significant media attention. They create microcosms of the world through global participation and individual state representation. Both are awarded to host nations through a process of international competition. In the case of the Olympic Games tendering progresses to hosting through a selection panel drawn from the IOC, based in Lausanne, Switzerland. The body overseeing the selection of host city for the World's Fair is the Bureau International des Expositions (BIE), based in Paris. Unlike the IOC, the BIE has no charter or unifying principles of membership, but both organizations express a desire to benefit humanity. Thus, Article Two of the IOC's Fundamental Principles of Olympism states: 'The goal of Olympism is to place sport at the service of the harmonious development of humankind, with a view to promoting a peaceful society concerned with the preservation of human dignity' (IOC, 2015: 12). Similarly, the BIE (2015) declares:

> Each Expo is a great opportunity to bring together experts and decision makers from the whole world around an important issue. Their thoughts, proposals and solutions are put together at the end of Expos in declarations, manuals etc. These documents constitute the core of the intellectual legacy of Expos and they aim at setting new guidelines for a more sustainable world.

As is commonly known, the Olympic Games date back to ancient Greece: founded around 776 BCE, they continued until 394 CE, when they were abolished by the Roman Emperor Theodosius I as part of his policy to impose Christianity as the dominant faith throughout the Roman Empire (Finley and Pleket, 1976). In antiquity the reach of the Games was quite small: participation was limited to free-born Greeks and the states taking part were all in close proximity to one another. During each Games a truce (*Ekecheiria*) between warring nations was called and the event itself would host political negotiations between the participating states (ibid.).

The modern Olympic Games, under the stewardship of the IOC, began in 1896, funded through a trust left to the Greek government by two entrepreneurial cousins – Evangelis and Konstantinos Zappas. After the first Games, the next few iterations were held as elements of the entertainment offered at the World's Fairs in Paris (1900) and St Louis (1904). The fourth Olympiad, held in London in 1908, was the first to feature athletes from every continent. However, even those early Games did not escape the political context in which they were staged. For instance, in 1908 Finland refused to participate in any competitions in which Russia participated; in 1916 the Summer Olympics, having been awarded to Berlin, was cancelled because of the First World War; and in 1920 Austria, Bulgaria, Germany, Hungary and Turkey were all excluded from the Antwerp Games because of their wartime allegiances (Guttman, 2002).

Prince Albert, the husband of Queen Victoria, had the idea for the first self-declared World's Fair, which took place in London in 1851. Described as 'an exhibition of the works of industry of all nations', the Great Exhibition – as it came to be known – was the first truly international exhibition of manufactured goods. According the Minihan (1977), it served the dual purpose of reinvigorating British manufacturing, which had been under severe pressure from the industrial growth on mainland Europe and in the United States, while robustly reasserting Britain's global political dominance.

Between 1851 and 1938, the primary theme of each World's Fair was the development of positive visions of the future through technological advancement. Their principal purpose was to promote the latest inventions and thereby support the manufacturing base of the host nation, with the focus a mix of international trade and technological spectacle (Finding and Pelle, 2008). They were industrialized variants on Matthew Arnold's principle for a civilized society (Arnold, 1999) – individual moral betterment through the display of the greatest and best of human (manufactured) achievement. After 1939, however, the focus of the events began to shift. While there was still a preponderance of technological innovation, each World's Fair began to draw on wider cultural themes to develop richer ideas for the formation of a better world. By 1967, the term 'World's Fair' was dropped and replaced by 'Expo' – a shortened version of the official full title, 'International and Universal Exposition' (Greenhalgh, 2011). This terminological shift also signalled a realignment: a movement away from the dual definition of 'fair', suggesting trade and spectacle, to a title that was more suggestive of sharing, learning and collaborative rationality.

Since 1988, there has been a clear move towards each host nation using Expo as part of its international relations/nation-branding strategy. For instance, de Groote (2005) suggests that Spain used its hosting of both an Expo and the Olympic Games in 1992 to position itself as a modern democracy and an active member of both the European Union and the wider global community (see also Martinez, 2010). This strategy is still prevalent, as can be seen in Brazil's hosting of the 2014 FIFA World Cup and the 2016 Olympic Games, as well as its (unsuccessful) bid for Expo 2020. The host of the next Expo at the time of writing – Astana, in Kazakhstan – could also be seen as following this line.

We have already noted that mega-events create a microcosmic world narrative, yet they also try to present a cohesive narrative of the host state. Such imaginaries of space, we argue, rest on unstated utopianism. Long-term conflict between states becomes concentrated into a temporary competition of style and imagineering (Expo) or elite national representatives (the Olympics). The highlight exhibit and the victorious athlete gain prestige for themselves and their home states for a set period, until a new challenger claims the title. Roles are clearly understood and demarcated: everyone knows their place in the structure of these imaginary spaces, and the contribution they should make to it. This is redolent of how Socrates portrays the utopian city-state he proposes in Book II of Plato's *Republic*. Described there, by Glaucon, as a 'city of pigs' (Plato, 1888), Socrates outlines how each member of this perfect state would respect the others' contributions, recognize how their part in the functioning of the nation benefits both themselves and others (as well as how others' contributions have the same effect) and, through that knowledge, collectively operate for the betterment of the whole community.

Significantly, Plato has his protagonist observe that such a state is an ideal. He continues by arguing that if we are to realize the best *possible* state, both appropriate administration and regulation are required. What legitimizes the operation of those functions is a shared vision. This leads Socrates to articulate what he calls a 'needful falsehood' (ibid.) – what has become known as the 'noble lie' – that sits at the very foundation of the state, rendering support for the actions of the state, and enabling its citizens to be self-regulating. In *The Republic* the Socratic 'noble lie' posits three characters of soul that are said to bear trace element of gold in its rulers, silver in warriors, and iron (or brass) in its labouring population. The resonance with sports mega-events seems quite transparent. Achievement is acknowledged through various metallic awards, with dope testing employed to ascertain whether the competitor has the mettle to deliver the output they have (or has the metal in their 'soul' been tainted?). But the principle that a binding set of ideals, which participants accept as truths, legitimizes the actions of those in positions of authority and opens up an expectation that participation requires self-discipline and self-governance runs through all mega-events. We have seen how the IOC has formulated a set of principles of Olympism to which all participating nations are meant to adhere, and how the BIE has devised a set of central aspirations that are meant to support every presentiment of an 'International and Universal Exposition'. But it is not just these events that suggest a connection between soft power and mega-events. In his discussion of the Burning Man festival – an arts and culture mega-event that places a philosophy of decentredness at the heart of its vision – Rojek (2013) points out that even this requires participants to adhere to ten key principles. The sharing of some form of Socratic myth not only works to unite participants but legitimizes the acts of those in authority while operating as a soft form of power that facilitates the self-governance of participants. It is a form of public diplomacy that makes a population governable through a means that is not overtly coercive.

The global character of mega-events means that soft power is articulated at a localized level, as public diplomacy in the host nation, but also transnationally, as an element of cultural diplomacy between states. Much of the literature that is interested in exploring the link between soft power and mega-events has tended to frame it within international relations – *place branding* as a means of realigning perceptions of a nation's place within the international community. For example, Grix (2012: 290) argues that the German hosting of the 2006 FIFA World Cup was accompanied by a 'series of long-term, carefully coordinated campaigns' that instrumentalized the event as a means of leveraging a more positive image of Germany across the world. This is contrasted with a more localized agenda of image building which Grix and Houlihan (2014) suggest was at work within the London 2012 Olympics. Meanwhile, Grix and Lee (2013) suggest that cultural diplomacy, as a form of soft power, is a primary contributing factor to the growing desire among emerging economies, such Brazil and South Africa, to host global mega-events. However, as Alekseyeva (2014) and Trubina (2015) have shown in their critiques of the Sochi Winter Olympics, the successful hosting of such events does not guarantee concomitant transnational credibility.

Though less abundant, a significant body of research indicates a strong connection between mega-events and soft power as public diplomacy. Gaffney (2010) suggests that from the announcement on 2 October 2009 that Rio was to host the 2016 Summer Olympics, the Brazilian government started to pursue its neo-liberalist economic agenda at an accelerating rate. This point is reiterated by Grix and Lee (2013) in their analysis of the 2010 FIFA World Cup in South Africa. Meanwhile, Bang-Shin (2012: 730) suggests that the rhetoric of a harmonious society, the public display of patriotic slogans and the creation of localized spectacles for regional and state consumption, which became progressively more overt in the lead-up to the 2008 Beijing Olympic Games, was a deliberate attempt to 'pacify social and political discontents rising out of economic inequalities, religious and ethnic tensions, and [an] urban–rural divide'. It is this use of soft power as public diplomacy to create an imaginary of the state as cohesive and united (which itself resonates strongly with the Platonic utopianism we discussed above) that Grix and Houlihan (2014) argue was the primary concern of the London 2012 Olympics.[6] However, as Maiello and Pasquinelli (2015) have suggested, event-based branding is a dialectical dynamic that also brings to the fore counter-hegemonic branding, articulated as dissent and protest. The relationship between mega-event, as governmental expression of soft power, and dissent is discussed in the next section.

Mega-events and dissent

In order to gain an enriched picture of the connections between mega-events and dissent, and consequently between power and *event*, we need to return to the discussions we had in the first two chapters which focused on conceptualizing *event* and developing a deeper understanding of its *spatial* relationships. By locating *event*, of whatever scale, in the operational concerns surrounding its delivery to an identified audience, anything that subverts that – challenges it, stands in its way – is necessarily problematic. Thus the close bonds between mainstream events management and event studies and an implicit neo-liberal agenda, by force of the logic of that very agenda, lead any analytic work in those fields to construe dissent as a factor that must be mitigated against – or in some cases, as we shall suggest shortly, commodified so that capitalist elites can create an imaginary of the dissenter as consumer and thereby strive to incorporate her/him within the wider paradigmatic frame of reference. CES replaces the operational construal of *event* with one that interprets it as something that intervenes in social structures, framing its spatiality as contested.

Events rupture and disrupt; they fundamentally expose discourses that are at work that are often obscured or hidden from view in our daily lives. Viewed in that way, dissent around anything portrayed as a 'planned event' seems a necessary concomitant. The grand narrative offered by the state that sits at the heart of the location branding for most mega-events is an abstraction that can be imposed only through violence – not necessarily violence expressed as some form of militarized intervention, although that is far from uncommon (Giulianotti and Klauser, 2010; Giulianotti *et al.*, 2015a), but cultural violence, whereby a hegemonic order is imposed (Bourdieu, 1992). Mega-events, by virtue of their scale and media presence, if nothing else, intervene extensively: land is acquired and reconfigured; new transportation programmes are developed and implemented; planning processes are reviewed and revised; colossal architectural investments are made with practical impacts on workforce practices, health-and-safety protocols and so forth. There are knock-on effects in design and associated developments in the fabrication of buildings, with new techniques investigated and utilized; security measures are evaluated and reinforced, where deemed necessary; restrictions on broadcast rights and media coverage are reviewed and amended; the list goes on and on. Many of these changes require revisions to policy and, possibly, new legislation.

A consequence of all this is that seeing the term 'event' as singular becomes increasingly problematic, because its character is more fractal than holistic. These and the myriad other interventions that form the framework for what might be called *the event* are themselves complex. They are multi-layered and bearers of multiple discourses around practice and how that practice interacts with the social and material world within which they operate. The characterization of *event* as 'that which intervenes' works seismically to shift the landscape of those discourses, made all the more pronounced by the articulation of the narrative surrounding the 'events', potentially exposing them to scrutiny and, thus, to challenge. These factors feature in Maiello and Pasquinelli's (2015: 116) analysis of 'the dialectical construction of city representation in Rio de Janeiro' during its preparations for the 2014 FIFA World Cup.

But the connection between mega-event and dissent (or more precisely between power, *event* and dissent) involves much more than simply the exposure of discursive relationships. A growing body of scholarship argues that the dialectical dynamics of representation proposed by Maiello and Pasquinelli (ibid.) are also, to some extent, co-created; that the hegemonic branding of the event and the counter-hegemonic alternate branding(s) – dissent – work to constitute the discourses of each other. At a pragmatic level Giulianotti *et al.* (2015b), in their study of public opposition to the London 2012 Olympic Games, hint at how the interplay between preparatory events in the lead-up to the Games and dissenting counter-events intensified how both of these were expressed. Liao (forthcoming) considers how a production depicting the siege of Troy presented by a national theatre company in an abandoned winery in Huashan, Taiwan, resulted in mutually defining hegemonic and counter-hegemonic articulations of space. The ensuing public protest and state counter-protest led, ultimately, to governmental policy change and the emergence of new narratives of space. Meanwhile, Pavoni and Sebastiano (forthcoming) critically reflect on two events – a large-scale regional event in Milan and the 2010 FIFA World Cup in South Africa – and suggest that event and dissent co-constitute a shared discourse, albeit a somewhat paradoxical one where there is no necessary connection at the level of ontology between the actors.

At the heart of these studies there seems to be a complex interaction between several theoretical frameworks. There are definite resonances with the ideas of Gramsci and his analysis of hegemony as cultural domination, which concluded that the power of a hegemonic culture is achievable only when there is a simultaneous formation of a counter-hegemonic, oppressed culture. Also at work are ideas of legitimation through a Habermasian instrumentalization of rationality, which attempts to frame communicative reason by compressing its three dimensions of validity – normative rightness, theorizations of truth and expressions of truthfulness (Habermas, 1997) – in the narrative of the state which the event is meant to present. There are also links to de Certeau's theorization of *strategy* and *tactics*. In *The Practice of Everyday Life* (de Certeau, 1988) the strategic domination of daily life and the *tactics* deployed in individual, and collective, subversion of that *strategy* are not causally connected – in the sense that one or the other causes its counterpart to come into existence. Both emerge from any analysis of daily life that is undertaken: they mutually constitute what counts as daily life. Similarly, an interpretation of event as 'that which intervenes in social space' – which is itself understood as contested and multi-layered, and thereby has the potential to expose those discourses that are commonly either obscured or hidden – would suggest that *events* that form the mega-event and *events* that constitute dissent associated with that 'mega-event' are not causally connected to each other; rather, they are co-dependent and co-emergent from some more primordial event/rupture.

We argue that the articulation of power constitutes that more primordial event. In order to gain a deeper understanding of that, we need to return to some core concepts which connect Foucault's formulations of governmentality, biopolitics and parrhesia with Habermasian ideas of instrumental and communicative rationality.

Communicative rationality

In his later lectures at the Collège de France Foucault (2011a, 2011b) claimed that governmentality was the *art of government*, but not 'government' in a sense that equated it with the politico-administrative functions of the state. Governmentality combines his previous analysis of panoptic techniques for control of the self through the presumptive gaze of the other – his focus in *Discipline and Punish* (1991) – the management of the other *en masse* (biopolitics, as developed in 2008) and power–knowledge, which formed the foundation of *The Birth of the Clinic* (1973) and the three-volume *History of Sexuality* (1976, 1984, 1986b).

Central to this project is the view that power, and the discourses that inform it, can manifest itself by becoming internalized. In so doing Foucault's interpretation of the body as a site of self-regulation is adjusted, framing governmentality not as externalized power but as 'the way in which one conducts the conduct of men' (Foucault, 2008: 186). The panopticon of his earlier work is relocated – moved from a position of individual behaviour steered by the ever-possible disciplinary gaze of those without, it is drawn *into* the subject, as constituted through power–knowledge relations of the dominant discourse, to become self-surveillance. In so doing a society is rendered governable.

Nikolas Rose and Peter Miller have developed these ideas further in their critique of neo-liberalism (Rose and Miller, 1992, 2008), which, they argue, develops technologies of control through structuring the boundaries – and setting the limits – of rationality to define the field of possible action. We thus become self-governing through the freedom apprehended through that frame of reference provided by the discursive context in which we act and interact. They write: 'Through an analysis of the intricate inter-dependencies between political rationalities and governmental technologies, we can begin to understand the multiple and delicate networks that connect the lives of individuals, groups and organizations to the aspirations of authorities in the advanced liberal democracies of the present' (Rose and Miller, 1992: 175–6). Those 'governmental technologies' reorientate the pragmatics of meaning that lie at the heart of the life-world by instrumentalizing communicative relationships within the public spheres in which we are engaged; hence the 'political rationalities' to which Rose and Miller refer. However, following de Certeau and Stuart Hall, we can be clear that such attempts to delimit the boundaries of rationality can never fully succeed. There is always a capacity for the disclosure of alternative world-views and, as Foucault (2011b) would put it, the possibility of speaking truth to power – parrhesia. This potentiality for alternative communicative rationalities is clearest in those communicative relationships in which we engage through activities associated with our non-work (leisure) time.

Stebbins (1982, 1997, 2006, 2009, 2014) identifies three principal nodes within a continuum of leisure engagement: casual, project-based and serious leisure. Casual leisure is short term and usually has an immediate payback for the individual's participation. It encompasses multiple forms of recreational activity, entertainment and sociable interaction that are intrinsically simple and not practised as part of some greater, longer-term, project. More complex forms of leisure, which can be single activities or multiple, but are always infrequent, are described as project-based. This form of leisure requires much greater planning and effort than casual leisure. It included such activities as purchasing and constructing an item of flat-packed furniture, attending a music festival, planning a dinner party for a special occasion, and so forth. The key difference between a casual and a project-based activity lies in the latter's connection to some wider project. Attending a theatrical production may be seen as casual leisure, but if you spend time planning and preparing for that visit for a particular purpose (for example, to celebrate an anniversary, to improve your understanding of the story, or to see a favourite celebrity who is appearing in the production), then it is more accurate to categorize it as project-based leisure.

Serious leisure is significantly different from both casual and project-based leisure. Participation in an activity as serious leisure means engaging with a distinctive social world – seeking out and acquiring specific skill sets in order to immerse oneself more fully in the interactions associated with the activity. Engagement at this level entails some understanding of hierarchies associated with the pursuit and the acquisition of the linguistic and discursive forms of interaction that are appropriate to it. Those engaged in such activity will be able to identify special benefits they construe as emanating from their participation, though they must also be prepared to persevere with the activity despite apparent setbacks. The activity carries with it a potential to develop some form of leisure career, and there will be a strong connection between regular, persistent engagement and both personal and interpersonal senses of identity.

Such characteristics were found in people who are active, at both national and regional levels, in anti-war movements (Lamond *et al.*, 2015). In every interview we conducted we found strong indicators in the narratives of engagement they offered to suggest that deeper involvement within the campaigning work of such social movements commonly turned on a Damascene experience. Such a thorough reassessment of the relationship between identity and the world in which the person lives marks a Žižekian *rupture*, a reordering of the *lifeworld*, a critical shift in the individual's *form of life*. The pragmatics of meaning may not be 'universal' in a strict Habermasian sense, but they clearly demarcate the formation of a public sphere, and a communicative rationality, that would indicate such deep-rooted serious leisure participation carries with it a change in axiological and ontological orientation, and inclusion within an epistemic community of practice that has the potential to challenge a dominant hegemony. It is thus through individual and collective engagement in serious leisure that participation can confront the connection between event and power. The emergence of alternative world-views which such activity, at that level, generates carries with it the potential for exposure of the discursive relationships, and *instrumental* rationality, that a governmental *conduct of conduct* might deploy to secure the governability of those whom it constitutes as subjects.

Conclusion

In this chapter we have considered the relationship between events and power. While that connection can be understood as taking place at all scales of 'event', we recognized that it can be brought into sharpest focus by concentrating on what mainstream events management and event studies categorize under the rubric of mega-event. Hence, it was important to clarify what might be classified as a 'mega-event' by discussing the various definitions that appear in the literature. While there is no broad agreement on scale, there are several points of commonality, especially concerning audience and media representation. We also noted that while some authors consider political factors, the perspective is distorted by both a preference for operational concerns and tacit deference to the perspective of a dominant elite.

When we began to investigate the messages mega-events attempt to convey we were led into a consideration of event as ideologically formulated place/state branding. Within developed and emerging neo-liberal economies we found echoes of this in Richard Florida's work on the mobilities of a 'creative class'. Through a discussion of two global-scale 'managed events' – the Olympic Games and the World's Fair/Expo – in which we considered their origins and most recent expressions, we discerned a connection between mega-event, utopianism and soft power. In establishing a link between how events are used to create an imaginary of the state – one that may be used as a form of international cultural diplomacy and national public diplomacy – and Plato's discussion of an (ostensibly realizable) utopia, we were also prompted to reflect on the dynamic dialectical relationship between event and dissent.

While our formulation of event as 'that which intervenes in social structures' enabled us to gain a better understanding of the complex and interlaced linkages between power, event and dissent, we were still faced with the problem of establishing how a pervasive governmentality, or politico-cultural hegemony, could be confronted. How is it possible to speak truth to power when hegemonic power itself establishes the framework within which we can articulate our freedom? In addressing that concern we turned our attention to a consideration of the communicative rationalities that are epiphenomenal to the discursive relationships that characterize serious leisure. The Damascene experience of people who are deeply engaged in any activity that could be described as serious leisure led us to suggest that such engagement may form new public spheres where alternative communicative rationalities could come to the fore. In consequence, the connectivity between power and event might be contested. Elements of the issues we have raised in this chapter are discussed further in Chapters 7, 8 and 11, where we will ask if an emancipatory event studies is feasible.

Notes

1. A term used in computational linguistics, 'n gram' refers to any continuous sequence of lexical items, where the number of items is specified by the search – i.e. it is not pre-set.
2. Note that we are still dealing with very small numbers. For instance, in 1979 the result for 'mega-event' was 0.000000003 per cent, and in 2008 it was 0.0000016309 per cent of Google's corpus in English. The dataset the Google n gram viewer used for this search ended in 2008.
3. Muller (2015) proposes a classification that extends to 'Gig-Events'. For the purposes of this Chapter we are merging 'mega' and 'giga' events under the same title of 'mega-events'.
4. Aspects of this will be addressed later in this chapter, and more fully in Chapter 7.
5. Data on the Olympics is drawn from various IOC reports, available through their portal: www.olympic.org; data on the Yeosu Expo is from Expo 2012 (2012).
6. Also discussed in a recent paper on the use of soft power by different political systems at various stages of economic development (Grix *et al.*, 2015).

5 Events and memory

Introduction

The expression 'If you can remember the sixties you weren't there', variously attributed to the clown peace activist Wavy Gravy, the singer–songwriter Grace Slick and the comedian and actor Robin Williams, is a trope familiar to many. Through multiple formulations, the phrase is applied to a peculiar inverse relationship between certain forms of event participation and the capacity to recall those events. It suggests a sort of authenticity to personal presence through the absence of memory. Alternatively, we have multinational businesses devoted to the creation of objects that formally and informally articulate, and frequently steer, the memory of events in particular ways. There seems no end of stuff churned up to concretize the memory of an event: T-shirts, DVDs, key-rings, memory sticks – the list goes on and on. As well as tangible products there are intangible opportunities to document your presence at an event. The social web is rife with event memory gateways. Scroll down any summer festival site and you will find links to Facebook, Twitter, Instagram, Pinterest, Google+ and YouTube,[1] as well as opportunities to tag photos from the event, post blogs, participate in forums, and many more activities. Events and memory are very intimately acquainted. In this chapter we explore the connections between event and memory in order to reach a clearer understanding of the part memory plays within CES.

The study of memory is a complex and multifaceted field that encompasses disciplines as diverse a neuroscience and the philosophy of mind, postmodern theories of space and postcolonial literary theory. A full analysis of the linkages between event and memory would be neither possible (within the restrictions of a single book chapter) nor desirable, as such detailed reflection would move us too far from our desired objective. So wide is the potential scope for a thorough discussion of the study of memory that such an undertaking would, in addition, be vastly beyond the shared competencies of the present authors. Instead, in this chapter we provide a somewhat idiosyncratic summary of the links between differing approaches to the study of memory and mainstream events management and event studies research. That overview is then combined with some alternative approaches, which come to the fore because of how they seem, in principle at least, to connect to the way we have been discussing a critical approach to the study of events.

In the first section we consider memory as an individual capacity. Beginning with a consideration of neuro-cognitivist approaches to memory, we develop this into a discussion of the *act* of remembering and remembrance. This takes us from the use of 'memory' as a biological process to its significant connection to the social world. If we adopt an internal and external metaphor, we move from memory viewed as inside the individual to how it is externally expressed. Next, we explore three key articulations of memory by pursuing this external-ization of memory metaphor. Starting with a consideration of how memory is externalized, as the articulation of individual and collective identity, we consider the linkages between memory and temporality before considering its connection to spatiality, and in particular some of those ideas of spatiality that were developed in Chapter 2.

The third section considers more closely the potentialities of considering the links between memory and event that emerge from adopting a critical approach to the study of events. We begin by considering the relationship between the experience/transformational economy and the commodification of memory in contemporary events management practice, as well as much of the work under-taken within the dominant paradigm within event studies. Having suggested a strong link between individual memory and mainstream events management and event studies research – through the latter's association with Pine and Gilmore's (1999) ideas on the *experience* and *transformational economy* – we conclude by asking if CES needs to have its own distinctive take on theories of memory, and discussing whether we now have a clearer understanding of the part memory plays within CES.

Approaches to the study of memory

Memory as an individual capacity

When discussing memory, it is common to associate it immediately with some capacity of the mind, although it would be more accurate to say, in our current era, that this has become synonymous with an activity of the *brain*. Pick up any psychology textbook[2] and you will come across a standard psychological inter-pretation of memory. Within that framework it is regarded as a central epistemic function of an individual's brain. So, in Gross (2015: 281), we read: 'We could define memory as the retention of learning and experience. As Blackmore (1988) says: "In the broadest sense, learning is the acquisition of knowledge and memory is the storage of an internal representation of that knowledge."' Within such a construal the study of memory becomes the analysis and modelling of three inter-connected aspects of information processing: encoding, storage and retrieval. While this metaphor resonates strongly with both bureaucratic and computational imagery, it is also consistent with how we commonly discuss memory: 'I know the answer to that, I read it only yesterday. Oh . . . it's on the tip of my tongue,' and so forth. But, as we shall see, this is not the only way we engage with and express our relationship to memory. Even if we accept a perspective that holds memory to be some kind of fancy filing cabinet, a mass storage device for a high-spec computer or a pantry of the future,[3] the simply stated format of encoding–storage–retrieval is only an abstract peak on a very complex iceberg.

Our common usage tends to focus on the storage and retrieval aspects of memory. Hence, we are more inclined to view it as a cognitive process, with our ability to reiterate details or our struggle to bring a piece of information to mind understood as a conscious act. However, by focusing on that aspect of memory most commonly identified as linked to the activity of thinking, the base structures of memory that are postulated as forming its ground level are overlooked. The development of CAT, PET and fMRI[4] has enabled us to produce detailed models of how the brain responds and reacts to a huge range of stimuli. Those models form the foundation for more nuanced descriptions of the functioning brain, going well beyond its capacity to store information in the short or long term.

Sperling (1963) hypothesized the presence of very short-term sensory memory. Such memory, he argued, sits outside of our cognitive control. It captures multiple source sense data within a fraction of a second and enables us to process that information in such a way as to render an object as an identifiable *something*. We are not necessarily conscious of the encoding and retrieval of such memories. This is similar to how Tulving (1985) characterizes 'procedural memory', in that there is less focus on the specifics of what make something a unique and *memorable* object and much more focus on motor skills and non-conscious motor skills. Usually it is only when something impedes or challenges such memories that we become aware of them. However, when this happens the process ceases to be sensory or procedural and becomes instead an element of other, more complex, memory processes. This approach is very similar to the use Bertrand Russell (1967) attributes to sense-data when considering the difference between appearance and reality in his early discussion of the basis for epistemology. In its application the principle struggles to overcome what are referred to as 'binding paradoxes': that is, how to account for our experience of objects as unique things composed of multiple sensations, which is the biological basis for how we are able to separate the different sensory elements of an object (known as the segmentation paradox) while also having the capacity to cluster those sensations into discrete objects (the combination paradox). While this capacity is apparent from our actual experience, the biological basis of it remains contested (Ding *et al.*, 2015; Kinsey *et al.*, 2011; Usher and Donnelly, 1998).

Experimental psychology began to investigate the biological basis of short- and long-term memory in the 1950s, around the time when advances were being made in the storage of data in computing. Consequently, much of the language associated with this research resonates with that of computing. Short-term memory is understood as an operational level of memory that (assuming no prior rehearsal) facilitates temporary information storage and quick retrieval of data for just a few seconds at a time. Experiments undertaken by Conrad and his colleagues in the mid-1960s (Conrad, 1964; Conrad *et al.*, 1965; Conrad and Rush, 1965) suggested that short-term memory relied on the existence of identifiable differences in the acoustic and visual nature of the material presented to participants. Material that was visually or acoustically similar was not retrieved as easily as material whose elements were recognizably dissimilar. However, as Singh and Bookless (1997) suggest, much of that research was based on what could be learned from single- and multiple-patient case studies: that is, conclusions were drawn from cases of impaired memory function in situations where there was some element of localized brain damage. By contrast, recent technological developments mean the functioning brains of healthy individuals can now be scanned. Kim's (2011) meta-analysis of seventy-four fMRI studies has highlighted areas where specific brain activity can be associated with subsequent memory or subsequent forgetting (which, interestingly, are termed 'encoding failures'). Long-term memory is most commonly associated with rehearsal and repetition. However, as we shall see later, significantly for the commodification of event experiences, there is also an identifiable connection between short, intense periods of emotion and the capacity to retain memories (Peters *et al.*, 2007; Wagner *et al.*, 2007).

Alan Baddeley's research into 'working memory' (Baddeley, 1966; Baddeley and Dale, 1966), which he defines as a combination of short- and long-term memory that encompasses the 'storage and manipulation' of information (Baddeley, 2012: 4), suggests that the basis of long-term memory is different from that of short-term memory. Our capacity to store substantial pieces of information and retrieve them, Baddeley argues, is rooted in semantic differences: that is, our ability to recognize and experience differences in meaning. This is significant because it hints that a richer understanding of memory demands more than a neurological description. We now move away from a consideration of memory as a straightforwardly internal operation of the brain, and instead focus on the link between memory and communicative relationships.

Communicative memory

The work of Baddeley and others – such as Johnson *et al.*'s (1974) research into the significance of contextual knowledge as a prerequisite for comprehending information (and consequently accommodating and remembering it) – has been instrumental in suggesting an experimental foundation for a contemporary turn towards communicative and collective memory within the field of memory studies. While much of the research done in psychology and neuroscience has concentrated on how memory works within the neural system – how it is *embodied* – its focus tends to omit any consideration of how memories become *embedded* within groups, communities and cultures. This is not to suggest that one is, in some sense, superior, or more representative of an assumed 'reality', than the other. It is rather to claim that both provide valuable descriptive insights that can help us make sense of the world, so a discussion of one without the other would be incomplete.

Drawing on a distinction suggested by Walter Benjamin, Griggio (2015) argues that meaningful memories go beyond the individual lived experience (*erlebnis* in Benjamin). Memorable experiences are enriched because they include elements of *erfahrung*: that is, they are more meaningful as a consequence of being shared and communicated with others. In her analysis of the experience of Vittangi

Moose Park in Swedish Lapland, Griggio (ibid.: 244) goes on to argue that it is by 'taking pictures and sharing them [that] ... visitors not only consume place, landscapes and experiences but also produce and reproduce them'. In other words, memory is not solely reducible to the neural pathways of an individual; another important aspect of it is the sharing and communicating of experiences with others.

That memory is a dynamic mix of the individual and socially communicative supports Feindt *et al.*'s (2014) suggestion that it operates across two layers of entanglement, both of which show it to have a strong connection to language and social action. Their work rests on a shift away from the encoding–storage–retrieval frame of reference and towards the act of remembering. Synchronically, they argue that every act of remembering locates that individual at a juncture of multiple social frames of reference – consequently, they become immersed in a polyphony of concurrent interpretation of the past. Diachronically, the re-presentation of the past, as an articulation of that which is remembered, becomes expressed through multiple, and shifting, modalities of reproduction. In order to support the study of memory through these entanglements they suggest the use of four heuristics: establishing chronologies; exploring points of conflict; examining generational change; and including elements of self-reflexivity. As Bietti (2009) has suggested, it is the interactional character of communicative memory that is central to how it is produced and reproduced.

Since the mid-nineties, Aleida Assmann and her husband Jan have suggested that communicative memory is insufficient for understanding more complex forms we might consider under a broader heading of 'remembrance'. In various articles and books (Assmann, 1996, 2008; Assmann and Czaplicka, 1995), written together or with peers, they have suggested that the events of the twentieth century, though not exclusively those of that period, are such that communicative memory is too everyday to be a useful framework. What is required, they suggest, is a conceptualization of collective or cultural memory.

Collective and cultural memory

Brockmeier (2010) maintains that the ideas that have dominated psychological and individualistic approaches to memory are falling apart. Earlier models, which construed individual identity in terms of it being some sort of organic archive, are evaporating. We are moving from an era when the primary conceptualization of memory was anchored in its epistemic functionality to one that understands it as more akin to participation in a cultural ontology.

Though most explicitly discussed within tourism, with the growth of thanatourism, sometimes referred to as 'dark tourism' (Jamal and Robinson, 2011), and within some sections of mobility studies (Hannam and Knox, 2011), such formulations of memory can be seen as undercurrents in events management's and event studies' interest in the 'experience economy' (Pine and Gilmore, 1999). As Brockmeier (2010) and others have argued, within all those fields the root of collective and cultural memory seems to be an association with, and sometimes participation in, a shared narrative. Tourism has been more overtly impacted by this construal of memory than research in events. For instance, in tourism a substantial volume of work has been done on sites of genocide and conflict (Causevic and Lynch, 2011; Smith, 2003; Stone, 2012). The impact of volunteer tourism in countries described as 'developing' has also been extensively studied, as has the dilution of cultural memory through processes of transculturation. Both Kaiser *et al.* (2014) and Santos (2015) suggest that the promulgation of strong narratives of national identity through various modalities, not exclusively tourism, has been applied to ease a perceived burden from the violent histories of authoritarian and democratic states.

An association between memory and narrative within events research has been more nuanced: its focus has relied on conflating a collective 'memory' with a shared 'experience'. The former, in mainstream events management and event studies, becomes synonymous with the individual buying into (in most cases literally) the narrative of a shared, highly orchestrated experience of the 'event'. Such an idea of *cultural* memory thus rests on a construal of *culture* that is framed by a presupposed 'way of life'[5] that the 'event' is ostensibly articulating. Of course, for the memory to work effectively for the 'event' the latter must be well managed – poorly maintained portable toilets and campylobacter are unlikely to lead to return visits or good word-of-mouth PR.

By equating the management of events with the creation of memorable experiences, memory becomes a commodity that can be articulated as something identifiable, to some extent measurable, and essentially marketable (sellable). It is, according to Hallmann and Zehrer (2014), the striving for 'authentic and memorable experiences' that enhances customer satisfaction and helps to 'create a unique selling proposition' for an event. Such a framing of memory abstracts it out from it being an epistemic function to becoming a means of commodifying individual ontic presence as part of the *culture* of the event. Guex and Crevoisier (2014) have argued that this forms the central economic driver in the experience economy. Yet it is also a crucial element in the next phase, identified by Pine and Gilmore (1999): the move from an *experiential* to a *transformational* economy. In that frame the objectification of ontic presence is not solely the selling of experiences but the documenting of a point of transformation. The DVD, T-shirt, flag and so on become more than the means of *retrieving* the memory of an experience; instead, they are signposts for memorializing a personal *transformation*.

While it is important to consider the commodification of memory[6] when developing an account of its connection to event, we will return to that later in the chapter. To lead us on, and deepen that discussion, the next section adopts a wider perspective and addresses the different social modes through which collective and cultural memories operate.

The modes of memory

Having discussed a number of approaches to memory studies, and how they relate to dominant attitudes in approaching the study of events in events management and event studies, we now turn to locating memory in the social dimensions that act as its modes of orientation. Though not exhaustive, or completely separable, we identify those modes as: temporality, spatiality and identity (both individual and collective).

Individually, memory operates through time as a central autobiographical element within our distinct personal identity. Consequently, it may well appear obvious to suggest that memory has a temporal mode. However, in addition to being central to cognitive models of autobiographical memory, temporality is manifest in the presentiment of the past in the present at communicative, political and cultural levels (Assmann and Shortt, 2012). Jan Assmann (2010: 122) suggests that each of these temporal aspects of memory has its own time-range:

> In the case of individual memory, this is equivalent to the time-range of an individual consciousness; communicative memory is typically limited to three interacting generations or 80 to 100 years; political memory lasts as long as the correspondent political institution, which may be as short as 12 years in the case of Nazi Germany, or over 200 years as in the case of the French Republic ... The typical time-range of cultural memory is 3,000 years, going back, in the West, to Homer and the Biblical authors and, in the East, to the Rigveda, the Buddha and other cultural foundations.

We need to be careful here. The argument is not that memory is seamlessly reproduced through lenses of such varying lengths; nor are Assmann's numbers meant to be absolute and definitive; rather, his suggestion is that the different modes of articulating the temporality of memory offer us various frames of reference through which memory echoes and reverberates. In the process it evolves, becoming distorted and skewed in different directions, and frequently forming an imaginary of that past rather than a re-presentation of it. Viewing memory in its temporal mode, examining the enunciation of a past within the present, is meant to allow us to make sense – that is, enable us to generate a relative coherent narrative – of how we behave, interact and interpret past events as part of a shared *way of life* (Williams, 1977).

Within the study of events, memory's connection with time is most apparent at points of memorialization and repetition. The State Opening of Parliament, 5 November firework displays in the UK, Holocaust Memorial Day, Remembrance Sunday, and the anniversary of the destruction of the World Trade Center in New York are just a few examples of how the past becomes embedded, through events, in the routines of the state. Examples of how memorialization is also apparent in routines of behaviour within events can also be discerned, such as the patterns of turn-taking at Prime Minister's Question Time, structures of politeness and hierarchies of order (for example, those found in familial rites of passage, whether religious or secular). Events that repeat also generate modes of temporal memory, both formally and informally. It would be absurd to imagine an opening ceremony of the Olympic Games where the head of the national organizing committee simply took the mike and said, 'Thanks for coming. Here are the teams.' Surely there has not been a single FIFA World Cup over the last fifty years when an English commentator (or pub philosopher) has not, at some point, referenced the national team's 'success' in 1966, or indeed its subsequent defeats to 'the Germans' on penalties.

Communicatively, institutionally, culturally and linguistically events articulate the past in the present. It is, however, not simply temporality that orientates the social mode of memory. Interlaced with it is an associated dimension of space. Memory's orientation to time is sustainable only in communicative, social and cultural interaction at the level of the organic body. A consequence of its rootedness in the body, or sequence number of organic bodies, is that it remains unstable. Stanković (2014: 89) argues memory remains in an unstable state until it is externalized: it requires 'specific material carriers and transmitters . . . apart from the living organism'.

Though not intuitively obvious, space is where traces of memory become deposited (Assmann and Shortt, 2012); where shared memories that may not be individually retrievable become articulated through their spatial traces. The French historian Pierre Nora (1996) suggests that space becomes place through the creation of *lieux de mémoire* (realms of memory), where memory becomes externalized and anchored as part of how communities and cultures enunciate their past. Paul Ricoeur (2004: 151) writes:

> It is on the scale of urbanism that we best catch sight of the work of time in space. A city brings together in the same space different ages, offering to our gaze a sedimented history of tastes and cultural forms. The city gives itself as both to be seen and to be read . . . its public spaces, its named spaces, invite commemorations and ritualized gatherings.

It is the connection between spatiality and memory that makes the city, in the terms we considered in Chapter 2, an urban palimpsest (Huyssen, 2003). Space is heterotopic (Foucault, 1986a), however, the traces of memory inscribed in space may not be erased but do become overwritten, presenting us with the 'sedimented history' to which Ricoeur refers. That overwriting, to borrow an expression from Proust, *sleeps* and waits to be awakened through, in Ricoeur's terms, 'commemorations and ritualized gatherings' – that is, events. To illustrate this further, let us consider an example: *Troy, Troy . . . Taiwan*.

Taiwan is an island off the east coast of the People's Republic of China (PRC). The twentieth century was a period of significant political turmoil in East Asia. Beginning the century with a predominantly Chinese population under Japanese occupation, the island became part of the Republic of China (RoC) after Japan's defeat in 1945. However, civil war resulted in Chiang Kai-shek setting up a one-party Chinese Nationalist government in Taiwan in 1949, with Taipei as its capital, seceding from the Communist Party-controlled PRC. Taiwan still maintains its status as the RoC. Tensions between the two states have frequently escalated into open conflict, usually centred on the sea that lies between the two nations – the Taiwan Strait. One-party, military rule was maintained on Taiwan until the mid-1980s, when a long period of increased political liberalization began. However, with increasing democratization came renewed claims from the PRC that the two nations should be reunited, with Taiwan coming under the dominion of Beijing.

Troy, Troy . . . Taiwan – a theatrical reinterpretation of Homer's *Iliad*, created by Wang Rong-Yu and the Golden Bough Theatre Company – was staged in the deserted Huashan Winery in 1997. The show premiered during a period of increased tension between China and Taiwan: over the previous two years the PRC had carried out military exercises in the Taiwan Strait, close to Taiwan. Built by the Japanese, the winery had become a playground for the RoC's Nationalist Party elite after the war. Abandoned in 1987, as that elite's power had started to evaporate, the site had been left unattended ever since, its dereliction echoing the embattled city of Troy and resonating with the ghosts of former occupations. Performatively, the production combined a faithful re-enactment of the mythic siege of Troy, as presented in Homer's epic, with traditional Taiwanese opera and costumes.

The prior inscribed memory of the space, its association with colonial rule and the militaristic repression of national identity, was not denied, but this was overwritten with deeper memories that transcended the relatively limited space of the winery to become an articulation of older cultural memories of pre-Japanese, Chinese and (even earlier) European occupation. Initially the state administration acted negatively towards the event. However, under substantial pressure from ordinary people, national media and artist activists, the penalties imposed on those involved in the production were eventually lifted and the site began its transformation into what has, since 2007, become known as the Huashan 1914 Creative Park.[7] Through the performance of *Troy, Troy . . . Taiwan* the space came to articulate multiple layers of memory – moving beyond those that could be identifiably located within the organic bodies of those present. While connected to the temporal mode of memory, it also moved beyond that – speaking to both a present and a future. The layers of time – both actual and (through the presentation of mythic events) imaginary – were compressed within the space of the deserted winery but simultaneously spilled out, breaching its geographic boundaries, to become expressions of cultural and individual identity. As Stanković (2014: 92) maintains, 'Apart from the active memories within the spaces of memory, other memories exist as well, but they could not be perceived without additional interpretations, whether because they are only partly obvious or are related to the group that once existed.' The performance thus became a spatial marker that facilitated a heterotopic space (Foucault, 1986a), where a *sleeping* memory – the absent past – was awakened to become part of a layered present (Huyssen, 2003). In so doing memory was expressed not just through a temporal mode or an externalized spatial mode, but also through an externalized mode of individual memory and identity.

Suggesting that one mode of memory is the externalization of individual memory might seem paradoxical. It seems to imply that we exist neurologically beyond our bodies. However, such a claim is only metaphorically correct. In the current age we are all highly networked. Such individual networked connections may be explicitly produced by ourselves through social media (via such established platforms as Twitter, Facebook, Instagram, Pinterest and so forth) or implicitly through the digital traces we leave by making mobile phone calls, online purchases, withdrawing cash from ATMs and such like. Such are the digital neural systems of which we are consciously and unconsciously a part that the means by which we encode–store–retrieve information can no longer be contained by the biochemical/ bio-electric systems bounded by the material body of the individual. Individual identity, as a product of autobiographical memory, like spatiality in *Troy, Troy . . . Taiwan*, is embodied in the organic body but simultaneously breaches its organic boundaries. The identity mode of memory, together with its temporal and spatial modes, results in what could be construed as a Jacquardian self:[8] that is, one that is a complex and shifting expression of the layered temporal and spatial modes of memory; organically stored and retrievable memories, as well as those digital connections that extend the neural network of the body. It could be argued, as Socrates does when extolling the god Theuth's[9] invention of writing – presented in the Platonic dialogue the *Phaedrus* (Plato, 1973) – that this is not really *memory* but managed *forgetting*. In Socrates' account Theuth claims that writing will make Egyptians wiser and give them better memories. Thamus counters that it will have the opposite effect: he suggests that humanity will become forgetful as it starts to rely on the written word over the spoken. This, however, is only partly correct, because those externalized individual, networked memories are not forgotten. As with memory in its temporal and spatial modes, they are merely *sleeping* – waiting to be awoken by some external stimulus.

Memory and critical event studies

Now, let us return to the central question that was set out at the start of this chapter: what part does memory play within CES? We have considered a number of ways of thinking about memory, and have suggested how they can be understood as operating within mainstream events management and event studies. That discussion hinges on the idea that the creation of *memorable experiences* is central to the dominant frame of reference within those fields. According to Pine and Gilmore (1999), 'developed economies' (for which we can read neo-liberal economies) are at a point of transition. Having grown through commodity-, goods- and service-based economies, we are now, they argue, in the age of the experience economy. But they do not view this as the end point. The eschatological goal, which they see as becoming ever more present, is the 'transformational economy':

> When you customize an experience to make it just right for an individual – providing exactly what he or she needs right now – you cannot help *changing* that individual. When you customize an experience, you automatically turn it into a *transformation . . .* [T]ransformations are a distinct economic offering, the fifth and final one in our Progression of Economic Value. A transformation

is what the out-of-shape person, the emotionally troubled person, the young managers, the hospital patient, and the struggling company all really desire.

(Ibid.: 165)

This goes beyond Manthiou *et al.*'s (2014) claim that it is by creating an experiential environment that events facilitate memorable experiences, and thereby provide their organizers with a competitive advantage. There are suggestions here that by producing what Hallmann and Zehrer (2014: 289; emphasis added) refer to as '*authentic* and memorable experiences', drawing on how memory is being framed internally through how participants are feeling (Calvo-Soraluze and Blanco, 2014), we not only consume, produce and reproduce places, landscapes and experiences (Griggio, 2015) but become complicit in co-creating the commodification of that transformational event-memory (Thrift, 2006), and thereby implicitly collude in the fabrication of aspects of our identity as products/services that can be sold back to us within a neo-liberal context.

Additionally, by placing the creation of memorable (and transformational) experience at the heart of mainstream events management and event studies we effectively commodify and depoliticize both events and ourselves (as event participants). We should not fool ourselves by thinking that the only reason to focus on the production of memorable/transformational experience is because events are managed by people with pure, altruistic motives whose sole objective is to ensure we all have a really good time. By focusing on each individual attendee's experience, and how it can best be *managed*, we ultimately anchor the context upon which we base the analysis and evaluation of the event in the organic individual attendee's memory. Elements of the wider setting become reorientated around the attendee's experience and whether the *transformation* they undergo results in further purchasing, repeat attendance and good word-of-mouth (including digital 'word-of-mouth') PR promotion to other potential customers. In such a context the triple-bottom line is diminished as a good thing in its own right, to become a way of servicing positive memories so that they can translate into greater consumption and a competitive advantage for any particular 'event'.

But is our discussion simply to construe the commodification of memory as some sort of 'capitalist evil' that should be avoided? No. This is not a trite leftist argument that equates commodification with capitalism. Even when we extend event studies to encompass forms of dissent, acts of protests, anti-capitalist occupations and various kinds of collective resistance, we still find memory commodified in the study and management of events. One a personal level, Lamond's jacket lapel sports a CND badge and an LGBT+ rainbow-striped triangle (bought, respectively, on an anti-war demonstration and during a Pride parade). On his wall is an Occupy Wall Street poster, purchased and displayed (temporarily) in his office to indicate solidarity with that campaign. In his bookcase are copies of various pamphlets, and in his CD and DVD collections are several artefacts that commodify the memory of his association, participation and activism within a number of causes that matter to him. It is important to recall that the Luddites were not opposed to technology per se. Breaking the frames of the textile machines that filled factories and the smaller, domestic equipment of the 'cottage' workers was a sign of revolt against the context of exploitation and inequity in power in which the technology was appearing (Conniff, 2011). Arguably, the Luddites tried to *emancipate* technology, not destroy it. Analogously, commodification of memory needs emancipation, not destruction. We will discuss this in greater depth in Chapter 11. In the meantime, the relationship between events and the dominant form of commodification in our current neo-liberal context will be addressed in Chapter 6.

Conclusion

The commodification of memory is a crucial attribute of events. So what does this mean for the link between memory and CES? At the core of CES are a number of interconnected concerns, which may be expressed as a series of questions. How do events intervene in the social? If they are disruptive, how are they, and what is thereby discursively exposed? What are the contexts in which the 'event' occurs? How do those contexts reveal different forms of contestation around the 'event'? What becomes identified as *the* dominant context (often equated with its narrative) of the 'event'? And who is framed, by that context, as managing it? These questions are neither definitive nor exhaustive, and we may add several others. In what ways does the 'event' suggest memory is contested? What form does the commodification of memory associated with the 'event' take, and for what purpose? And who becomes framed within that dominant 'event' narrative as responsible for managing that event-memory commodification? Therefore, in adopting a critical approach to event studies, no specific model or theory of memory and 'event' is required – part of its value, as an attitude and an approach, lies in recognizing contestation and commodification, and questioning both.

Notes

1. These websites are now so ubiquitous that the software used to write this chapter highlights 'Facebook', 'Instagram', 'YouTube' and the rest as misspelled if the companies' capitalization and spelling preferences are ignored.
2. In remembrance of Lamond's own past as a psychology student we consulted two textbooks he used in college: *Atkinson and Hilgard's Introduction to Psychology* (Nolen-Hoeksema *et al.*, 2014), now in its sixteenth edition, and Gross, who produced the seventh edition of his textbook in 2015.
3. Anyone who has seen a hospital's automated pharmaceutical dispensary at work will know what we mean.
4. CAT or CT – computerized axial tomography; PET – positron emission tomography; fMRI – functional magnetic resonance imaging. These are all means of generating cross-sectional images of the brain, and its functioning, in a living participant. Three-dimensional models of the functioning brain can then be constructed through the computational layering of these images.
5. Thus tentatively drawing on Raymond Williams's (1977) wider construal of 'culture'.
6. On the commodification of memory and events, there are some interesting discussions on the use of digital media and social media and the 'event experience' in Luxford and Dickinson (2015) and Calvo-Soraluze and Blanco (2014).

7. The discussion of this case study is indebted to the fascinating research done by Dominique Liao (forthcoming). Any errors of fact are entirely our own.
8. We use the term 'Jacquardian' to allude to the loom invented by Joseph Marie Jacquard in 1801. This produced complex patterns in woven fabric through the decoding of hole-punched cards. While the loom remained the same, changing the card resulted in the creation of a different pattern. Analogously, by changing the content of the layers in the modes of memory, the complex pattern of individual identity is altered.
9. In the *Phaedrus* Plato uses the names Theuth and Thamus in place of Thoth (god of the underworld) and Ammon (king of the Egyptian gods).

6 Commodification of events

Introduction

Rugby league is a version (or 'code') of rugby football that split away from rugby union in 1895 in the north of England (Collins, 2015; Spracklen, 2009; Spracklen and Spracklen, 2008; Spracklen *et al.*, 2010). The initial split was a matter of governance, but also related to disagreements over the rise in the commodification of sport in that period. The northern English rugby football clubs had thousands of supporters who were willing to pay money to watch the matches, and as such the clubs attracted sponsors and benefactors who were willing to bank-roll supposedly amateur players signed from around the country. The people who ran the game in the south of England (the Rugby Football Union – RFU) strongly disagreed with this increasing professionalization of the sport in the north, but also did not like the idea that working-class men were seeking greater control of their sports careers. For a number of years the Northern Rugby Football Union (NFU) continued to play rugby under the same rules as the original RFU. But then the entrepreneurs who ran the northern game experimented in a bid to make it more entertaining, more of a spectacle: the number of players was reduced from fifteen to thirteen; overt professionalism was allowed; and line-outs, rucks and mauls were all abolished in favour of 'play-the-ball', which restarted play as soon as a player was tackled. Australians used the term 'rugby league' for this version of the game, and this was then adopted in the north of England (Collins, 2015).

Throughout the twentieth century rugby league continued to experiment with its rules in order to sell itself as a modern spectator sport, and later a modern television sport. Its struggle to gain political and cultural respectability in England was – and still is – hindered by its perceived parochialism – a game for working-class people in the marginal north – even though its elite competition is part of the corporate sports package that is now owned and shaped by transnational media corporations (ibid.). In 1995, UK rugby league signed a long-term broadcasting deal with Rupert Murdoch's Sky TV, part of News Corp, which heralded an attempt to transform the game into a global mega-event – the Super League. Teams were established in new cities in mainland Europe and Australia, and a rival league was founded in the latter in direct competition with the Australian Rugby League.

In Australia, rugby league has fared much better at the level of corporate, commodified events. The game has expanded from its New South Wales base to become one of the principal national sports, challenging Australian Rules for dominance and pushing rugby union into relative obscurity (ibid.). The Grand Final is watched by millions of people on television, and it is as big and as corporate an event as any national final in any professional team sport, from the Super Bowl to the FA Cup. But even the Grand Final is seen as second-tier in rugby league when compared to the 'State of Origin' matches between New South Wales and Queensland. Australian Rugby League was thus a key target for the Super League takeover in the 1990s, and for some years two competitions ran alongside one another. But the huge amounts of money to be made from the corporate events of the State of Origin series and the Grand Final remained in the hands of the Australian Rugby League, so inevitably News Corp had to make a compromise deal with the ARL to gain a cut of the profits from the big events. This led to the creation of the National Rugby League (NRL), which emerged from the struggle even stronger (financially) than the ARL had been back in the early 1990s. The State of Origin series increased its viewing figures and its sponsorship deals as it evolved from an annual event that was loved by working-class rugby league fans in New South Wales and Queensland to a mega-event followed by all classes throughout Australia (Brawley, 2009). In the 2010s cities and venues started to compete with each other to host the State of Origin matches. In 2015, for example, the second match of the series was held in Melbourne, the capital city of Victoria, the heartland of Australian Rules football. Nevertheless, it attracted a record (sell-out) crowd of 91,513 spectators (Total Rugby League, 2015).

In the previous five chapters the arrow of time has pointed to an increasing commodification of events as we enter the present and start to move into the near future. Commodification is the focus of this chapter. Events have been part of the history of commodification. They have been constructed as commodities, and they are increasingly sold as commodities to consumers. This has certainly happened with rugby league: capitalism and commodification have been ever present since the game was founded, but it has now grown into the spectacle of State of Origin, which has become so all-encompassing in Australia that it is viewed as more important than test matches featuring the national team (Collins, 2015). State of Origin is now so big that it is influencing the development of British rugby league, and the ways in which British rugby league events are marketed and packaged. It is rugby league's mega-event – a commodity that is greedily consumed by sports fans, watched in awe by newcomers to the game and with pride by long-term devotees.

In this chapter, we focus more closely on the processes through which events become commodities, and event participants become consumers. In the first section we return to the key theories of Gramsci, Adorno and Habermas relating to the rise of capitalism and the power of capitalism and other instrumental rationalities in the period of modernity in order to analyse sports mega-events such as the Olympics and the FIFA World Cup. Then we discuss the shift to postmodernity and the supposed decline of the power of nation-states, and explore how this has increased commodification in the events industry as one part of the wider cultural and entertainment industries. Finally, we investigate the ways in which commodification might be resisted though events.

Gramsci, Adorno and Habermas revisited: commodification as modernity in modern mega-events

What is a mega-event? Maurice Roche (1994: 1), one of the first scholars to develop a social critique of mega-events, neatly captures their essence by arguing: 'Mega-events (large scale leisure and tourism events such as Olympic Games and World Fairs) are short-term events with long-term consequences for the cities that stage them.' In the same paper, he sets out an explanation for why cities feel the need to stage such events that goes beyond the reductive, economic arguments that these events generate money from tourism and/or development. A successful mega-event brings with it a sense that the host city or country has gained admission to an elite circle: hosting such an event generates parochial pride, nationalism and, among cities, the feeling that one has joined the ranks of global cities, in which the post-industrial economy is founded (Sassen, 2011).

It is easy to describe sports events such as the Olympics and the FIFA World Cup as mega-events. They generate billions of dollars in contracts, sales and sponsorship deals, and the stakes are so high that corruption has followed both events over the years (Rowe, 2012; Thornley, 2012; Tomlinson, 2014). They are global spectacles, watched by people around the world who buy their branded gear and drink their official partners' beers, while competitors spend billions of dollars searching for tiny advantages over their rivals. In other cases, however, what may be classified as a mega-event is less clear, with arguments raging in the academic literature over the identification of particular events as 'mega' (Horne, 2015).

Following Roche's initial definition, just about any event that is staged for the purposes of making money and selling the event host in some way could be termed a mega-event. In this section, we shall focus on sporting mega-events, and especially the Olympics and the FIFA World Cup. Sporting mega-events are tied to the rise of modern sport as a part of the entertainment industry (Horne, 2015; Roche, 1992; Spracklen, 2011a). That is, modern sport has always served a role in perpetuating the hegemony of the Western, Global Northern elites. Modern sports are part of the media and cultural work of the elites who, following Gramsci's analysis, maintain their power despite the contradictions of the bourgeois revolution and the material inevitability of the proletariat revolution (Gramsci, 1973; Spracklen, 2009, 2011a). Sports number among the Gramscian cultural forms that make people think they are free when in fact they are not, and deflect the anger and agency of the working classes from political action. Football has been global and professional in scope since the start of the twentieth century, when it was spread through the efforts of British and other European teachers, traders and engineers to countries that were linked economically and culturally to the West

(Collins, 2015). Although it was associated with the bourgeois and lower classes in the UK – and ignored by the ruling elites of the British Empire – it became a vehicle for the hegemonic interests of other countries in Western Europe (Tomlinson, 2014). FIFA's development of the World Cup in the 1930s, and its transformation of that competition into a commercial success of sports broadcasting, made the organization and its officials rich while also creating a cycle of expensive bidding wars for media rights, sponsorship deals and hosting.

The World Cup continues to serve as a hegemonic distraction. The naive football fan believes football is the greatest game in the world because they have been told so by their friends, their families and their newspapers and television channels. The game is easy to follow, and easy to play. But it creates solidarity based on narrow forms of belonging – a club or a country – and that solidarity is constructed at the expense of shared international working-class consciousness. Extending Gramsci's hegemonic lens to the gender order, we can see that the World Cup as mega-event also constructs and affirms a hegemonic masculinity (Connell, 1987, 1995; Messner and Sabo, 1990). The footballers who take part become the best of men, emulated by other men, role-models in their egregious relationships with women as they are in their ability to bond with other men (and score goals).

As we briefly discussed in an earlier chapter, the philosophy of Olympianism runs against the grain of commerce and capitalism, but the growth of broadcast media in modernity soon made the Olympic Games the site for similar commercialization, instrumentality and commodification. By the 1980s the idea that the Olympics was a celebration of the amateur ideal had been undermined by the money to be made from endorsement deals and secondary contracts, and amateurism was quickly replaced by a full embrace of professionalism (Guttman, 2002; Lenskyj, 2015). The Olympian ideal became commodified, and the belief in taking part was replaced by a belief in winning and making a profit. The Olympian ideal also became a marker for elitism and privilege, but instead of the cultural capital formed by aristocratic amateurs, the hegemonic power in the Olympics was the new wealth of modernity: transnational corporations, the United States of America, the bankers of Switzerland and the oligarchs of Russia, the Middle East and beyond (Lenskyj, 2015; Rowe, 2012). The Olympics became a brand to be defended from those who sought to exploit it for their own financial gain. The IOC became a source of clandestine legal powers, able to impose its own restrictions on existing laws in any country where the Games were held (Lenskyj, 2015). It followed FIFA in the distribution of largesse, the buying and selling of contracts, the buying and selling of services, and the personal enrichment of the new elites. And while this was happening the Olympics as an event was transformed into a global mega-event, just like the World Cup, where nation-states exercise their sovereignty and create myths of national superiority through their athletes' endeavours.

This points to a possible paradox in Gramscian hegemony. The organizations that own such sporting mega-events are transnational in nature, and the bidding processes for the Olympics and the World Cup generate global headlines and interest in every market. But any success is measured in *national* terms. National sides compete to win medals or the World Cup, and nation-states take pride in successfully bidding for and hosting such events. But again, it is Gramsci who can help us resolve this. In trying to understand the realities of the Italian Fascists' seizure of power, and the imposition of their bourgeois hegemony on Italian culture and politics, Gramsci realized that the capitalist world order relies on such nationalism. Mega-events need the interests of nation-states to make them successful, and to make them aspects of everyday life, even as they take millions of dollars from nation-states and transfer them to transnational corporations.

We have discussed commodification a number of times so far without really defining what we mean by the term. Historically, capitalism in all its forms has reduced social and cultural forms to commodities. In the rise of the British Empire and the West, humans were turned into physical commodities – slaves who were bought and sold by owners to generate profits. It is no exaggeration to say that the wealth of the West is built on the proceeds of slavery, and the fine stately homes of the United Kingdom, for example, owe their creation to the enormous sums of money accrued by capitalists and elites in the eighteenth and nineteenth centuries. Although slavery was ultimately abolished in the West, the unequal power relationships between owners and slaves continued into the hegemonic power of capitalists over their workers in the factory systems of high modernity. Factory workers may have had limited social freedom and regular incomes, but they were subject to dehumanizing rules and constraints, and they received unfair remuneration for their labour, as Marx described so forcefully (see Hobsbawm, 1988, 1989). The condition of capitalism, then, is the way in which workers are turned into commodities that can be used and discarded subject to the whims of managers, capitalist owners and the modern economy. This commodification of labour and the workplace then creates tensions between the workers, who compete with one another to turn themselves into valuable commodities that are useful to the bosses, when they should work with one another to fight collectively for better conditions and wages.

The trends towards commodification in the factory systems of the late nineteenth century continued into the first seventy years of the twentieth century, when the United States' industrial economy gave it political and cultural dominance. According to Adorno (2001), this was the period when developing technologies created the culture industry – a commodified version of high culture. This culture industry, as we discussed in an earlier chapter, was a product of the concatenation of US imperialism, late modern capitalist practices and the construction of popular culture as something that was given to the masses by their 'betters' (ibid.). In essence, it extended the notion of commodification into culture and leisure. Instead of being judged by aesthetic or ethical qualities, the new cultural forms of pop music, cinema and television were reduced to a commoditized reckoning: a good film or pop song *sold* well; a good television programme attracted sufficient regular viewers to generate significant advertising revenue. Adorno shows that the creators of popular culture in modernity are forced to play along with the rules of commodification even if they believe that their work is inspired by higher things.

Such auteurs still regard their work as potential sources of income, and their audiences as consumers. Criticism becomes a way of giving works of art the seal of approval in the market place. On the other side of this equation, the consumers are encouraged to spend money on art that keeps them happy, and to shun anything that challenges them or shows them how to change society. The entire public sphere is commodified, polluted by the belief that all human interaction can be reduced to financial transactions, and all worth is measurable in profit and loss. In late modernity this belief system comes from neo-liberalism, but it was a dominant ideology in the culture industry from its very creation (Bauman, 2000, 2007; Beck, 1992).

Events are one small but significant part of the culture industry, and they are thus tools for the normalization of this ideology of commodification. Adorno (1967: 81) believed strongly that sports belong to the realm of 'unfreedom'. For him, sports discipline people as slaves and passive workers, and shape them to behave as commodities and as consumers of commodities. There is strong evidence from the sociology and history of modern sport that this process lies at the heart of the construction of modern sports, and that it is crucial in the ongoing centrality of sports in modern society: sports show men how to be men, teach people to obey rules, and make people embody social and political norms (Messner and Sabo, 1990; Spracklen, 2009; Spracklen *et al.*, 2010). Sports events are extensions of this, but made more problematic by their connection with modern, global capitalism. The Olympics and the FIFA World Cup provide spectacles for television audiences as humans are transformed into commodities for the purposes of entertainment. Some might argue that the athletes choose to participate and they are well paid for their efforts. We would counter that most athletes become athletes because they have few meaningful life-choices as children or are unaware of the consequences of their choices as children, and that most athletes are poorly rewarded and retire with debilitating, long-term health problems (Waddington, 2000). Athletes are only marginally better off than the slaves who trained to be gladiators for the amusement of the Romans.

These sporting mega-events don't just turn the athletes into commodities. They turn the audiences and workers into commodities, too, and ultimately transform the activities themselves into commodities. The audiences watching through the process of mediatization embody the constraints of passive consumerism. They drink beer, eat snacks and watch the adverts. They get excited only when 'their' athlete or team is winning or losing, coupled with a sense of local or national pride if it is the former. By buying subscriptions and the products sold by the sponsors and advertisers, the mediated viewer is the perfect consumer. The audiences who attend the events are just as passive, and just as commodified, only they have paid for the expensive tickets to prove that they are acceptably rich. Their presence in the host city comes at enormous financial cost to them: they have to pay for transport, hotel rooms and food at inflated prices because of the presence of the mega-event. And this commoditization continues inside the event itself, as attendees are restricted over where they can go, herded by security officials as ruthlessly as slaves by their foremen. The workers at the events are reduced to commodities, too. Mega-events rely on recruiting hundreds if not thousands of volunteers (as any payment would impact on profits). These volunteers might feel as if they are taking part in the adventure of a lifetime, and there is some evidence that they look back on their volunteering with fond memories (Nichols and Ralston, 2012). But what does this volunteering actually comprise? You volunteer your free time to help the organizers of the mega-event run it efficiently so that it hits their financial targets. You volunteer your labour to allow the organizers to make more money. For the Olympics and the FIFA World Cup, volunteers give up their holiday leave to work for nothing for weeks. This is exploitation and commodification of the social relationships these volunteers have with the sports they love. They are athletes themselves or keen supporters who are excited to be chosen. But that does not alter the fact that the sense of belonging and community is transformed into a commodified exchange based on unpaid labour. In the nineteenth century some defenders of the slave trade argued that the slaves were happy to be slaves, and benefited from that status. Volunteers at mega-events are happy to be volunteers, and they gain some benefits from their involvement, but sports mega-events are still exploiting them, just as slave owners exploited their slaves.

Habermas (1992a, 1992b, 1992c) helps us make sense of the commodification of events in modernity. As mentioned in Chapter 1, Habermas believes that modernity emerged in the West at the moment when the urban bourgeoisie freed themselves from feudal and religious oppression. Given the freedom to think and act communicatively, says Habermas (1992a), this class constructed a public sphere in which new ways of thinking about the world were generated. This is a rather simplistic view of the Enlightenment and the rise of science and capitalism, but Habermas is essentially correct in showing this public sphere was constructed in the Enlightenment, and it did allow new ideas such as liberal democracy, secularism and science to appear. But the public sphere and the Enlightenment also created the idea that humans are individuals – rational agents who buy and sell goods. Adam Smith's theories of the free market were turned into a new way of thinking that legitimized modern, imperial capitalism and its post-imperial, global variant (Gramsci, 1973; Hall, 1993). For Habermas (1992b, 1992c), this is the seed of destruction in the public sphere, the instrumental rationality that is justified by the communicative rationality that allows the public sphere to be cultivated in the first place. Communicative rationality has led to the end of feudalism and the rise of modernity, but in turn this has led to the rise of capitalism and the reductionist logic of instrumentality.

In late modernity, this instrumentality operates as a system colonizing the lifeworld of social activity in two ways. First, instrumentality has reduced every action to its economic value in the market. Our leisure lives, leisure spaces and activities have become managed by commercial transactions (Spracklen, 2009, 2011a). Second, instrumentality has turned human interactions and social spaces into bureaucracies and rationalized encounters. Nation-states have become all-powerful machines calculating and assessing our every move, and every modern organization mirrors the structures and bureaucracies of the nation-state. In our leisure lives, we might see this in what Habermas would call the juridification of informal leisure activities, such as games and socializing. We now have to agree to complicated terms and conditions we do not understand just to play a game online, and when we socialize in a bar we are subject to stringent licensing laws that limit the amount of alcohol we are allowed to consume.

Instrumentality commodifies the everyday and the social. Sporting mega-events, if they are to have any meaning, should be things that bring some moral or social value to the world. This is the claim that they make. For example, as we saw earlier, the IOC's Olympic Charter includes what are called the 'fundamental principles of Olympism', the first two of which are:

1. Olympism is a philosophy of life, exalting and combining in a balanced whole the qualities of body, will and mind. Blending sport with culture and education, Olympism seeks to create a way of life based on the joy of effort, the educational value of good example, social responsibility and respect for universal fundamental ethical principles.
2. The goal of Olympism is to place sport at the service of the harmonious development of humankind, with a view to promoting a peaceful society concerned with the preservation of human dignity.

(IOC, 2015: 12)

These goals owe their origins to the ideals of the founders of the modern Olympic movement, and there is of course nothing wrong with some of the underlying aims. There is no doubt that we need to create a world where universal, fundamental ethical principles are respected, and maybe even developed through our leisure lives. And who does not want to support the idea that we need to work towards a peaceful society where human dignity is respected? But can modern sports achieve these aims? Let us allow the Olympic movement this claim, though. If sports are a vehicle for bringing people together to help them understand ethics and the joy of participation, how can this happen when the Olympics has become a hyper-commodified mega-event? The instrumentality at work in such commodification means that the only values that are truly respected are those that reduce human activity to winning or losing, to buying, and to making money. The founders of the Olympic movement believed that participating in sport made people better human beings, and that the endeavour mattered more than the financial reward, or even the place in the competition (Guttman, 2002). The values associated with this muscular Christian amateurism have now been lost to the instrumentality of the bottom line. The IOC would probably argue that the money generated from the sponsorship deals and the bidding and the events themselves is always put to good use in sporting and educational development work around the world. But the power of instrumental rationality, according to Habermas, lies in how such rationality is able to normalize itself, and how it then mimics the lifeworld it colonizes. Olympism has not only been colonized by the instrumental rationality of commodification; it also relies on such instrumentality to maintain its commitment to its communicative values. A similar sleight of hand operates in

FIFA, though its goals and values were never so ideally written as those of the Olympic movement. FIFA exists to promote football and the various communities and individuals who make up the global footballing family. The profits made by the World Cup are justified by the need to fund the development schemes FIFA delivers in the Global South (Tomlinson, 2014). Instrumentality is thus justified by reference to communicative values and social goals, which are then used to justify the excesses of the World Cup's sponsorship deals and bidding processes.

The postmodern turn in commodification: the rise of hyper-realism

We have discussed the postmodern turn elsewhere in this book, so we will not spend much time defining it here. Many scholars have argued that there has been a shift to postmodernity and a decline in the power of nation-states. For instance, Zygmunt Bauman (2000) claims that we live in a world defined by global capitalism and the power of global elites, where nation-states have less power over their citizens, but where identity and belonging are liquid. In this definition, postmodernity becomes merely a stage in the development of human societies – one that some or all of the world may have reached. This is a fairly modest claim that can be tested through observing changes in societies, and assessing whether the period of high modernity has been replaced by something different: something post-industrial, post-Fordist, post-national, postmodern (Spracklen, 2009).

Another way of thinking about postmodernity is to elide the idea of a stage in society with the cultural and philosophical theories collected under the term 'post-modernism' (Foucault, 2002). These theories question the status of knowledge about the world and the notion of universal truth. There is some truth in the notion that truth is mediated by the powerful, and some truth in the idea that our knowledge will always be incomplete, but we do not need to abandon epistemological certainty for the ontological darkness of relativism. The turn to postmodernism can warn us about the embeddedness of power in discourses, but we can still write critiques of that power based on our knowledge of how it works. Here we want to explore how this postmodern turn might have increased commodification in the events industry as one part of the wider cultural and entertainment industries.

It might be argued that the FIFA World Cup is a *prima facie* case for the shift to postmodernity. Because association football has never been associated with US cultural and political hegemony, FIFA has managed to develop a power structure and base that reflect the international reach of the sport. The internal committees and decision-making systems offer every national governing body of football parity in terms of voice and power (with some exceptions around the division of power in the UK; see Tomlinson, 2014). The World Cup has been hosted around the globe, and has been the subject of intense bidding, which has resulted in new economic powers in the Middle and Far East securing the hosting rights. The markets for the broadcasting deals and bidding processes for sponsorships are also suitably globalized. As a result of all this the World Cup has become a symbol of the power of globalization in commodification. Local and national differences have been squeezed out by the enormous marketing spend of the World Cup, its media partners and its sponsors, who make sure every nation-state is sold the same global products (ibid.). If this is true of the World Cup, it is also true of the Olympics. Both of these sporting mega-events create global audiences and global tastes, and both have international organizations that transcend and overpower nation-states, whether in dictating the terms of domestic television deals, insisting on the construction of new facilities at enormous social cost to the host nation-states, or demanding that the hosts change laws to give the organizations more power and immunity from the checks and balances of democratic oversight (Thornley, 2012).

Sporting mega-events, then, are clear evidence of the turn to postmodernity. They could not exist in the forms they do today without globalization and the redistribution of power from nation-states to transnational corporations and organizations, or the redistribution of power from the West to other parts of the world. They could not exist without the global markets that happily consume the mediated products and the products of sponsors, who would not invest so much money in the events without the certainty that they will get their money back – and make substantial profits – through the viewers' conspicuous consumption. Of course, capitalists do sometimes make mistakes about profits, and it is not unknown for individuals to take personal cuts of cash to ensure their companies sign expensive sponsorship deals, but the instrumentality of the logic of the market nearly always ensures that the corporations win.

So do people really buy a particular carbonated, sugar-filled soft drink just because they have seen the name of that beverage during a televised football match? Are people really that stupid? We all like to think that we are not subject to the pressures of marketing and the entertainment industry, but we all fall for it (Žižek, 2010). We choose books, movies, music, television, food, drink and numerous other products because we read reviews, hear about them, or see adverts for them. We might think that reading reviews or hearing about something is more of a free choice than being influenced by a cute advert, but in fact the industry spends a great deal of time and effort shaping what is reviewed and what is discussed. Nearly every aspect of our lives is shaped by the instrumentality of the industries that want to sell us their products. Those industries have become so dominant because we have become postmodern. That is, our lives are no longer shaped by the constraints of work, family and local cultures – we have more disposable income, relatively speaking, but we are individualized, atomized, and alienated from one another. With no community or workplace to give us a sense of belonging we buy belonging through liking stuff: our musical tastes, our events, our fashions and our eating and drinking habits are shaped by our need to find belonging and meaning through commodification, and by the work of the industry in constructing and marketing products which meet that need. So sport mega-events allow us to purchase some kind of ephemeral belonging, whether we drink the beverage of the corporate sponsors, buy the sneakers endorsed by the top athletes, or wave flags branded with a make of car we will never be able to afford, but which we dream of buying if we manage to move up the corporate ladder.

Pop festivals might be viewed as products of postmodernity, and as spaces for commodification. In the first few decades of popular music's history, the music was created – as part of Adorno's (2001) culture industry – as a form of distraction for the masses. Quite quickly, young people developed their own subcultures and fashions associated with particular forms of pop music, and these were each in turn incorporated into the pop music industry. Following Hebdige (1979), we might argue that pop music is always a leisure site for the construction of alternative, subcultural identities, but at any moment in the history of pop music some subcultures are alternative and resistive, some are co-opted into the commerce of the industry, and others are disappearing. So when Hebdige wrote his book on subcultures in British music, the mainstream music and fashion industries were already in the process of co-opting punk, while Teddy boys were fast becoming half-remembered folk devils. However, the final years of the twentieth century saw some important structural and cultural changes to pop music, which have continued to the present day. First, the industry started to lose control of its copyrighted material, and the internet allowed anyone to listen to anything for free (Spracklen, 2014b, 2015). Second, the internet and globalization have led to the growth of pop music mega-stars but also to a reduction in the genres and spaces available to resist the controlled forms of pop music: rock, heavy metal, rap and dance – all in their time underground musical forms – have been mainstreamed (Spracklen, 2014b; Spracklen and Spracklen, 2012, 2014). This means, on the one hand, that the pop music industry is struggling to respond to a loss of power while music listeners have an infinite range of choices. But on the other hand, music's political and cultural edge has been subverted by omnivorism and playfulness.

Pop music, then, has all the hallmarks of postmodernity. And festivals are a form of event that evidences this postmodern turn. In their original forms these festivals were associated with deviance, law-breaking and subversive subcultures. They were unfashionable spaces that attracted marginal – mainly young – people who followed whichever musical genre was represented on the festival bill, be it jazz, rock or heavy metal. Consequently, festivals were associated in the mainstream public sphere with bikers, drug-users and hippies. In the UK the Glastonbury Festival was perceived as a dangerous combination of left-wing politics and drunken rock fans, and politicians and media commentators called for it to be banned, just as they called for the end of free festivals at Stonehenge (Flinn and Frew, 2014). In the 1980s and 1990s festivals were cleansed in the public imagination through stronger security measures and stricter local licensing, the introduction of corporate sponsors, and increases in ticket prices. In this century they have come to dominate and shape the music scene. For many smaller or unsigned artists, the festival circuit is now the only way they can find new audiences and fans, so they are willing to pay to play. For big artists, festivals are all they need to do to pay their bills, so the number of tours and gigs outside of the festival season has declined. Festival owners and promoters now make huge profits from their events, because people are willing to pay huge amounts of money for tickets.

Why do people want to attend festivals? They go because they have been sold the idea that festival-going marks them as hip, important individuals who stand out from the crowd. Glastonbury has become part of the British urban bourgeoisie's social calendar, part of the establishment's 'season', sandwiched between Royal Ascot and surfing in Cornwall (ibid.). Hipster boutique festivals cater for rich people who want to play at being alternative individuals for a weekend. The Leeds and Reading rock festivals have become safe playgrounds for lower-middle-class students who want to prove they are cultural omnivores. The idea of going to a festival is as important as actually attending. This is commodification as it turns into Baudrillard's (1994, 1995) hyper-real. The logic of the postmodern music festival is ironically the dissolution of the link between the music scene and the festival. Glastonbury sells out long before any act is announced, because people want their friends to know they are going to the festival. The bands that are then signed up cover the broadest possible tastes, with even heavy metal acts such as Metallica performing there. Other festivals aspire to this end-point of making the festival experience more important than the music, and increasingly sell whole experience packages. So Bloodstock, a small heavy metal festival, encourages attendees to buy VIP tickets so that they can jump the queues at signings and have access to a real-ale bar that sells metal-themed beer. According to this logic, music consumers have become cultural omnivores (Friedman, 2012): they know everything about every form of music, so they merely need plenty of stalls where they can buy things that prove, in their cost, that the festival-goer is actually at the festival, doing festival-related things.

This hyper-real turn makes attending music festivals a cannibalistic form of commodification. With the focus on the experience rather than the music, the danger is that the music will be lost altogether, or replaced by something else. Moreover, this hyper-real commodification is not limited to music festivals. All mega-events aspire to this same end-point, where the attendees believe they are doing something amazing (so they return in future years), yet that something is actually a hyper-real, fake, watered-down version of the original experience, because the mega-event is controlled by the entertainment industries, which are key components of the culture industry. As Adorno (2001) says, festivals are merely sites where our choices relating to how we listen to and make music are circumscribed by the economic practices of capitalists and ruling elites. We cannot escape the fact that sporting mega-events and music festivals are recent social constructions, made by hegemonic elites in the period of high modernity.

The turn to postmodernity has supposedly made the purpose of the culture industry more ambiguous. In *America*, Baudrillard (1986) reflects on the ways in which US cultural spaces have been transformed into mythic spaces by the hyper-reality of Disney, while, on the other hand, Disney and its hyper-real spaces are in turn shaped by the stories, symbols and discourses of US life. In postmodernity it becomes possible to be playful and ironic about belonging by picking and choosing the cultural artefacts that we use to define ourselves, reinventing and shaping our identities in polysemic ways (Bauman, 2000; Foucault, 2002). Furthermore, the postmodernists argue, the power of the centre has been overturned or reduced, enabling all of us to participate in this play of polysemy. Leisure and culture have become places where we find meaning, rather than control. Even if the elites try to impose their will through social structures and culture and leisure, we have the agency to transgress their norms and values. So the commodification of mega-events in postmodernity might be read as a way of making different meanings from these cultural spaces.

The State of Origin might be identified as a mega-event that does not fit the structural view of such things. First, rugby league is a marginal sport associated with rough working-class communities; even in Australia it is not part of the history of the ruling elites, and even now it is often dismissed as a sport that is played by stupid, lower-class white men in the western suburbs of Sydney (Brawley, 2009). So rugby league is not instructing spectators to be good citizens. State of Origin is parochial, pitching the states of New South Wales and Queensland against each other. It is a recognition that rugby league does not really exist beyond those two states. The matches are hyped by rugby league journalists and supporters for the 'biff' – the confrontations and fights that take place when club-mates forget their team loyalties for eighty minutes and instead focus their aggression on their state rivals. State of Origin should never have become a mega-event, because it is a marginal contest in a marginal sport. But the 'biff' and the hype have turned it into the biggest rugby league contest in the world, and one of the biggest sport events in Australia (Collins, 2015). For the working-class white men of western Sydney and the towns on the Queensland coast, State of Origin represents everything they hold dear. It is also something that they enjoy in an un-ironic way, something that provides them with a reaffirmation of their heteronormativity (Butler, 2006). The State of Origin sells them a commodified, working-class hegemonically masculine identity (Connell, 1995).

But for the middle-class hipsters who hold State of Origin parties, or the elites in suits with corporate tickets for the matches, something else is happening. They cheer on the teams with a sense of play, having decided to commoditize their identity for the evening by supporting either Queensland or New South Wales. They have a few drinks, just like the working-class men, and curse the 'Cockroaches' or the 'Cane Toads'. But they consume this cultural form for just one night. The following day they shed this identity and find another one. For instance, the evening after State of Origin the banker and the hipster might run into each other at an electronica festival. They will not carry any symbolic representation of State of Origin into the boundaries of that festival, unless they do so to mock the working-class men who are standing at the bars discussing any upcoming rugby league matches. For the hipsters and bankers, the State of Origin is a simulation (Baudrillard, 1994) of working-class Australian masculinity, something they can enjoy because they are sufficiently hip to be omnivores. For them, the State of Origin is a hyper-real moment that is soon forgotten and replaced by the next commodified event experience. They do not really care who wins. By contrast, for the working-class men of western Sydney, the State of Origin is extremely important, and victory for the Blues (New South Wales) allows them to sleep soundly without caring about their problems.

Conclusion

There is a clear trend in events. As modernity moved from its high to its late stage, events became commodified, and that commodification made commodities out of the people who used those events – as artists, workers, visitors, spectators or viewers. All active participation in such events is transformed by the power of instrumentality into passive consumption or docile obedience. This commodification has continued with the continued rise of mega-events, such as the FIFA World Cup, the Olympics, music festivals such as Glastonbury, and spectacles such as the State of Origin. This rise has been particularly noticeable in the first two decades of this century, and may be related to the idea that we have shifted from a state of modernity to one of postmodernity. Commodification still exists in this postmodern phase of mega-events, but it is accentuated by the different ways in which people embrace such hyper-real commodification: with irony and play for the hipsters; with feeling and meaning for Bauman's (2000) 'poor consumers', who do not have the cultural or economic capital to make the right choices.

Is it possible to resist such commodification? Some people certainly reject it, by choosing to disengage with mega-events. That is, some people have stopped attending music festivals, or refuse to subscribe to the television channels that screen the Olympics and the FIFA World Cup. One can make an instant objection to commodification by not consuming. We have much sympathy for this stance: much of the academic scholarship about sports mega-events and music festivals is weakened by the fact that the authors rarely advocate outright rejection of consumption and engagement with these capitalist events. We believe strongly that we have to act as we theorize, and as such we have no desire, paraphrasing Adorno (2001), to eat the 'baby food' of commodified events. The fortunes of Olympic athletes are as immaterial to us as conversations about who was the best headliner at Glastonbury this year. So we reject commodification by choosing not to buy it – as much as possible – and we hope our readers will follow our example.

But *rejecting* commodification is not the same as *resisting* it. Is there a way in which people might actively engage in resisting commodification? Paradoxically, the language, practice and symbolism of events offer a way of resisting commodification in events. When a sport mega-event comes to any major city these days, there is likely to be some sort of local campaign against it, even if that campaign is restricted by stringent local laws and brutal police suppression. People who do not want to see local resources wasted in the construction of facilities can and do organize and host their own events: protests, fundraising gigs, direct action and social media campaigns (Castells, 2012). In the next chapter, we will say more about how protest can be seen as a form of event. In this conclusion, we just need to note that such campaigns can be highly successful. In the run-up to the London 2012 Olympic Games campaigners tried to stop the event from happening from the start. When they failed to halt construction of the Olympic Park they challenged the organizers over freedom issues and damage to the environment. One campaign condemned the involvement of ATOS, a French company that assessed disability claimants' fitness to work. ATOS had been strongly criticized for the undue harshness of its judgements and for its ruthlessness when assessing people with long-term health problems. Some campaigners managed to gain access to the Olympic venues with stickers condemning ATOS, while others organized vocal jeers and boos for Conservative members of the British government. This required considerable organizational effort on the part of the anti-ATOS campaigners. They had to secure tickets in the lottery, then find the money to pay for those tickets, then sneak past security with the stickers. Did any of this make a difference? Well, their actions were reported in the mainstream media and online, which raised awareness of the problems with ATOS, which eventually lost its government contract. But it is difficult to argue that the protest at the Olympics directly resulted in ATOS losing that contract. Nor did it result in ATOS losing its Olympic contract. At best, the protest helped to raise the profile of the wider campaign against ATOS, and raised awareness of the continuing problems people were having with the company.

Finally, whenever anyone tries to resist commodification in events through staging counter-events or actions, there is always a danger that they will end up being co-opted into the events industry. Various fringe festivals – such as at Edinburgh – started out as counter-cultural, unofficial (or semi-official) rejections of the mainstream tastes and commercial practices of the main festivals. But they soon end up being just as organized and commercially proficient as the mainstream festivals. Achieving success in counter-cultural or fringe activities entails embracing Habermasian instrumentality, which turns the counter-cultural into just another commodity. The Olympics were initially a rejection of modern bourgeois capitalism by an aesthetic elite, but this Platonian ideal did not survive the growth of sports media. Glastonbury may have been launched by a hippy farmer who loved music, but the festival now makes deals with events corporations such as Mean Fiddler to maintain and increase its profits.

The seeds of commodification were present at the birth of modernity, and commodification continues into postmodernity and the seeming eventization and festivalization of leisure spaces. Commodification is in the discourse of the hyper-real. It is there in every mega-event by definition, by practice, and by the fact that such systems have colonized our lifeworld. Every event that is not a mega-event now is a mega-event in the making because all events have the potential to become commodified, to grow and to be part of instrumental leisure. The State of Origin started out fairly marginal, reasonably low-key, but it may soon be watched by a global audience. We cannot escape the instrumentality through copying it. The only way we can actively resist it is by subverting it in some way.

7   Protests as events

Introduction

This chapter develops our framework (Lamond and Spracklen, 2015) for understanding protests as events, events as protest, and activism as leisure. In the introductory section we introduce readers to various forms of protests as events, including organized 'chaos', non-violent direct action, and protests that are tangential to other events. We draw on new case studies on these practices and situate them in our deeper theoretical framework. The next two sections then acquaint readers with our own framework and situate it in broader studies of new social movements. The penultimate section focuses on activism and protest as communicative and serious leisure, drawing on the work of Spracklen and Stebbins. Finally, we use the work of Žižek and Bauman to explore the ways in which protest events might be understood as interdictory spaces, using the Occupy movement as our example.

Typologies of protest

One does not have to go far to see protests in the media or on the streets. As we write this chapter in July 2015, the deals over Greece remaining in the Eurozone are the focus of anti-austerity protests in Germany, while Athens remains the site of a number of protests from both left and right, with people accusing the Syriza-led government of giving in to the bankers of the Eurozone. Closer to Leeds, there are ongoing camps, actions and protests in Lancashire over the possibility of fracking. We have no doubt more are taking place elsewhere. It is impossible not to notice the growth of social activism this century (Bennett, 2012; Castells, 2012).

   Protest is nothing new. There is literary evidence of riots and protests throughout the Roman world: Rome itself was infamous for its angry mob, while the city of Alexandria was riven by protests about paganism and different creeds of Christianity in the fourth and fifth centuries (MacMullen, 1999). Later, pre-modern city-states developed strong systems of control through religion and standing armies, so they must have been aware of the possibility of challenge from their own citizens. Cities, with their public urban spaces, have always allowed individuals unhappy with political and social conditions, and many a pre-modern hegemony faced loud protests whenever the citizens overcame their fear of divine vengeance. But it was the age of modernity – with its rigid class structures and capital's exploitation of labour – that shaped protests as we know them today.

In the twentieth century, large-scale, mass protests were organized by trade unions and political parties that were not elements within the political hegemonies of nation-state establishments. Fascists, nationalists, socialists, communists and anarchists all organized in similar ways to bring their supporters onto the streets (Gramsci, 1973; Hobsbawm, 1989). Local committees marshalled their protesters and joined with colleagues at rallying points. When everybody had gathered there would be music, the waving of flags and banners, and a formal march through the streets. At the end there would be speeches, rallies and often violent attacks from police and violent confrontations with political rivals.

With the decline of trade unionism in the Global North, caused by the shift to post-industrialism and the rise of globalization, some political commentators predicted the 'end of history' and the end of protest (Fukuyama, 2006). The era of non-centrist politics is supposedly still at hand in the Global North: in the United States, there is allegedly little difference between Democratic and Republican policies; in the UK, we are told that all politics has been reduced to manager-politicians trying to prove that they are more efficient than their rivals at maintaining the instruments and processes of neo-liberal capitalism. But while the era of general strikes and mass pickets outside mines may have ended, activists are still using protest as a form of political expression in every corner of the globe.

Protest, then, is still an important part of political discourse and practice (Carter, 2014; Gerbaudo, 2012; Lamond and Spracklen, 2015). It comes in a variety of forms, the most famous of which is the formal march or rally, carefully controlled by the security services and the police. It is immediately obvious that these are events, governed by legal restrictions over the spaces through which they move and over who is allowed to be there. They are also constrained by security regulations, which are often brutally enforced by security agencies. Associated with the march and the rally is a type of protest that is renowned for its refutation of violence: the non-violent demonstrations associated with Gandhi in colonial India and CND in Britain (Carter, 2014; McKay, 2003). For those protests that are non-violent, there is a question of how far to take the peaceful protest. Should one break the law by taking the protest into a space associated with corporate or state wrongdoing, or a public space where the protest will be highly visible? Non-violent direct action involves taking over such a space and risking arrest. Environmental activists might sit down in front of lorries leaving an oil refinery, or they may climb over the refinery's fence and hang banners from the machinery.

Protests may be seen as successful if they generate a degree of chaos. Stopping lorries from leaving a refinery is one thing; stopping rush-hour traffic by organizing plays and clowning on a high street is another. Many activists deliberately organize their actions and protests to cause maximum disruption for the widest spread of actors. Of course, security agencies do not like such protests, and rarely allow them to occur, unlike marches and rallies that can be managed and 'kettled' – constrained – by police action. For activists, however, such protests are a great way of getting a message across and causing real damage to the workings of corporate and/or state structures.

We hope that it is already apparent that all forms of protest are events, as we will theorize in more detail in the rest of this chapter. But can mainstream mega-events – what we might call commodified events – be forms of protest? While Glastonbury is used to protest against the environmental consequences of capitalism, and about the appalling living conditions in many developing countries (another consequence of capitalism), it is a rare exception. The normative ontological state is that mega-events are products of capitalism and hegemonic power; as such, they are generally used to maintain that power. Such events typically attract protests that become associated with them but have no formal relationship with them. So large-scale protests are organized whenever the Olympics comes to town, often supported by a group of transnational anti-Olympics campaigning organizations (Rowe, 2012). These protests depend, in a sense, on the Olympics and other mega-events like them, but they focus on the expense of such mega-events to protest about inequalities more generally. As such, we might say that events become a form of protest only when people organize and protest about the inequities of bidding systems and the impact on local communities and economies of winning the right to host such events.

Protests as events

We have already written about protests as events (Lamond and Spracklen, 2015). From a conference with the same theme, we compiled an edited collection that showed how academics from a range of disciplines were exploring the idea that protest is a form of event. In the introduction to that book we set out the key connections that exist, and the key connection that needs to be developed, between different disciplines and subject fields. For us, the connection between the cultural-analytical disciplines of politics, protest studies and cultural, social and political protest and the functional subject fields of event studies, events management studies and leisure studies is an underdeveloped area of research and scholarship. We recognize that the subject field of leisure studies is critical in its grounding in sociology, politics and cultural studies, but such criticality is missing from events management and its relations. The 'protests as events' framework is an area that is ripe for development in events management, but such development will need encouragement: that is, although individuals are working to develop CES (the people who are reading this book!), the notion of studying protest as a form of event might seem novel or strange even to them. We argued in our book on protests as events that the related fields of CES and critical leisure studies, and their convergence around questions relevant to the study of protest and social movements, offer a new dynamic that has the potential to supplement and enhance the interdisciplinarity of politics and protest studies. Our edited collection was the first book to contribute to this interdisciplinary endeavour. Part of our aim was to explore how leisure studies might help resurrect criticality in event studies. So our edited collection includes papers that explore activism as leisure, and protest as event. The two ideas are central to our framework. Anyone who participates in a protest is an activist. To be an activist is to participate, during one's leisure time, in a protest that is an event. Therefore, activism is a form of leisure that takes place within an event. The edited collection brought together new research from around the world which explores the idea of protests as events, and activism as serious leisure, to engage in developing a new critical politics of events and leisure.

Events management as an academic subject field is situated firmly in the neo-liberal marketization of higher education. We talk about this in more detail in other chapters in this book, but here we need to remind readers of this fact. Events management courses teach students how to become efficient workers in the corporate events industry, and how to make their strong links with that industry a key part of their marketing and their curriculum. Events management researchers generally have aims that correlate to the aims of corporations and policy-makers. The conduct impact studies and cost–benefit analyses that conveniently reach conclusions that help the corporations make even more money. The whole purpose of events management degrees is defined by the way in which they create knowledge and workers for the events industry. This means that students do not receive any sociological or cultural training, although they may get a taste of ethics. They are not told about the problematic nature of big events, the consequences of the eventization of modern life (Spracklen, Richter and Spracklen, 2013), or the ways in which protests might be seen as events, or how activists might protest against events.

In our edited collection, and indeed in this book, we attempt to make what might seem to be an impossible connection between social movement studies, political studies and events management. Social movement studies and radical political studies are critical in their analyses of capitalism and modernity. They use similar critical lenses to theorize the nature of politics, agency and constraint in the world today. Can we resist the capitalist structures and power that shape our everyday lives? Or are we doomed to become completely enslaved? How does power operate in the (post)modern state – in the world of technological networks, mobilities and transnational corporations (Urry, 2002, 2012)? For researchers in social movement studies, what is at stake is the agency of activists in social movements, and the limits of that agency in the networks and groups that form new social movements, most of which are aligned in a radical political position against global capitalism, hegemony, governmentality, patriarchy, neo-liberalism and structural power in general. Radical political studies researchers and theorists seek to use their (relative) academic freedom and their skills and knowledge to critique political structures and systems that work against equality and social justice, such as global capitalism. Some radical theorists in political studies argue that there is no escape from capitalism, and that social structures remain fixed in the inequalities of power sketched out by Marx (Blackledge, 2006, 2009). By contrast, others feel that recent changes mean we are now living in a postmodern political landscape, where class has become less important as a constraining structure, or just one among many that intersect with one another (Bauman, 2000; Beck, 1992; Urry, 2012).

So how can these subject fields meet events management? If events management continues as it is, and the industry continues as it is, the only thing these subject fields might have to offer events management in its neo-liberal guise is an instrumental understanding of how informal social networks might operate, which might be of some use to corporations that are looking to profit from such networks. One might imagine a corporation being very pleased with Marxist researchers who can explain how to make money from protest! But this is not what we want to happen. We want events management to change. Looking at the discourse from another perspective, we suggest that many of the spaces and activities that surround social movements and activism might best be understood as events, or at least as activities shaped by the corporate events against which people are protesting. Protests are events, and events are sites of protest. If nothing else, we hope that our critical friends in social movement studies and political studies come to recognize that the idea of events is a useful analytical lens.

But we want to go further. We want events management to learn from social movement studies and political studies. Our suggestion here, which we will discuss further in the Chapters 8 and 13, is that events management, as it is currently constructed and constituted – as a university course and as a subject field – is in desperate need of radical reform and overhaul. Students need to develop critical thinking in universities. Academics need to do critical research and be ethical beings. One way in which this will happen is through events management embracing our theoretical framework about protests as events.

Forming a theoretical framework that can accommodate protests as events

The acculturation of events management as an activity that operates within a neo-liberal field emerges from a commonly unquestioned assumption, which suggests that the question of what constitutes an event has an economic answer within a neo-liberal frame of reference. Hence questions that are pertinent to events management are framed by the horizons of that paradigm. Following a constructivist epistemology of knowledge at this point, one can see that such a paradigm rules out any attempt to situate knowledge about events in anything other than an instrumental rationality. Following Habermas, we would say that this is a deliberate attempt by the events industry and its supporters within academia to control what counts as 'true' knowledge. Issues of relevance to the analysis of events, what they are, how they are organized, their development, sustainability and so forth become ones that implicitly or explicitly support and promote the dominant political hegemony. Concerns around the instrumentalism of events and their commodification, such as the arguments developed by Rojek (2013) and Andrews and Leopold (2013), while rightly generating critiques of that hege-monic position, rarely address the acculturated conceptualization of event within events management.

Also missing from their accounts is an understanding of the importance of seeing protests as legitimate spaces and processes of events. That is, these critiques of events have critiqued only the kinds of events defined by the events industry and its supporters in higher education. So, to accommodate protest in event studies, we need to remind ourselves of issues we have raised so far in this book, and introduce some concepts that will be outlined in more detail later. To develop a framework that is able to accommodate protest we need to begin by contesting the dominant construal of 'event'. Such a project requires the explora-tion of several trajectories that can begin here but require the extra space of the rest of this book for their complete development. Indeed, we want this book to be the start of something called CES that transforms events management teaching and research. As discussed earlier, Badiou's and Žižek's conceptualization of event as radical rupture offers us a way of developing an alternative perspective on events that can support a realignment of events management that can incorpo-rate protest and acts of civil disobedience. A valuable concurrent aspect of their theorization of event is its essential connection to identity and the subjectivization of the subject. Recognition that at the heart of reconfiguring events management to incorporate protest is a requirement to review processes of subjectification critically draws us into a further important step in developing a theoretical frame-work. Protest as event might be understood as a way of rupturing the neo-liberal categories that shape events management, and a way of rupturing in the streets the power of the neo-liberal forces that shape those spaces. By thinking about the legitimacy of protest as event, we tell the student that not all events are marketized. By thinking about the centrality of protest as liberatory, rupturing events on the streets, we can give legitimacy to the work of activists who are trying to make the world a better place. As researchers studying protests as events, we can begin to map the successes and failures of protests and social movements, and help activists learn about the work of others who are engaged in the same struggle.

Adorno's (2001) critique of the culture industry, which has informed two previ-ous chapters, is a powerful indictment of how capitalism commodifies the human subject while reproducing itself through a cultural lens. As we have shown, his critique of the mass reproduction of culture presents us with a further trajectory along which we are able theoretically to reframe one of the culture industry's most recent incarnations: the similarly named events industry. Adorno's view of events such as music festivals informs our view of mega-events. We suggest that the production of standardizing models within events management education evokes the dominant hegemony, which either ignores protests as events or construes them as risks to be mitigated. Of course, we are not suggesting that protests as events might be a part of the culture industry, though they face the danger of being co-opted by political and cultural hegemonies. Politicians, for example, have long used protests to show that they are on the side of the people against the establishment, or faceless bureaucrats, or distant transnational corporations (Carter, 2014). In the United Kingdom, for example, politicians such as David Cameron and Boris Johnson have joined Plane Stupid activists in publicly arguing that Heathrow Airport should not be granted a third runway. The shameless populism of this can be seen in Cameron's endless prevarication on the matter once he had to make a firm decision on the expansion. There are also examples of corporations using direct action and social activism to sell their products and fashions (Castells, 2012). But that does not mean protests as events are inevitably co-opted by the culture industry. Protest–events have the legitimacy of agency, voluntarism and radical politics at the heart of their creation, making it much more difficult for hegemonic power to take them over outright.

Associated with the industrialization and commodification of events are the communicative practices that augment the construction of the subject with an articulation of relationships of power and constitute the prevailing colonization of events management discourse within a neo-liberalist paradigm, as we have highlighted in earlier chapters on mediatization and commodification. The works of Habermas (1992a, 1992b, 1992c) and, in the English cultural studies tradition, McGuigan (2009a, 2009b) contribute substantially to how we may interrogate those discourses. McGuigan's (2006) formulation of 'cool capitalism' in particular suggests a prism through which the elements of the events industry can be clearly diffracted and carefully assessed. His definition of cool capitalism as the new norm epitomizes how the depoliticization of events frames much of the events management literature. A conceptualization of events that construes event as a contested referent, which critiques the commodification of the event industry, acknowledges and goes beyond Badiou's and Žižek's formulation of event as rupture to encompass the event as a potential arena of dissensus.

Protest seen as event allows us to see ways of writing new stories about leisure and events. People participate in protests as a form of leisure, and because they are attracted to the protest as an event. The excitement of marching and cheering gives people a sense of belonging and a feeling of satisfaction and happiness. Direct action might give people even more than community and satisfaction – the nature of the action gives people an authentic feeling of excitement and purpose in an otherwise mundane world. In being part of such protests and actions, individuals find personal fulfilment, even if the protests and actions do not achieve their stated goals. The purpose of protest, after all, is to make known one's objections to the world as it is, to the ruling classes, to their hegemony, to traditional and conservative ideologies, but especially to the capitalist instrumentality around us. Protests may be angry, populist or right wing in nature, but they are always about expressing a profound dissatisfaction with the narratives of the global, capitalist order. When protesting, people know they are making a difference, even if all they change is the opinion of one bystander on the street. Protest makes the world more purposive, and it makes establishments aware of the anger generated by their policies and plans (Carter, 2014). Operating at a point of convergence between aesthetics and politics, events as protests, protests as events, radically reconfigures the ontology of events management, widens its reach and facilitates epistemological approaches that currently do not figure within the field. The theoretical framework necessary to accommodate protests as a valid part of events management and event studies research and scholarship problematizes event and articulates a critique of the events industry. In so doing it locates an understanding of those two terms within a critical perspective that challenges a neo-liberalist construal of them and frames them as valid ground for the discussion of concerns regarding emancipation and oppression.

So how does this play out in practice? Let us look at some protests in more detail. One previously mentioned example, which has been researched by Neil Gavin (2010), is Plane Stupid. This social activist group uses direct action to generate publicity for its campaign to stop the rise in the use of airports in the United Kingdom. Governments and the airline industry argue that airports are essential for business and the economy, and that the country needs more capacity – specifically, a third runway at Heathrow Airport – to accommodate more passengers and more flights. The pro-expansion lobbyists claim the country will be harmed economically if that does not happen. Plane Stupid counters that this is plain stupid – expanding capacity will mean more environmental damage, and not just in the immediate vicinity of airports, but globally as a result of climate change caused by increased carbon-dioxide emissions. Plane Stupid is clearly right, but the travelling habit is hard for people to break. It is not just business leaders who want to fly more; almost everybody wants cheap flights for foreign holidays. To get their message through to people, Plane Stupid's activists need to plan and deliver direct action as a media spectacle. Their protests become media events, but this entails finding new ways to say the same thing. So they broke into Heathrow Airport, knowing this security breach would become a story in itself, which allowed them to raise their campaign's profile even as the mainstream media concerned itself with the threat of terrorists doing something similar (ibid.).

Another example is the SlutWalk (Miriam, 2012). While women have more rights in liberal democracies in the Global North than they used to have, they are still living in societies that are shaped by and created for hegemonic masculinity. Struggles for a truly equal society are hindered by the power of traditions, assumptions made by men in power and on the fringes of power, and continuing gender violence and repression. SlutWalk activists took as their cue for protest the views of politicians, judges, police officers and others in positions of authority (nearly always, but not exclusively, men) who condemned victims of sexual abuse for wearing 'slutty' clothing. These are not the thoughts of obscure preachers, but the opinions of high-profile commentators and judicial officials in many countries of the Global North (ibid.). Their view is that women who are sexually abused when they are wearing 'sexy' clothing are at least partially to blame for inciting their own assault. In response to this horrendous ideology of patriarchal oppression SlutWalk organized a series of marches during which women dressed outrageously, often playing with notions of femininity and female sexuality. For some feminists, the marches played into the hands of heteronormative views, especially when images of the protests were reproduced in newspapers and on television. But the activists behind SlutWalk were making a serious point about sexual violence on the streets, and sexism and misogyny in popular culture. The spread of the protests and the organization showed young women that it was possible to challenge and ridicule sexism.

Castells (2012) and others (Lotan *et al.*, 2011; Willis, 2014) have explored the meaning and purpose of the protests dubbed the 'Arab Spring'. For many academics studying social movements and protest, these protests were a lost opportunity. Led by young, educated protesters with Western and/or secular leanings, there was much hope at the beginning. These were people 'like us', so politicians and journalists in the West were keen to show their support. On the streets people organized their protests carefully, with support systems established to bring water, food and materials for barricades and potential missiles. Teachers and activists ran classes on democracy and free speech. Musicians played to encourage the protesters. People of all ages, classes and genders assembled on the streets and in the squares. Theirs was a true, authentic outpouring of dissatisfaction with the corruption and repression of the regimes that governed them. The urban middle classes were unhappy about the lack of freedom. The urban working classes were unhappy about the lack of jobs and opportunities. Their protests grew spontaneously across a number of Arab countries, with varying degrees of democratic legitimacy and retaliation from the ruling elites, and the outcomes were markedly diverse.

In Tunisia the protests started when people expressed their anger at local corruption and economic mismanagement. The end result was the downfall of the regime, the drafting of a new constitution, and democratic elections. In Egypt the protests saw a wide range of political groups unite to oust the regime of Hosni Mubarak, but this 'rainbow alliance' was fundamentally split between secularists and the Muslim Brotherhood, who wished to introduce an Islamic state. When the Brotherhood won the subsequent elections the secularists returned to the streets, and Egypt was riven by violent protests both for and against Mohamed Morsi's new government. In the end the military intervened on the side of the secularists, arresting Morsi and hundreds of members of the Brotherhood. The ongoing violence and repression in Egypt represents a prime example of the ugly side of protest. Similarly, there was brutal state repression of protesters in other Arab countries, while in Syria the protests led directly to civil war, millions of refugees and hundreds of thousands of deaths.

The events of the Arab Spring and its aftermath followed a pattern seen in countries in Eastern Europe and Central Asia, such as Ukraine, Georgia and Turkey, as well as in earlier protests for freedom and democracy, such as those in China. Nation-states ruling through oppression and manipulation of the media and the constitution inevitably become places where educated, liberal, left-wing people grow increasingly unhappy and angry. It is impossible to keep such people sheltered from the truth of their condition and from the knowledge that other countries respect human rights, including freedom of speech and freedom of assembly. Protesting can result in death, torture or imprisonment, but sometimes it generates real change. For instance, in Tunisia, there has been a genuine shift to liberal democracy. Meanwhile, in Turkey, despite the state's brutal repression of activists, the protest movement continues to operate. It has created a public sphere in which people learn about their rights, learn how to organize and learn how to protest. Radicals in the Global North should remember that their colleagues in left-wing parties and groups are leading this activism in Turkey and in other countries where freedom of speech is curtailed.

For those of us who live in liberal democracies, it is sometimes easy to forget the importance of protest as a civic right. The French Revolution emerged out of one of the first popular protest movements of the modern era, and that movement's demands (liberty, equality, fraternity) were ultimately enshrined in international human rights legislation. The Chartist movement campaigned over many years in the United Kingdom for the abolition of privilege in the corrupt Houses of Parliament and the introduction of a universal franchise. Suffragettes campaigned for votes and rights for women. Trade unions campaigned for employment rights. All of these campaigns and movements included protests on the streets and direct action. Everything we take for granted in our democracies has been earned by the blood of protesters.

Activism as leisure

This book is situated in the wider critical subject field of leisure studies, which explores the meaning and purpose of leisure. It is interested in the status of leisure in society, the ways in which different people and social groups access leisure spaces and practices, and the ways and forms in which people pursue leisure. The academic investigation of leisure began as far back as Durkheim, Marx and Veblen, but the modern subject field arose in the second half of the twentieth century, when academics started to debate the contested status of leisure in modernity. For some academics, leisure studies was a way of demonstrating the importance of leisure, and specifically forms of active recreation and physical activity. It also allowed them to research the optimal forms of leisure for motivation, healthiness and well-being. For others, leisure studies was a way of critiquing the very notion that leisure was unimportant or uncontentious. These scholars came from sociology, politics and geography backgrounds, and they were strongly influenced by Marxism and radical feminism. They saw leisure as something that might be free in theory, but dominated by the logic of capitalism in practice. From their perspective, it was given to some people and not to others, a space where men could play while women stayed at home and looked after their families, and where elites could take long holidays while the working classes were constrained by poverty to the occasional week at the seaside or bank holiday.

One of the most important early theorists of leisure, Robert Stebbins (1982, 1997, 2009), argues that to understand the importance of leisure we have to have a typology of leisure: for him, there is a crucial distinction between casual leisure (Stebbins, 1997) and serious leisure (Stebbins, 1982, 2006). The former is what we do when we are not actively thinking and positioning ourselves, such as watching television or drinking with friends. We do these things because they give us pleasure, demand little effort on our part, and are easy to fit into our working and family lives. A form of casual leisure activism might be signing an online petition a friend has posted on Facebook: it takes seconds and we neither know nor care much about the consequences of the protest. By contrast, serious leisure demands effort, knowledge and skill if we are to do it well, so sustained, intrinsic motivation is a prerequisite. Classic examples of serious leisure activities are playing a musical instrument and running. It takes time to do these things well, and once you have achieved that level of competence you need to sustain your effort thereafter; but the rewards are high both psychologically and sociologically. A form of serious leisure activism might be joining a campaign group, becoming its treasurer, devoting time and effort to understanding its internal systems, and playing a role in the group's direct action and protest–events.

Over the last thirty years leisure studies researchers and theorists have become more aware of wider sociological and cultural ideas relating to the state of modernity. For some academics, this has meant a full embrace of the implications of postmodernity and postmodernism. They believe that the old structures that governed modern society have been swept away by the tide of post-industrialization, mobilities, globalization and increasing equality across the genders and ethnicities. The consequences of this process are greater individuation and choice, and a greater realization that leisure lifestyles are important in giving people belonging and identity. Leisure spaces and forms are said to be places where people can perform identity and belonging. Doing leisure, to paraphrase Rojek (2010), involves the labour of work. In an age of liquid modernity, we have liquid leisure (Blackshaw, 2010). The lucky few in the Global North are allowed to play at being all kinds of leisure consumers while everybody else has to look on in a combination of anger and envy. In the leisure journals and at leisure conferences, the exploration of lifestyles seems to be a dominant theme. Researchers are exploring how individuals create identity and belonging, meaning and purpose, through the music scenes they inhabit, the spaces through which they move, the leisure activities in which they engage. Some of this work explores the marginal and the liminal. Who is allowed to be free with their leisure choices? Who is excluded from this postmodern performativity? But much of this work celebrates the people who do the leisure performances. The research declares that such people get to do all sorts of things in their leisure time, but it fails to explore the moral asymmetry of global capitalism's takeover of leisure. It might be good for people to travel to distant places, but only rich Western people are able to do so for a holiday, or during a sabbatical from work. Global flows and mobilities might be open for those with the money to buy visas, but for the global poor mobility is restricted and discouraged by Western governments that continue to erect walls and fences alongside the symbolic walls of immigration sheds.

So there are huge problems with this postmodern turn in leisure studies. But it could be argued that activism is a form of performative leisure identity. One joins a campaign group because one finds belonging and community among one's fellow activists. One then performs the role of the good activist by turning up to meetings, posting material on social media, and attending actions and protests.

Moreover, in playing this performative role, one learns the right things to say, and even the right things to eat and wear, from others.

Despite this turn to the postmodern, leisure studies as a subject field is still dominated by structural and post-structural discourses that are indebted to Marxism and feminism. There is still a strong awareness of the inequalities of modern life, the historical nature of capitalism, modernity, imperialism, racial hierarchies and the gender order, to name just a few of the important issues that remain pertinent in leisure and society (although this too is in danger of being overshadowed by the rising tide of management and instrumentality, not least in the new curricula of university leisure courses). Leisure studies still produces research that shows that the notion that leisure is freely chosen and freely given in a free leisure space owned by no one is a myth (Bramham, 2005; Spracklen, 2009). We are all borne of our circumstances, and the leisure spaces we inhabit, and the leisure activities we choose to pursue, are dictated by those circumstances, even when we think we are able to change them. Someone who chooses to like heavy metal rather than rap music might think they are being alternative and rebellious – and they are right, in many ways – but fundamentally there is no difference between the two genres. Both of these forms of music are created by the culture industry for our entertainment and our subjugation. Someone who thinks running every day makes them a better person than someone who watches nightly repeats of *Jersey Shore* is right only in the sense that running (in moderation) is a healthy activity while watching hours of television is likely to be unhealthy. Running is not necessarily *morally* better than watching television. We live in a culture that gives running an elite cultural capital, whereas watching television is seen as a lower-class pursuit. Even bourgeois omnivores, when they consume television, do so with a knowing irony about their tastes sliding down a couple of classes.

Leisure, then, is never something we do *just* for fun, even though we might enjoy the things that we do. We do things in our leisure time because they are aspects of our cultural norms and values, and of the expectations of our class. We do things that are given to us by the culture industry in the name of political hegemonies; and subcultures and alternative, counter-hegemonic resistance are always limited. This is why events are so important to us now. They have been constructed as normal parts of our lives, and they are designed to control our freedom of choice and restrict us to deciding whether to spend our money on the cup final or the boutique festival.

Where does this leave social activism and protest? Taking a pessimistic view, we might argue that social activism is the preserve of younger middle-class elites before they assume the establishment leadership roles they expect of themselves. This might be a form of cultural omnivorousness or fetishism, where young members of the ruling classes get a visceral thrill or social satisfaction from engaging in the counter-cultural public sphere. There are many examples of mainstream politicians in the West who were involved in radical politics and direct action before rejecting radical change for compromise and centrist/right politics. In the United Kingdom Tony Blair's New Labour government was filled with such activists turned defenders of the establishment: Peter Hain, a member of cabinet under both Blair and his successor Gordon Brown, was a famous campaigner against apartheid in South Africa, leading the campaign that eventually resulted in a number of sports boycotts; Harriet Harman, deputy leader of the Labour Party on a number of occasions, was an activist for and employee of the National Council for Civil Liberties; and Blair himself was a member of the Campaign for Nuclear Disarmament. In the campaigns against road-building in England in the 1980s and 1990s, a popular story circulated that the protesters were drawn largely from middle- and upper-class backgrounds – privately educated hippies who were free to protest thanks to their trust funds. This extended to New Age travellers who journeyed from free festival to free festival, and even inspired the new portmanteau word 'trustafarian': white, upper-class young adults with trust funds and dreadlocks who slummed it in camps and squats for a few years (Martin, 2002).

There is some truth to the pessimistic view of social activism as a form of instrumental leisure – something provided as a diversion that is useful to the hegemonic powers that control us. Instrumental leisure, as mentioned elsewhere in this book, serves Habermas's (1992b, 1992c) instrumental rationalities: the rationalities associated with hegemonic powers (i.e. nation-states and global capitalism). But social activism is a legitimate form of serious leisure that allows individuals to resist the invasion of instrumentality in society at large. It is always in opposition to hegemonic powers, whether it is radical left or populist right. It might be used by people with hegemonic aims, such as politicians who wish to divert or control dissent; it might even be a place where elites impose their own performativity of resistance, as we have just seen in the case of the trustafarians. But social activism is a legitimate form of communicative leisure (Spracklen, 2009) because it is nearly always constructed against the tide of instrumentality. People stand up to fight against capitalism and its effects, and against racism and sexism. These are all worthwhile causes. Social activism is an important place where individuals can protest about the inequalities caused by the evils of global capitalism and its political establishment (Castells, 2012; Habermas, 1987). We contend that activism is a form of leisure activity and leisure lifestyle, and protests (and events) are leisure spaces. Following Habermas (1992b, 1992c), Spracklen (2009) argues that as the world has become ever more commodified and commercialized, leisure has become more instrumental. But leisure still provides a small communicative space in which humans can work to resist the colonization of their Habermasian lifeworld.

Activism as leisure, then, describes this communicative rationality and action, the resistance and counter-hegemonic struggle. Social activists choose to take part in their activism, and they make their protest space in discussion and agreement with other activists. This is the Habermasian public sphere at work. There is no compulsion to be an activist. One joins in and participates in whichever way one can, and one co-produces the cultures, the actions and the events associated with the spaces. Social activists are working in their leisure time to become better social activists. They are using the public sphere to protest, and the private spheres of social media and community networks to maintain a Habermasian lifeworld of communicative rationality and action. Protest and campaign groups might take on the tools of instrumentality, through professional marketing campaigns and fundraising systems, but they still rely on the goodwill and free choices of volunteers, activists and members. Social activism is like volunteering at a corporate mega-event, but here the relationship is not analogous to slavery. Social activists operate within a logic and discourse of communicative action. They freely choose to give their leisure time and their labour to the protest and the actions. They do this because the defence of the lifeworld – the social and physical world around us – is so important to them that they are prepared to relinquish some freedoms to preserve it.

Conclusion

The Occupy movement has been the subject of a number of academic studies (Costanza-Chock, 2012; Gamson and Sifry, 2013; Razsa and Kurnik, 2012). It first made headlines in 2011 when its activists took over streets and squares in hundreds of cities around the world. It was inspired by the Arab Spring and ongoing takeovers of public and semi-public, privatized spaces in Spain. Occupy targeted spaces close to financial centres, such as Wall Street in New York and the City of London. Many of these spaces were privatized: that is, they were public spaces that had been sold to private landlords and were now regulated by private security agencies as a way of distancing the financial elites from the public. This did not stop Occupy's activists, who built camps (and barricades around those camps) in defiance of the private security firms and the police. All of the Occupy campaigns were organized through social media, and technology was used to maintain the camps' viability and media presence. Some of the protesters were veterans of radical protests and direct action against capitalism, but many of those involved were persuaded to protest for the first time by growing social inequality exacerbated by the global recession (Costanza-Chock, 2012). Occupy organized collectively to manage and run the camps and any related actions through a system of participatory democracy that was reminiscent of anarchist protests and communes (Razsa and Kurnik, 2012). Campaigners came up with the catchy slogan 'We are the 99%' to highlight the proportion of Americans who had seen their personal wealth fall during the recession, compared to the top 1 per cent who increased their wealth. The movement gained global headlines, and inspired more Occupy camps throughout the Global North and beyond. But the movement's momentum was hindered by the growing use of police violence: protesters were forcibly evicted from camps, beaten up and arrested, while tents and banners were torn down. Occupy continues to inspire protests, and it has transformed into an umbrella organization for many anti-capitalist campaigners, but the takeovers of city spaces have slowed to a trickle, and bankers continue to make enormous profits.

When Occupy was in full swing, the camps became spaces where the rules of capitalism and social order, the by-laws and regulations that limited freedom in these privatized spaces, were abolished. Following Žižek, we suggest that the Occupy protesters intended to overturn what Flusty (2005) calls 'interdictory space' – semi-public space that has been designed in such a way as to repel the public from venturing into it. In modern cities these spaces feature spikes and studs where one might otherwise sit or play. Policy-makers and landlords introduce these design elements to ensure that the homeless, young people and other undesirables, such as skaters and social activists, move away from the city centre. In their study of Leeds city centre, Spracklen, Richter and Spracklen (2013) note that policies to make the city centre desirable to the middle classes also make it eventized, gentrified and privatized, with alternative subcultures and political action forced to the outskirts. Clearly, Occupy activists would take pride in reclaiming such interdictory space by physically living and protesting within it for such a long period of time. In that sense, events as protests can be seen as a way of reclaiming and overturning interdictory spaces and transforming them into spaces of interaction and dissent.

However, Bauman (2007) argues that these interdictory spaces are also designed to segregate, alienate and marginalize people from one another. Following him, it could be said that the Occupy activists allowed the ruling authorities to turn their camps into interdictory spaces where they were marginalized and controlled, surrounded by police and private security firms. In that sense, such static protests might serve the purposes of the rulers. Inside, the Occupy camps may have been exciting places of transgression and hope; but outside, the authorities ensured that the interdictory space taken over by Occupy became just another kind of interdictory space – the kind suggested by Bauman. The police and media guaranteed that the protesters were marginalized and alienated from wider society, and from the businesses that continued to buy and sell around the camps.

Events as protests therefore have the ability to be spaces where the norms and values of society are transgressed. They carry all the hallmarks of third spaces, or heterotopias, to use Foucault's (1991) term. But while these heterotopias might physically challenge the materiality of interdictory spaces in urban centres, they risk becoming fenced-off, kettled and surveilled interdictory spaces in their own right, serving as temporary prisons for the people who live inside.

So was Occupy a waste of time? No, it was not. Politicians have had to take notice of the growing anger of the people who have suffered through the global recession. Hegemonic control of the media makes it difficult for people to see the true social and economic costs of global capitalism, whereas Occupy's protests and actions make such issues known to everyone who watches television or browses the internet. The growing inequality caused by the system we are told is the best solution for our problems is increasingly apparent. The mood in the public sphere has changed, with the left re-energized around the world. Saying nothing and accepting the inequalities that surround us equates to giving up on the Habermasian lifeworld and our communicative actions and rationality. People now understand that they have to protest if they want some part of humanity to remain free from instrumentality.

8 The colonization of event discourse

Introduction

We seem to be living every second of our waking lives as if we are in some sort of event, watched by spectators and other participants. Sometimes this feels as if the event is life itself, which has become a game in which we accumulate things to win some kind of immortal prize. On our train journeys into work, people casually take out their expensive new phones and other gadgets and share their mundane thoughts. This phenomenon is just an expression of the performativity of fashion in general – people see public spaces as opportunities to compete and show that they have more money or more style (Bourdieu, 1984; Hebdige, 1979). The fashion and communications industries nurture this gaming of life because they see their profits rise on the back of it. This game is an event in which every commuter has to be involved, either as a ruthless competitor acquiring and consuming the right goods or as a passive spectator giving silent approval to the blinking phone or the fancy shoes. We are driven to be part of this game because we enjoy the spectacle and the competition. We want to show that we are winners, better than those around us, more successful or wealthier (Bauman, 2000; Bourdieu, 1984; Spracklen, 2013, 2015). We approach the business of interacting with others on a purely individual level, seeking to gain some advantage for ourselves alone, adding up the points we have accrued by virtue of our number of sexual partners, the number of dollars in our bank account, or the number of downloads on our devices. In the religious past people endeavoured to do good deeds to ensure their place in heaven. In our secular age people think only of the abstract balance sheet at the end of their lives, and the scoreboards of the event in which we exist.

This might sound exaggerated, but it is not just fashion-conscious office workers on commuter trains who obsess over the accumulation of points in the game-as-event of life. Academics, including the present authors, are judged by others for our research output, and careers are won and lost on the number of studies we can deliver within certain time-scales. In the United Kingdom we are subject to the scrutiny of the Research Excellence Framework (known as REF), set up by the state to ensure academics are doing the 'right sort' of research – that which generates money and/or has a significant impact in wider society. The people who sit in judgement on the panels and sub-panels are world-class experts in our areas. They review all the work submitted to them by universities, then decide who is best, who is second best, and so on. We submitted to a range of sub-panels in the latest REF (audited in 2014), but our strongest submission was for Unit 26: Sport and Exercise Science, Leisure and Tourism. We had previously come third on the table that combines the rankings awarded and the number of people submitted. This time, we came second: that is, we had lots of people in our submission, and the work they submitted was very good. Our university was very pleased with our efforts and has trumpeted the fact that we moved from third to second. But we still scored quite low on quality of submissions and some other indicators. Moreover, we remain behind Loughborough, the biggest and richest sports-dominated university in the country. We have no choice but to take part in the REF, because our university is scored on various league tables for its research strength, and these league tables strongly influence parents' decisions about where to send their children to study. The REF results also attract additional research money, which is useful; and doing well makes us feel good as individuals.

But REF is not a good thing for us as academics. Each researcher who wanted to be a part of our Unit 26 submission had to present four 'outputs' that were judged to be of at least 3* ('internationally important') quality. Reducing research to something called an 'output' is instrumental, and evidence of the game-as-events of the REF. Some universities insisted that the only measure of quality was if a research paper was published in a journal with a high impact factor. Some people in our own university shared this view. One of us was not submitted to the REF, and this may have implications for him securing grants internally. We also know of a colleague who had a fourth output knocked back because it was published just before the deadline and the manager who was assessing quality did not think it was a definite 3*. Colleagues in other universities were told their work would not be submitted because it was in the form of book chapters. Some colleagues at other universities have been made redundant after poor REF results led to departmental closures. No one is allowed to know what their individual scores are, but individuals are 'in' or 'out', and departments are 'good' or 'bad'. As academics, all we should ever want to do is conduct interesting research and then write about it. But now we have to justify our choices and play the REF event because our lives (or at least our livelihoods) depend on it.

In this chapter we look at the ways in which the norms, assumptions, practices and discourses of events management have been extended into two separate but related fields: leisure and popular cultural spaces; and the pedagogy and curricula of undergraduate degree courses. The first section of the chapter returns to the idea of eventization, introduced in Chapter 2. We show that this is not only pro-gressing at the level of public spaces but proceeding in a hegemonic fashion to shape all manner of spaces and activities that are only loosely connected to events management. In the second section we concentrate on how leisure and cultural spaces are being eventized through a process of colonization. Finally, we focus on the ways in which the academic study of leisure has become eventized.

Eventization of life

Put simply, everything is an event in the life of something, whether that something is a quark binding other quarks to it inside a proton, a galaxy expanding in the vast depths of the universe, or a heart beating. All life forms, whether they are bacteria, trees or humans, go through a series of related events that mark their life course. We are born, we live our lives, we grow older, and we die. Human life and culture are shaped by the events that mark them. All human cultures have recognized the stages in our life cycle, the structures that govern families and tribes, and the events associated with those stages and structures. The importance of rituals surrounding birth, coming of age, marriage and death show that humans in pre-modernity placed utmost importance on the place of individuals in their communities, and expected everyone to participate in these events in the correct way. Religions emerged from the human concern with making sense of the world and people's place in it, and religious events soon became the accepted ways of marking the life course and identifying belonging and community (Eliade, 2013). Events came to mean special moments in time, points when the everyday and mundane might be marked by something important or unusual (even if the unusual was regular). Rituals became ever more elaborate as human culture became associated with agriculture and villages, and the cycle of the seasons became important in the cycle of events that shaped each year (ibid.). In *The Golden Bough* (Frazer, 1922), J.G. Frazer's impressively large synthesis of anthropology and history, the importance of these events in the lives of pre-modern cultures and the cultures of European history is made abundantly clear. Humans everywhere need ritual, and they need to mark the passing of time through different events. Rulers (the priests and kings of Frazer's theoretical framework) need such events to impress their subjects about their divine right to rule. That is, rulers need to use events to prove that they are divine, or at least have been granted power by gods, so they take possession of the cyclical festivals and claim they are responsible for the return of spring. For everyone else, the rituals and festivals mark the passage of time, the return of the sun and a chance to experience the liminal through feasting, drinking and other transgressions (ibid.). As formal belief systems with holy scriptures emerged out of pre-history, rituals and calendars of events became aspects of the *habitus* of a majority of the world's inhabitants. In Christianity, this appeared in the fixed cycle of saints' days, with their accompanying festivals and carnivals. Some belief systems use the phases of the moon to set the dates of their scared events, so these drift across the modern calendar year, but their adherents cling to the lunar calendar because it was used to mark the most important religious festivals in the first place.

Events, then, as special moments in time when the mundane is suspended, are parts of our human cultural memory. As human societies entered modernity the events that shaped people's lives continued to combine the personal, the communal and the religious. Even as modern society has become secular, religious belief has continued, and religious events continue to shape lives: in the West, Christmas still dominates the calendar as an end-of-year festival when we swap presents, meet up with family and old friends, and eat and drink to excess. But there are other events too, such as graduations, which did not exist in the shapes that they do now, and ultimately connect to the idea of coming of age. In our university we have a week-long graduation event each July, in which students who have passed through the final year of their degree course get to walk across a stage and receive their certificate. The students dress up in their suits and dresses, wear mortar boards and gowns, and wait their turn while their parents cry and cheer. We wear our robes and our senior managers stand on the stage and say nice things about the students and the university. At the end of the week thousands of students have walked across the stage and into their new adult lives. Of course, students graduated in pre-modernity from the few universities that existed in that period, but the enormous growth in higher education since around the world since the 1960s means that obtaining a degree is now open to a large section of the population. The rituals of the medieval university have been reinvented for our times and popularized by the adoption of fancy American graduation ceremonies and subsequent US influences in popular culture (Hebdige, 1979; Williams, 1977). Graduation is now acted out in the US style, and our students throw their mortar boards in the air because they have seen a hundred Hollywood films that present this as normal behaviour. This Americanization of global coming-of-age ceremonies can also be seen in the spread of the end-of-school prom. This used to be seen in the United Kingdom as a weird US peculiarity, seen only in movie theatres and on TV screens. Now it is a coming-of-age event for our children, too.

As we enter the era of late modernity or postmodernity, the centrality of events in our lives is becoming ever more salient. The language of the event is applied to every aspect of our everyday lives. We are saturated by the norms and values of events management. We minimize risk, plan operational activities, have strategic goals and plans, and set our financial budgets. We become our own managers, running our own events. We assume that every day is one day in the event of our lives, during which we have to compete and do well under the public's gaze. Even when we choose to brush our teeth or wash our hair we are making decisions about how to maximize our gains in the public sphere, or responding to feedback we have received from others in real life or on television. We modulate the way we walk, the way we talk and the way we think as we try to compete against others in the workplace, school or college. The game of life we have set ourselves is to find a well-paid job, climb corporate ladders and make more money than we will ever need (Bourdieu, 1984). This might be related to the other main aim of trying to find a life partner, someone with whom to build a home and raise a family, but our work status – and our place in the event of work – comes first. Whether we are religious or secular, we approach the acquisition of status as the most important life goal. This planet is the main stage of our festival, and we are our own headliners in our imagination, with our cheering fans filling the space in front of us. But we are not making music. We are making money.

Marriage was always an important stage of our lives, complete with appropriate solemn rituals and drunken events. In this new order every wedding is now the subject of strategic, instrumental planning and management. Wedding planners are hired to maximize the spectacle while pandering to the desires of the couple and the requirements of fashion's ever-changing trends. Many students who study events management at university dream of becoming wedding planners, and many others do work experience in that industry. These late modern weddings are among the most egregious examples of eventization. Guests are expected to pay thousands of pounds for hotel rooms and to travel to some fancy location. The presents that appear on extensive lists are all extortionately expensive. The contractors who provide food, entertainment and even flowers charge outrageous sums for their goods and services, as do the wedding planners themselves. Why is this tolerated on such a sacred and important day for the couple who are getting married? Because this is just how weddings are these days. Anyone who dares to make a stand against such eventization is criticized for turning against family and close friends, who expect us to legitimate the latest move in their monetized, instrumentalized game of life.

Within families, this eventization has transformed parents' relationships with their children, and with others' children. It is not enough for us to be merely happy parents. There is now enormous social and cultural pressure from the eventization of family life to show that we are *successful* parents (Golombok, 2015). So we invest time and energy in showing off our parenting skills to others, through the choices we make for our children. In the playground, in the park and at the school gate we flaunt our children's experiences in front of other parents. We hothouse our children through extra tutorials, music lessons, sports activities and educational trips to museums and stately homes in a desperate bid to increase their intelligence and boost their extra-curricular activities. We do this because we know such things are necessary for our children to succeed in the 'getting into a good university' event. In the United Kingdom ideally that means Oxbridge, although we might grudgingly accept a Russell Group institution. In the United States ideally it means an Ivy League college. Every country has a similar hierarchy of universities. We tell ourselves that winning this game is all about giving our children the best start in life. But, of course, if our children get into one of these universities, *our* scoresheets improve too. We can tell our neighbours and our work colleagues that our children are now at Oxford or Harvard with a smug little smile, as if we are not bothered at all as long as they are happy. But we *are* bothered, because we are always trying to prove that we are better than those around us. As with social media updates, we are constantly writing our own heroic narratives, showing the world that we are the winners in this event.

Over recent years there has been an increasing eventization of life as a result of the accelerating trends of late modernity: increasing commodification; increasing individualism; increasing competition; the fracturing of communities; and increasing mobility (Rojek, 2013, 2014; Spracklen, Richter and Spracklen, 2013). We have discussed all of these issues in previous chapters. There is, we suggest, a feedback loop at work between the events industry and society and popular culture. Mega-events have made society and popular culture more like mega-events. They have given society and culture a set of instruments and metaphors to apply to them, so everyday life and work have both become eventized. But the increasing competition and individualism in everyday life and work have in turn fed into the increased importance of mega-events in society and culture. Because we are more instrumental, more neo-liberal in our relationships and families, we seek the forms of leisure and culture that mirror such instrumentalization. So we prefer to spend our money and our time on mega-events, and on turning our everyday leisure and culture activities and spaces into events.

The eventization of leisure and culture

As we have already discussed, in leisure studies there is an ongoing debate about the meaning and purpose of leisure, and the possibility of free choice in modern leisure (Rojek, 2010; Spracklen, 2009). While leisure studies scholars argue about how much free choice there is, and whether anybody had that choice in the past, they generally agree that such free, communicative leisure has moral and social value. People like to do the leisure things they do because they get some sense of self from them. This search for an authentic leisure experience predicated on free will and free choice is paralleled in urban studies and cultural geographies – specifically in discussions about the politics of space and the adoption of neo-liberal cultural policies that limit the use of that space. We can see here that the eventization of these public spaces is being constructed by a combination of neo-liberalism and a lack of public sector resources. Put simply, local government has been starved of cash and forced to sell off public spaces – valuable areas of urban real estate – to landlords and developers. They, in turn, transform those public spaces into private ones, and more events and private security are the consequences. Cultural policies are shaped by the wider political consensus of neo-liberalism. Mainstream political parties at the local and national levels in the West write manifestos that promise greater economic choice, more market liberalism, more 'partnership' with the 'dynamic' private sector, and tougher action against criminals and others who are viewed as 'poor consumers' (Bauman, 2000). This consensus serves the interests of global capitalism and the few who have the capital and/or job security to enjoy private shopping malls and their homogenized food halls. But even before the global recession such policies excluded and marginalized a great number of people. In urban spaces the hegemony of global capitalism in late modernity has seen an increasing gentrification of city centres, ever more exclusion of independent retailers by outpricing them, and the displacement of the poor and the marginalized – the unemployed, the working class, minority ethnic communities, alternative subcultures and counter-cultures – away from the spaces that politicians identify as being part of their 'outward-facing' branding strategies.

Spracklen (2012: 121) notes that Prime Minister David Cameron continually boosted the London 2012 Olympics through press releases and public statements in which he stressed the importance of 'legacy' and 'regeneration': 'with the British economy stalling, unemployment figures rising and cuts to public services affecting millions of marginalized people up and down the country, naturally Cameron wanted to find some positive message'. Our lives, we are told, depend on bidding successfully for events, hosting those events, and embracing the neo-liberal, managerialist ideology of events. For corporations and governments, events are a key way to make profits. For governments, they are also a way to normalize nationalism (or regionalism or parochialism, depending on the size of government and the event, as discussed earlier), the ideology of neo-liberalism, the idea that we need to pay to be at leisure, and the notion that we need to work hard to succeed as a performer. Eventization turns all forms of leisure and culture into events, stages in a series of projects, with profit margins and ideological, hegemonic status (Gramsci, 1973). Eventization, we argue, is the transformation of (free or cheap) communicative leisure activities and spaces into (expensive) corporatized spectacles and privatized spaces. There is a crisis of thinking at the centre of global politics: blind belief in events as transformative; determination to turn public spaces over to private events corporations; and wishful thinking about legacies that leads to cynicism among people who are struggling to pay their household bills while billions of pounds of public money are spent on hosting a mega-event. This should come as no surprise, but we need to think a little deeper about this eventization's impact on leisure and culture today.

Sport is an obvious way in which eventization and its instrumental logic have changed leisure and culture. For much of the last century active recreation and active leisure were the norms for most young people in the West. They had sports and physical education lessons during school hours, then played outside, participating in all kinds of informal play activities, interspersed with loosely organized sports (Spracklen, 2011a). Alongside these communicative, self-regulating activities, local councils, sports clubs and associations provided opportunities for more formal active recreation. Admittedly a series of power relationships – especially around gender – restricted such participation, but working-class and elite men in Western countries typically found ways to become actively involved in sports and recreation (ibid.). These were mass *participation* movements. Sports spectatorship existed in parallel, but it complemented the physical involvement. Then, in the second half of the twentieth century, the balance started to shift as ever more people became fans, consumers and critics of professional sports, rather than active participants. Football in the United Kingdom, for example, became a huge part of the entertainment industry, with star players earning millions of pounds a year – all supported by the mainstreaming of fan culture and the rise of subscriptions to watch the sport on television. Some of the growth in football in the UK is due to changing demographics and the appearance of the bourgeois postmodern fan. But it is also fed by a relentless eventization of every match. It is not enough to read a match report after the event. There is intense pressure to attend the match, whatever the cost, if one wishes to feel authentic. Failing that, one should at least watch the game live through one's satellite box. All sport is reduced to watching an event, and paying to watch that event. All sports fandom is a privatization of community and identity, with fans obliged to purchase belonging through viewing the event and consuming the sponsors' products.

If the Olympics and professional sports such as football represent particularly egregious examples of the privatization and commodification of culture, as well as the eventization of urban spaces, they are nonetheless typical of the kind of instrumentalized leisure that transforms cities from spaces of belonging into spaces of exclusion (Bauman, 2007; Flusty, 2005; Spracklen, Richter and Spracklen, 2013). Politicians, policy-makers and their partners in global capitalism are keen to transform city spaces into commodified, eventized spaces because their hegemonic power is threatened by counter-hegemonic movements. They do not want to see alternative people, minority ethnic groups and the lower classes enjoying the spaces on their streets, so they create interdictory spaces that are designed to discourage people from 'hanging around' (see Chapter 7). The owners of these eventized spaces do not want youngsters playing on bikes and skate-boards, because older and wealthier bourgeois people – whom the corporations wish to attract to these urban spaces to spend money – fear the young as a source of antisocial behaviour. Young people's leisure and culture are sanitized from the urban space as if they are plagues that will kill off the consumers before they reach the cash register. Others are similarly stigmatized and excluded by the corporations, too. Because these spaces are now private spaces, the private security firms have the power to eject anyone they do not like. In practice, though, poor consumers do not even enter because they are made to feel so unwelcome. The notion that one can simply hang around on a street corner or in a public building, talking to friends and enjoying a pleasant summer's evening, is now a form of heresy against the instrumental logic of eventized culture.

This transformation of urban space into consumer space has shifted the way we participate in everyday leisure activities, such as going out for the evening. In the West urban residents of all classes have traditionally gone out to delineate the working day from the leisure evening; and in the last century the opportunities to do this paralleled the growth of towns and cities. For elites, going out typi-cally meant eating out in a fancy restaurant, or paying to attend a theatre production. For the lower classes, a lack of money and a lack of cultural capital limited their evening pastimes to pubs and bars, coffee houses and tea shops, cinemas and music halls. Again, there were enormous inequality issues with this form of leisure, especially in relation to the notion that women should not visit such public leisure spaces (Spracklen, 2011a). Nevertheless, going out allowed working-class people (or at least men) to socialize, create a sense of community and belonging, and educate themselves about and possibly even act against the hegemony of the ruling classes. Conversely, going out allowed the ruling elites to police their status and sustain their political hegemony through contracts, marriages and the dissemination of information (ibid.).

Now, however, going out has become completely eventized for everybody. It is not enough just to find somewhere to have a quiet drink with one's friends. We are expected to process from chain-bar to chain-bar, drinking to excess to prove to our friends and potential friends that we are winners. We are expected to recount stories of our excesses and boast of our drinking prowess. Drinking has become a competition sport, an occasion when we are expected to excel, especially if the consumption of alcohol forms part of an event such as stag party (Thurnell-Read, 2012). If we decide to eat out, we have to eat at the 'right' restaurant – whether that is a transnational corporation or a *faux*-traditional hipster pie-and-mash joint – and behave in the instrumental ways we have learned from the media and each other. So the food and the company become less important than the décor and the sexiness of the serving staff, because this is an *event* in our life. If we leave the house for some cultural nourishment, we no longer go to a library, to the back room of a pub, or to a free museum filled with quiet statues. Cultural venues have turned themselves into events, attractions that shout about their importance through slick marketing campaigns and then take our money. Whether it is a festival, a gig at an enormous stadium, an opera or a play, we are told that this experience is so important that we need to pay a huge amount of money just to be there. We then validate our existence, and our place in the eventized modern world, by posting pictures of ourselves at the event on social media (Spracklen, 2015). By doing so, we show that our entire life consists of one corporate event after another. We display our good taste, or at least the taste that others tell us is good. We let everybody know that we are having the time of our life because we have had the latest exclusive experience. Learning from television and newspaper reports about celebrities, we shape our Facebook profiles as if we ourselves are celebrities: our children are the subjects of conversations about fashion; our choice of bar is recorded by a thousand photographs. Every selfie we take proves to the world that we have made it, that we are the winners of our life event. Every 'like' constructs our identity and manages that identity as if we are a multinational corporation's marketing manager. Our number of friends on Facebook becomes the instrumental measure by which our failure or success is judged. So Facebook becomes both a means of validating our eventized lives and an event in itself.

Eventization of leisure studies and leisure education

Events management degrees have emerged from the leisure studies subject field, and they are still identified as elements in the cluster of sport, leisure and tourism degrees in many universities and funding bodies (for the basis of the arguments in this section, see Spracklen, 2014a). In the Research Excellence Framework, mentioned earlier in this chapter, events management is seen as an area within the tourism management section of the sub-panel Unit 26. Publishers position events-related publications, such as this one, in their tourism or leisure portfolios. In our university events research is carried out within the International Centre for Research in Events, Tourism and Hospitality, which itself is part of the larger Institute for Sport, Physical Activity and Leisure. We both belong to the Centre for Research in Events, Tourism and Hospitality, and Spracklen is also a member of another research centre within the institute called Diversity, Equity and Inclusion, which concentrates on socio-cultural critiques of inequalities in sport and leisure. So, events is a sub-set of leisure, although the phrase 'leisure studies' (and indeed 'leisure') has fallen out of favour in management structures. Lamond teaches in the School of Events, Tourism and Hospitality on events management degrees; Spracklen teaches in the School of Sport on leisure degrees (although only one of these has the word 'leisure' in its title). Both schools, along with the School of

Education and Childhood, were in the Carnegie Faculty at the time of writing. One might argue that such a faculty should be called the 'Faculty of Leisure', but this was ruled out in our last management reshuffle. In the higher education academy all of the courses and subject fields in the two schools where we teach are identified as belonging to the long-winded Hospitality, Leisure, Sport, Tourism and Events area.

Leisure-related courses first appeared in the United States. Designed and delivered by enthusiasts for active recreation and kinesiology, these vocational, practical degrees included some psychology, physiology and biomechanics to stimulate student interest in recreation and sport (Rojek, 2010). Before long they also incorporated management, pedagogy, sociology and policy into their curricula to create the classic North American leisure studies or leisure management course. At the same time in Europe, universities were beginning to develop degrees in physical education, or sport science, as ways of developing sports teachers, coaches and athletes (Spracklen, 2009, 2014a).

In the United Kingdom tourism studies was originally linked to and often sold as tourism management, a vocational degree that was designed to educate tourism planners and managers. Tourism studies has since become a mature subject field in its own right, drawing on leisure studies but also on policy studies and geography. Tourism management courses emerged in leisure departments where there were concentrations of scholars who aligned themselves with tourism studies. By calling their courses tourism management, they followed global trends of reducing the critical social science content of leisure courses and boosting the vocational or professional content. The secession of tourism studies from tourism management was driven by academics who were keen to create a particular niche for their own research, consultancy and teaching. As Aitchison (2006) suggests, an intellectual case can be made for the emergence of tourism studies.

Leisure studies emerged in Europe in the 1970s. From the beginning, this subject field combined critical social science research about what people did in their non-work lives with more practical content relating to leisure management and leisure policy. The impetus to bring people together to study leisure came from a number of places. First, there was the growth of North American active recreation and leisure courses. Second, a number of important books were published in which leisure was used as a lens through which to analyse changes in modern society (Rojek, 2010; Spracklen, 2009). Third, European government agencies were beginning to conceptualize leisure as activities that local councils deliver or manage – from organized sports through to libraries – to improve the lives of local people. Sports and active recreation ran through both the critical sociological debates about leisure and the practical debates about how to improve people's leisure time. The foundation of the Leisure Studies Association in 1975 and the creation of the journal *Leisure Studies* in 1982 established leisure studies as an exciting multi-disciplinary subject field that focused on increasing knowledge about the function of leisure and sport in everyday life, and helped policy-makers to make leisure central to their planning. In the United Kingdom local authorities took on the role of providing leisure opportunities by building leisure centres and delivering programmes of leisure and sport. Leisure studies attracted support in the educational establishment, and in the 1980s degree courses in the subject started to appear throughout Europe.

These first leisure studies degrees were all very similar. They included critical sociology, a policy and management core, and practical elements associated with sports and active recreation that came from physical education. The critical sociology was there to give students an understanding of the deep structural biases in society that made accessing leisure difficult for some people. For instance, women's leisure lives were constrained because of cultural assumptions about their responsibilities and domesticity; and working-class people's leisure lives were constrained because they did not have the money, the cultural capital or the power to engage in anything other than a small range of activities. Critical sociology also gave leisure studies a solid theoretical foundation in radical feminism and Marxism. Meanwhile, the other elements of leisure studies courses grounded the theory in practice: the policy and management core gave students the training and skills they needed to become leisure planners or leisure managers; and the practical aspects of the curriculum helped them to develop leadership skills and acquire some knowledge of the science of human movement. So there was some vocational and professional content in these early courses, but it was connected to and contained within the socio-cultural content. The ideal leisure manager – the person who attained a leisure studies degree – was not a free-market ideologue driven by neo-liberalism. She or he was a critical policy-maker who used professional skills and knowledge to plan a better society.

There were also some engagements with other social sciences and humanities, such as economics and philosophy, as well as a sport-studies focus that rolled together leisure studies and sport science at many colleges. Similar courses emerged in other parts of the world, especially North America – where leisure courses started to adopt some of the content but not so much of the critical sociology – Europe, Australia and New Zealand. These were mainly called leisure studies degrees, although some were termed sport studies or recreation studies. Crucially, whatever they were called, they were often the only form of leisure study possible in each higher education institution that offered them. There was no internal competition from leisure management, sports development or events management courses.

The success of these undergraduate courses rested partly on their links with policy-makers and the opportunities they generated for graduate careers in the leisure industry. But they also catered to young people's interest in the problem of leisure in post-industrial societies. Some students wanted to learn how leisure might be used to make sense of community and belonging, and how it might be used to favour some groups over others. Many others, however, embarked on leisure studies courses primarily because of their keen interest in sports or other forms of physical activity. In the 1980s leisure studies courses became legitimate routes for sporty students to enter higher education. They were often the only courses on which students could learn a little about sport *and* participate in it.

Since then, sport has become all-pervasive in society. Watching it has become an acceptable part of global popular culture, and the radical critique of it as another opium of the masses has been lost in the chatter about who will win what this year. Playing sport has once again become a moral good rather than a residual element of elite culture (Spracklen, 2011a). As such, over the last twenty years leisure studies courses have had to face challenges over their content and even their existence. The rehabilitation of sport has led to claims that the critical sociology aspect of leisure studies was too anti-sport or too generic. In response, many leisure studies courses have been reworked so that they focus more on sport. Consequently, some are now known as 'leisure and sport studies', while others have done away with 'leisure' altogether, becoming simply 'sport studies' or even 'sport and community development'. The neo-liberal politics of higher education in recent years has also led to brand-new courses that have included some leisure studies content from the old courses when creating degrees in 'sports studies', 'sports management' or 'sports development'. These new courses fit more easily with prospective students' interest in sport, sound better to parents who are concerned with post-university employability, and make life easier for university marketing managers who are uncomfortable with the criticality of leisure studies (Spracklen, 2014a). In our university a wave of new degrees joined leisure studies in the 1990s and 2000s. The first of these was titled 'sport and recreation development'. This specialized course is strongly vocational, but it shares some elements with the old multi-disciplinary leisure studies. The next couple of new courses – 'sport business management' and 'sports marketing' – tapped into the neo-liberal zeitgeist of the 2000s. More recently, a 'sports coaching' course has also been launched. All of these courses attract students who might otherwise have applied for the leisure studies course. As a consequence, the latter first struggled to attract students and then disappeared. Ironically, it is now being rebranded as 'sport and social sciences', partly because sport is so popular.

So leisure studies has been a victim of its own success: it attracted people who are interested in sport into higher education, but over the years such people started to demand degrees that contained more sport and less critical sociology. Meanwhile, at the other end of the leisure subject field, leisure studies was threatened by the emergence of leisure management, tourism studies and tourism management, and ultimately events management. Leisure management degrees take as their ideal graduate student someone who works in the private sector – the chief executive of a gym or a marketing consultancy. Here, leisure is reduced to the neo-liberal instrumentality: if you want it, you can pay for it. And if you do not want it, they will find ways to make you want it. Just as leisure management creates pliant leisure industry workers, tourism management and events management produce pliant leisure industry workers.

Tourism is at least a large employment sector in most developed countries, with government agencies, national strategies and action plans all designed to make it more economically successful. In that sense, the demand for tourism management might be a top-down pull from the industry and from policy-makers. But where is the events industry? Where is the focused sub-set of the leisure industry where these graduates will find work? The graduates of events management courses are trained to manage events, and while the eventization of the public sphere and popular culture has been occurring, it has not yet become so dominant that these graduates are becoming leaders in cultural policy-making. Rather, they move into jobs that allow them to impose their neo-liberal views of management and leadership in the workplace. Instead of finding community and solidarity in collective bargaining, they act as self-motivated individual entrepreneurs, demanding their own rights but ignoring those of their colleagues.

The emergence of events management and its secession from leisure studies seems both pragmatic and ideological. It is pragmatic because the academics and university managers who create the courses are well aware of the inadequacies of their content, but they know that they meet the demands of prospective students. Such applicants typically enjoy attending festivals and events, and they may well have helped to organize something locally. The universities promise that events management is a thriving industry, and insist that finding a job within it is easy with a good degree. The 'events' part of the title inspires the prospective student to apply, but the 'management' aspect is also appealing – to the student and their parents – because it denotes a well-paid, suitably bourgeois, graduate career. Managers are respectably middle class (Bourdieu, 1984), and enrolling in a degree with 'management' in the title suggests one will acquire the requisite skills and knowledge to become a manager, without having to face a daunting workload. Most prospective events management students expect an easy degree, especially once they have read the student feedback and learned how much fun the course is. And, in fact, events management courses *are* easy. There is little or no critical content. Students are not prompted to feel uncomfortable about events. Instead, they are told events are great, the events management industry is cool, being an events manager is fun, and all of the practical stuff that is taught on the course will pave the way to becoming one. So the students work through modules on running this and planning that, but they rarely learn any social theory, or indeed much management or leadership theory.

Events management's emergence is also ideological because, as a subject field, it does not question neo-liberalism or its instrumental logic (Rojek, 2013). Rather, it promotes such contested issues as facts of life and morally good because making profit is a good thing. The whole questionable status of leisure in our modern society is reduced to embracing the narrow instrumentality that is currently colonizing our lifeworld (Habermas, 1992b, 1992c; Spracklen, 2009). In events management courses leisure is reduced to an industry that is fixated on profit. They normalize neo-liberalism to such an extent that students hear dissenting voices about the value of events and capitalism only when they stumble on books like this one. Events management breeds ignorance of the current state of affairs in the world, globalization and mobilities, climate change and environmental destruction. There is no moral compass in events management, no ethics, no critical lens. This is because events management curricula are deliberately shallow and superficial. The theory goes that if students actually learn about any of the problems and issues associated with events, they will no longer wish to become events managers. Even worse, they might stop buying into the discourse of eventization, and refuse to buy tickets for the next big event. So, by helping us to validate our programmes, the events industry – our friends in the private sector – ensure that we do not present our students with such difficult content.

Conclusion

Eventization is happening in everyday life, in leisure and culture, and on our university courses. People think in ways that are delineated and constrained by the discourse of events. Popular culture has become eventized (Žižek, 2014), packaged up and sold back to us as experiences we cannot afford to miss, films we must see, or festivals that define who we are (as long as we have the funds to buy a ticket). People are trapped in an instrumental view of leisure, where all spaces and all activities become events that must be bought. Eventization is a form of privatization of space, leisure and life. This is why we need to fight back and push for CES: critical event studies. This is the purpose of this book: to help academics and students realize that the assumptions about events do not have to be accepted. We want to help events develop a critical lens. This is why we are proposing a subject field related to events management called critical event studies – the subject of this book but hopefully also a subject field in university programmes, a research network and maybe even a journal.

This new subject field rejects the notion of management training and instead places events in the ongoing political, social and cultural struggle against injustice and inequality. This has already happened in the tourism and leisure sectors, where the dominant paradigm of management has been critiqued and partly replaced with critical tourism studies and leisure studies. The proposed critical event studies will respond to the interest young people have in events. They want to learn about events. So CES will help them gain that knowledge in a way that allows them to evaluate and assess the impact of events, the nature of events, and the relationship between events and capitalism.

9   Resilience and events

Introduction

Attempts to conceptualize resilience initially emerged in the physical and life sciences. Within material science, for example, resilience is understood to be the capacity of a material to absorb energy when it is being deformed elastically (such as when stretching, compressing or twisting) and to return to its prior state. This is associated with, though different from, a material's tensile toughness, and it is measured in the joules per cubic metre (J/m^3) that a material can absorb before it is irreversibly deformed or fractures (Campbell, 2008). The SI unit for resilience is *Ur*. In the life sciences the concept of resilience is also associated with a capacity to withstand stresses and strains, though in these areas the focus is on biologically complex systems rather than simple materials. While it is found across a wide spectrum of disciplinary areas within the life sciences – from anatomy to zoology – it is arguably most fully developed within ecology. Here it is understood as the capacity of an ecosystem to resist damage and recover (Hallegatte, 2014). Because this recovery does not necessarily entail a return to the exact state that preceded the damage, it incorporates the possibility of a system's adaptability – an aspect of resilience that is not addressed in the material science definition.

In this chapter we discuss the connections between resilience and events management/event studies as well as its place within critical approaches to the study of events. We start by showing how the concept of resilience has been increasingly used within the social sciences. Beginning with an outline of the relationship between resilience and vulnerability, we address the issue of resilience as an individual, group and community resource. That leads to a consideration of how it is construed within mainstream events management/event studies – a construal that we find problematic as it frequently places resilience in opposition to resistance and, as such, exposes the conceptualization to post-structuralist critiques through the application of Foucauldian theories of governmentality and biopolitics. Additionally, Žižek's (2014) and Badiou's (2003, 2005) conceptualization of 'event' as 'rupture' has a negative connotation. Consequently, we can discern concerns about the possibility of legitimately employing resilience in any analysis of events that attempts to understand them in cultural, social and political terms. In trying to address these concerns we return to Bourdieu's (1984) theorization of the social field, *habitus* and symbolic violence, while also considering the relationship between resilience and his less commonly discussed formulation of *habitus clivé*. When we combine these ideas with an interpretation of resilience as a defence of difference (drawing, in part, on Deleuze), we feel we have grounds for suggesting, within certain contexts, that resilience can contribute to a form of eventful protest (della Porta, 2015). That, in turn, leads us to consider more carefully the relationship between resilience and resistance. In conclusion we reflect on the different strands discussed in the chapter and ask what they might mean for those who want to adopt a critical approach to the study of events.

Resilience and the social sciences

Within the social sciences, resilience can be understood as the process by which individuals and groups adapt to adverse conditions that impact on them personally or collectively (Bahadur *et al.*, 2010). As such, it is frequently associated with some form of trauma and placed in contradistinction to vulnerability (Jenkins, 2011). Some of the earliest work in this field was done by the social and developmental psychologist Emmy Werner (1987, 1989). In the mid-seventies she began a longitudinal study into the developmental psychology of children whose background was thought to place them at high risk of encountering personal and societal problems in later life. In a number of articles written in the late 1980s she argued that some children grew into fully rounded and caring adults despite lacking the familial, social and emotional support that is normally associated with successful development. According to Werner (ibid.), the children who flourished possessed the trait of *resiliency*, which mitigated the trauma of their deprived childhoods.

A further wave of research into individual resilience started to appear in the academic literature after the first Gulf War of 1990–1. This was principally due to an upsurge in interest in how those affected by conflict manage the profound emotional distress they have experienced. Although the term 'post-traumatic stress disorder' (PTSD) first appeared in the early 1980s in a paper that considered anxiety-based disorders among Vietnam veterans (Fairbank *et al.*, 1981), it was not formally recognized as a diagnosable condition until the American Psychiatric Association included it in the third edition of *The Diagnostic and Statistical Manual of Mental Disorders* (DSM-III) in 1987 (Robert *et al.*, 1987). For much of the following decade, empirical work that concentrated on resilience and vulnerability (Aldwin *et al.*, 1994; King *et al.*, 1998; Sutker *et al.*, 1995) centred on the impact of psychological stress encountered by people who had been exposed to traumatic situations because of their proximity to the harsh realities of war zones. The application of PTSD, and resilience/vulnerability, beyond a paradigm that highlighted its association with sites of military action began to develop following the terrorist attacks on the World Trade Center on 11 September 2001 (Bonanno *et al.*, 2006). Bonanno (2004, 2005) suggests that resilience should be understood as a process by which an individual returns to a place of relative emotional stability, rather than as an innate personality trait. Meanwhile,

Ong *et al.* (2006) have argued that a positive emotional context is important in supporting resilience by mitigating against reactivity, and aiding recovery, following psychological trauma.

More recently, resilience as an attribute of groups and communities has become a dominant trope within research into disaster relief, whether that collective trauma is the result of a natural catastrophe (e.g. earthquake or tsunami), environmental 'accident' (e.g. the Bhopal gas tragedy of 1984, the Deepwater Horizon oil spill of 2010, or the Fukushima Daiichi nuclear disaster of 2011), political instability (e.g. arguably the Ethiopian famine of 1984; see Franks, 2014) or more overt forms of conflict and violence. In their analysis of how the Emergency Operations Centre (EOC) continued to function during and after the attacks on the World Trade Center, despite the destruction of its facilities, Kendra and Wachtendorf (2003) suggest that resilience cannot be fully understood unless it incorporates less tangible attributes, such as communication strategies, patterns of cooperative behaviour and a clear understanding of roles, responsibilities and capabilities. The significant contributions made by communication, information and social capital are also highlighted in Norris *et al.*'s (2008) study of communities that are at high risk of suffering natural disasters.

By realigning the focus of resilience to how communities rebuild themselves after a crisis, the discussion has shifted from trying to discern the capacities of individuals or the cognitive and emotional attributes of groups of individuals – that is, a concentration on psychology and social psychology. Now the discussion is concerned with social environment and intersubjective group capabilities, focusing, as Chandler (2015) puts it, on 'concrete social practices'. Resilience, Ijzerman and Lindenberg (2014) argue, cannot be understood fully if we do not locate the agent in what they refer to as their 'begin-state' – that is, to understand the individual as inseparable from its relational connections. While tentatively supporting earlier cognitive and emotive models, they go on to suggest that a focus on resilience as a facet of the individual is to ignore that agent's relational context; furthermore, to do so actively undermines a person's ability to recover, which can lead to additional strains and even greater stress. However, this means they sustain a discourse of the individual over the social, which thereby overlooks the possibility of resilience being a collective experience and something that may be articulated at a communitarian level. In their attempt to get a better grip on understanding collective adaptive responses to climate change, Pelling and High (2005) consider a number of approaches that draw less on cognitive/emotional or psycho-social models. They suggest a better approach would be to concentrate research on critically engaging with theories that are more concerned with assessing social capital.

Though *Bowling Alone* is not explicitly concerned with resilience, Robert Putnam (2001a) does suggest that the ties which once bound together identifiable communities in the United States – and effectively made them resilient – have, in some sense, broken down, while other forms of community are emerging. Specifically, *Bowling Alone* discusses the decline of family-and-friend bowling clubs, which reached a peak of popularity in the 1950s. Putnam suggests that their subsequent decline is symptomatic of wider breakdowns in the social fabric of communities across America. In his later work, such as 'Social capital: Measurement and consequences' (Putnam, 2001b) and *Better Together* (Putnam *et al.*, 2005), he develops the conceptual underpinnings of *Bowling Alone* by postulating two principal forms of social capital: bonding capital and bridging capital. For Putnam, community should be understood as a network of social relationships that become observable, and thus open to enquiry, through their articulation as forms of social capital. While wider external forces – social, cultural, environmental and so on – place those relationships under considerable strain, the links that exist because of both forms of social capital sustain the community. Unfortunately, though, that connectivity cannot last for ever: at some point it will be deformed out of any previously recognizable shape. However, the social capital is not lost when this happens; rather, it is transformed into new kinds of relationship. For Putnam, bonding social capital refers to the networks of social relationships that hold together homogeneous groups of people: families are prototypical of this, although neighbours, class/socio-economic groups and certain psycho-demographic categories may also exhibit such a connection. By contrast, bridging social capital binds together heterogeneous or different homogeneous groups. As such, it could be argued, it strengthens diverse communities during periods of crisis (Putnam, 2001a). More recently, Daniel Aldrich has extended Putnam's ideas by adding linking capital, by which he means those social relationships that connect individuals/groups/communities to governmental resources and governmental power (Aldrich, 2010, 2011; Aldrich and Smith, 2015). As such, he argues that social capital underpins community and collective resilience, particularly in times of crisis and environmental disaster.

In this section we have devoted considerable time to developing an understanding of how resilience has migrated from its original domain of material and life sciences to areas that are more closely associated with the social sciences. Central to this discussion has been the idea that, as a concept, resilience is closely connected to responses to – and mitigation of – crisis. This notion tends to dominate whenever resilience is discussed within the mainstream events management and event studies literature. In the next section we look at how resilience is addressed in those fields.

Resilience in the discourse of mainstream events management/event studies

Though it is rarely discussed as such directly, resilience plays a significant role in the academic discourses of events management and event studies. In both fields the concept draws on a variety of characteristics associated with those we have identified as emerging from its incorporation into the social sciences. However, the two fields have taken quite different trajectories when applying resilience to their respective perspectives. Because of that difference – in contrast to the approach adopted in most of this book – events management and event studies will be treated as separate fields within this section.

Resilience in events management

A quick survey of the literature associated with degree-level events management suggests that resilience does not have a significant role to play.[1] That, however, is a false impression. Across much of this literature, either explicitly or implicitly, there is an operational framework that is known as the 'events management body of knowledge'. As a framework, it splits the management of events into five core values, which intersect five knowledge domains, each delivered through five processes over a five-stage timeline, which runs from the initiation of an event project to its conclusion. The management and mitigation of risk forms one of the five domains of knowledge required by the framework for the successful delivery of an event. In one of the few events management texts to feature the word 'resilience', Bowdin *et al.* (2012: 610–11) write:

> Experienced event companies are adept at minimising . . . exposure profile by identifying the critical points. They focus on the exposure profile and control the risks. A similar approach to risk is found in vulnerability profiling and building resilience . . . This process stresses the process of risk planning, as distinct from the risk plan as a document, and the community's capacity to deal with hazards.

Here, as we considered earlier, the possibility of risk draws on the twin, entwined, concepts of resilience and vulnerability. The capacity required to mitigate risk is understood as a combination of a prepared risk mitigation plan together with familiarity with the community context in which the event is taking place. Interestingly, a connection is also drawn between exposure (how the event is perceived) and vulnerability profiling, suggesting an association between resilience and an imaginary associated with the event (at the very least this might be at the level of its 'reputation'). As we saw in our earlier consideration of space and event (Chapter 4), the imaginary of an event is central to its potential for marketization/commodification and its capacity to generate an income (if not necessarily a profit). Those operational tasks associated with risk management in event planning, such as risk assessments and emergency action plans, are ultimately reputational (i.e. grounded in sustaining an imaginary of the relationship between space and the event; see Kostov and Lingard, 2003) and, crucially, require judgements of likelihood and severity that are implicitly framed by making that imaginary financially viable.[2] A veil of depoliticization, through the managerialization of a hegemonically dominant construal of likelihood, suggests that risk (and thus resilience) within mainstream events management is actually socio-politically constructed (Beck, 1992; Klein, 2007) as a biopolitical means of domination (Rabinow and Rose, 2006).

Resilience in event studies

As we have found, the connection between resilience and risk in events management is dominated by operational concerns; as such, it has only a marginal connection to how resilience is discussed within event studies. Within that field, as Getz (2012) suggests, the discourses within which the studied event is engaged, rather than the operational elements of it, are highlighted. The dominant discourses of resilience with which mainstream event studies is concerned are associated with sustainability, which incorporates and exceeds the baseline financial concerns of events management, and community capacity-building. Derrett (2009) provides good illustrations of both of these trajectories. She writes (ibid.: 109):

> Festivals and events are seen to build social capital and in community development terms showcase the strengths of a community at play and demonstrate its capacity to cope with external stresses and disturbances as a result of social, political and environmental change . . . Festivals demonstrate how individual and cooperative strengths can be harnessed and deliver outcomes that can be replicated in the future to meet diverse community needs.

The event studies literature relating to sustainability and community capacity-building is substantial and multifaceted. Discourses on sustainability draw on a range of approaches, including arguments that are more closely associated with economic impact and business competitiveness (e.g. O'Sullivan and Jackson, 2002; Dwyer and Jago, 2014; and, to a degree, Henderson, 2011[3]). While not always excluding issues of competitive advantage, alternative discourses also connect sustainability with an increased awareness of events' environmental and social impact (Getz, 2009; Winsemius and Guntram, 2013).

Derrett's (2009) suggestion that events can empower communities is also a substantial trope within the event studies literature, suggesting a link to resilience through the development of socially cohesive communities and, in some cases (such as the legacy claims made for the 2012 Olympic Games), more physically active citizens (e.g. Misener and Mason, 2009; Smith, 2014). However, in a pattern initially recognized by cultural policy scholars, the empirical basis of such claims is frequently weakened by prioritizing rhetoric over substance when it comes to substantiating events' capacity to deliver substantive results (see, e.g., Belfiore, 2004, 2009; McGuigan, 2009b; see also Kohe and Bowen-Jones, 2015). Conceptualizing resilience as a resource (of either processes or communities) risks overextending it as a metaphor. As Hobfoll (2002) notes, overusing the resource metaphor in its connection to resilience has the potential to distract us from some underlying principles that might help us better understand how individuals and groups respond to disruption.

In discussing resilience within the social sciences we saw it conceptualized as both individual trait and collective process. In discussing its role within events management and event studies, while we found that it resonated with both of those characteristics, we also learned that it may be understood as a resource to be managed and/or developed. However, all of these rest on a construal of resilience as countervailing, or mitigating, vulnerability. This leaves the very idea of resilience open to a much deeper critique, to which we now turn.

The post-structuralist critique of resilience

Though not overtly rooted in a critical discussion of events management/ event studies, a post-structuralist critique of resilience can be discerned at the heart of arguments such as those developed by Rojek (2013), which suggest that those fields support (at least tacitly) a neo-liberal agenda of socio-cultural manipulation. In order to understand that perspective and move on from it, we first need to return to some of the ideas relating to the conceptualization of 'event' that were discussed in Chapter 1, and specifically to the idea of 'event' that is found in the philosophies of Badiou and Žižek. Therefore, we will begin with a very short summary of those ideas.

For Badiou, 'event' is fundamentally bound to truth *qua* truth. In *Being and Event* (Badiou, 2005) and *Philosophy and the Event* (Badiou, 2013), among many other publications, Badiou sets out his view that philosophy works through a rigorous examination of the truth procedures of four primary ontological conditions – art, love, politics and science – without permitting itself to be wholly subservient to any one of them. Truth, he argues, remains invariant even when the purported truths or those individuated conditions shift: it cannot be refined to the truth of any one condition because it is, in contradistinction to Plato's idea of the ultimate, ontic unity of truth, multiple. Any dominant ideology strives to contain the multiplicity of truth through its articulation of the ultimate ontic foundation of our being-in-the-world as singular. For Badiou, 'event' is the rupturing of that singularity by the multiplicity that is truth, which enables it – if only for a fleeting moment – to be glimpsed. Within such a framework resilience is the imbuing of a society or culture (community, group or individual) with the capacity to manage that rupture so as not to disrupt the ideology's dominance.

There is a similar presentation of the tension between event and ideology within Žižek's political and cultural theory. In *The Sublime Object of Ideology* (Žižek, 1989) he takes as his starting point a critique of the dominant Marxian view – as presented in *The German Ideology* (Marx and Engels, 1987) – that ideology works as a filter through which reality is distorted. He counters this by arguing that ideology acts as the final justification of the prevailing social order, and thereby constructs the reality of which we are a part, rather than acting as a distorting lens. The reality of our daily lives is inscribed by the ideology that constructs it; opposed to this is the Real, which can never be articulated by that reality. So the Real stands, in some sense, outside the fabricated reality of our daily lives, yet can rupture it at points of resistance to it. Resilience is thus placed in opposition not to vulnerability but to resistance, as it is the means by which ideology attempts to repel the incursion of the Real as the presentation of that which ideology cannot justify (Žižek, 1989).

While the foundations of this critique – and the consequent problematization of resilience as a characteristic of ideological and hegemonic domination – have been grounded in much discussion within the wider social sciences and humanities, it has yet to find an expression within event studies. In part that is due to the limited overt discussion of resilience in this discipline. However, that limited discussion can be understood as an attribute of the successful hegemonic colonization of the concept within this field, not as evidence of event studies' inability to generate an adequate rebuttal. According to Joseph (2013), resilience is actually a form of neo-liberalist governmentality in that it attempts to depoliticize systemic shock by refocusing attention away from the political structures in which events occur and instead emphasizing individual and community adaptability. That point is reinforced by Welsh (2014), who claims that resilience supports citizen acceptance of a system where shocks become naturalized in a post-political space, and change becomes allied with contemporary governmental discourses that responsibilize risk away from the state and onto individuals and institutions. Juntunen and Hyvönen (2014), Corry (2014) and Hardy (2015), in their various discussions of security policy, develop those ideas further. Each argues that resilience is a tactic of a neo-liberal regime of processually driven self-governance, where political action is replaced by standardized procedures that are framed as apolitical.

However, the dissolution of resistance through its inculcation into procedural governmentalized technologies of resilience need not be total. Juntunen and Hyvönen (2014) and Corry (2014) both conclude that the structures of collective action are in need of revitalization, while Schulz and Siriwardane (2015; emphasis added) argue that a 'deeper engagement with politicisation in the context of *transformative adaptation*' is required for a more nuanced account of the relationship between resistance and resilience. Laying the foundations for that requires a reconsideration of Bourdieu's notions of social field and *habitus*.

Conceptualizing resilience in cultural, social and political terms

Bourdieu's central concern is to develop an understanding of the dynamics of power that constitutes society as that space where we act and interact.[4] The social spaces we inhabit, he argues, are structured with rules that frame the behaviours we exhibit, establishing the contours of domination and the criteria of legitimation within them, and demarcate those options that are open to us in terms of the choices we make and the character of our interactions. Those structured social spaces – or, as Bourdieu calls them, fields – are relatively autonomous within a wider social context – or space – of the social world as a whole. The dispositions we display – from our preferences in cuisine and music to the language we use to express our political views – develop as a result of the struggles and complex connections in our social relationships within our field. Importantly, these dispositions develop as a result of the objective conditions that are encountered by the individual. They are therefore not predetermined traits of someone's personality or cognitive process that can be understood independently of the contexts in which the individual participates. As a consequence they are quite different from models of resilience that focus on it as something that is innate to a person and transcends the environment of which they are a part.

'*Habitus*' refers to those dispositions, acquired modes of perception, ways of acting and so forth that we express (which makes them amenable to empirical study); these reveal us as particular participants within a social field. Our state of *doxa* is all that we view as self-evident, natural common sense. Our dispositions in this state are deeply held values, beliefs and thoughts that inform our actions and connections within that field. But as *habitus* is not innate, nor reducible to an existing set of processes, but learned, what supports its foundation and development? It is here that Bourdieu introduces three types of capital: cultural, social and economic. Within this framework 'cultural capital' refers to those assets that enable an individual agent to muster authority within a specified and appropriate context within a field. Such assets might include skills, qualifications, or clear evidence of ability within a range of actions/interactions. These can act as forms of legitimation within a field for the actions associated with their holder.

There are some similarities between Putnam's use of 'social capital' (as discussed earlier in this chapter) and Bourdieu's, but also some significant differences. Putnam views this principally as a group attribute, whereas Bourdieu also connects it with individual dispositions within a *habitus*. However, Bourdieu sees it as more than simply an attribute of individuals: the relationship between the individual (and the group) and *habitus* is understood as mutually co-constructive. Social capital represents those resources accrued by virtue of the networks of mutual acquaintance and recognition in which the agent participates.

Bourdieu uses 'economic capital' in much the same way as it is employed in economic theory. It is associated with the economic leverage an agent can muster. Consequently, the resources/assets that are identified with this form of capital include the economic goods that are held by, and the resources that are accessible to, the agent, their financial position and their place within the economy of the wider socio-political setting in which they live.

In addition to these three types of capital, Bourdieu identifies a fourth – symbolic capital. According to his long-time collaborator Loïc Wacquant (2011), this can be perceived as being of value (or not) within a *habitus* only when it is viewed through the lens of one of the other types of capital. The concept of symbolic capital is important because of its connection to symbolic violence. For Bourdieu, this occurs when an agent (either an individual or a group) uses the symbolic capital they possess to alter the actions, modes of thought and perceptions of others (who usually possess less symbolic capital). In so doing the instigator(s) restructure the modes of cognition and action of those agents, imposing criteria of legitimation that the dominated come to accept as a self-evident social order.

In his critique of *habitus*, Anthony King (2000: 427) argues that the definition developed by Bourdieu and Wacquant undermines its capacity to admit social change, making it, in his terms, 'formally immutable'. King (ibid.: 428) argues that the social and psychological stability which a strong *habitus* imbues on agents who are active within a social field means that 'every individual is constrained by his habitus ... objective conditions will simply be reproduced [by the *habitus*] and no social change will take place'. In a sense then, King construes *habitus* as some form of social resilience: that is, it has a capacity to make agents resilient to the impact of wider societal changes on the field in which they participate. However, this does not seem to acknowledge the important role – which Friedman (2015) claims Bourdieu accepts – that abrupt change can have on *habitus*. In his paper on *habitus clivé* (cleft *habitus*), Friedman discusses the full impact Bourdieu thought sudden change had on the connection between *habitus* and field. Though he accepts that this is in part due to a lack of empirical research in this area, *habitus clivé* is understood as playing a significant role in Bourdieu's thinking on the composition and changing properties of *habitus*, as well as some of the possible effects of symbolic violence. This opens up the possibility of the resilience of *habitus* acting as a form of resistance.

Bourbeau (2013), in a context of securitization studies within the field of international relations, proposes three types of resilience: resilience as maintenance (which is concerned with the maintenance of stability, no matter what); resilience as marginality (which accepts some degree of minor adjustment to change); and resilience as renewal. The last of these interprets disturbance as an opportunity for renewal, which may be difficult and challenging, resulting in 'important shifts in interpretation and meaning in an agent's power relations, as well as institutional and organizational reconfiguration' (ibid.: 16). Linking this to our earlier discussion of *habitus*, echoes of systemic shock intrinsic to *habitus clivé* can be seen in Bourbeau's 'disturbance'. Resilience does not necessarily equate to passivity or acquiescence. When *habitus* is significantly disturbed – or, to use some of the language we have employed in other chapters, when an event disrupts/intervenes in a social field – resilience can act in the form of *resilience as renewal*, seeking redefinition in the face of the apparent new order, articulated as resistance.

In the next section we briefly consider how elements in the theoretical frameworks of de Certeau, Foucault, Gramsci and Deleuze can be brought to bear on the connection between resilience and resistance.

Connecting resilience and resistance through event

We have now got to a position where 'event', understood conceptually as disruption and that which intervenes in a social field, means certain forms of resilience can be understood as resistance. This moves our discussion of the conceptualization of resilience forward, and draws it closer to the construal of 'event' within CES at a theoretical level. However, it does not really help us progress our thinking about the connection between resilience and events management/event studies. Beginning with some reflections on how key ideas developed by four theorists might give us greater insight into the linkages between resilience, resistance and event, we will consider whether the role of the latter in resilient resistance is one way of achieving this: that is, if events can make resilience an act of resistance, can acts of resilience, as resistance, also be understood as events? The four theorists are arranged in a very rough order of scale when it comes to considering the event of resilient resistance.

Resilience as resistance: de Certeau, Foucault, Gramsci and Deleuze

In his analysis of the practices of everyday life Michel de Certeau (1988) discusses small acts of resistance he calls *la perruque* (the wig). These are those daily events in which we engage in minor acts of subversion. They are deployed, often unconsciously, as a means of tactically managing that which strategically tries to dominate us. As an example, de Certeau suggests someone writing a love letter while sitting at their office desk and ostensibly working on a task determined by their role in the organization. Such small acts of tactical management form an articulation of resilience as difference from the organizationally defined context within which that individual works; they are disruptions/interventions in a social field bounded by the work role defined by those individuals and institutions that are in dominant positions of power with respect to that individual.

The first substantial discussion of parrhesia (the speaking of truth to power) to appear in the work of Michel Foucault occurs in the publication of his lectures at the Collège de France in 1982 (Foucault, 2011b). In a wide-ranging discussion, which builds on a consideration of the structures of Athenian democracy and the role of truth-telling in the myths and philosophic traditions of ancient Greece, he presents the parrhesiac as someone who disrupts while standing firm. Such people are resilient in their commitment to speaking out as they know that this confronts power and disturbs it through its very steadfastness. As an example, he discusses Socrates' defence during his trial for corrupting the thoughts of the youth of Athens. Socrates claims that he is a gadfly whose purpose is to arouse,[5] persuade and reproach the state so that it is continuously reminded of the truth. His resilience becomes his act of resistance: 'I know that my plainness of speech makes them hate me, and what is their hatred but a proof that I am speaking the truth' (Plato, 1988: 33). Socrates is an event that disrupts power and intervenes in the social field of the political elite of ancient Athens.

Where the example drawn from de Certeau is concerned with the small scale, and that taken from Foucault considers a lone voice speaking truth to power, Gramsci can be read as articulating the class struggle as a series of acts of resilience as resistance. Hegemony works by *colonizing* – to borrow a term from Habermas (1992b) – the culture of those whom it dominates, distorting meaning and human relationships. It is through the development of a working-class culture that hegemony can be opposed, because that culture's resilience through the *event*ful expression of itself acts as a mode of resistance against oppression.

A central characteristic of Deleuze's early philosophic project (Deleuze, 2014 [1968]) was the inversion of the relationship between identity and difference. He argues that all prior metaphysical frameworks rested on an assumption that identity has precedence over difference. First you have things; then you identify the differences between them. By contrast, for Deleuze, the differences are central, and identity, as we encounter it, is an expression of those differences. Our experience always has and will exceed our capacity to conceptualize it. It is experience's capacity to surprise us as already and always different that forces us to think in new ways. Whereas de Certeau addressed disruption at a micro level,

Foucault focused on the lone voice speaking against power, and Gramsci located disruption at the level of hegemonic struggle, Deleuze portrays it as a fundamental metaphysical quality. Resilience is a declaration of difference, and as such it can become the expression of resistance. Articulated as dissentful action, eventful protest (della Porta, 2015), resilience as resistance is both constructed through event *and* central to the formation of an event.

Conclusion

This chapter has covered a substantial amount of material. Beginning with a basic construal of resilience as found in the physical and life sciences, we explored the transition of the term into social science discourses. Within those academic areas conceptualizations of resilience were dominated by two central points of opposition: it was either opposed to vulnerability or, within a post-structuralist critique of its formulation, placed in contradistinction to resistance.

In considering the relationship between Bourdieu's conceptualization of *habitus*, field, species of capital and (crucially) the place of the little-explored concept of *habitus clivé* (*habitus* cleft), we discerned a connection between resilience and event. We used these ideas to establish their centrality in developing an alternative conceptualization of resilience, one that showed its potential as resistance. We then considered a number of theorists as a means of exploring the extent to which resilience could be viewed as resistance. We found aspects of the theoretical frameworks of Michel de Certeau, Michel Foucault, Antonio Gramsci and Gilles Deleuze that it was possible to see as events, at various metaphysical levels, as significant for the constitution of acts of resilient resistance.

At a mundane level we can see that all events which proclaim an identity – from the village fête, to events that claim to have regional and/or national significance, to global media-centric events – can do so only in terms of exposing their character as one of difference from that which surrounds them. That difference might be as local as an individual's daily routine or as global as media scheduling; similarly, the disruption/intervention that is the event parallels the difference in scale. What is significant for CES is to understand how resilient resistance is being articulated by the event as it is studied – its variety, the discourse it is exposing and the acts of realignment that occur as a result.

Notes

1. This claim is based on a simple index and contents-page search of the following texts: Bowdin *et al.*, 2012; Raj and Walters, 2013; Bladen and Kennell, 2012; Shone and Parry, 2010; Ferdinand and Kitchin, 2012; Conway, 2009; and Capell, 2013. While not exhaustive, this does seem to be a good spread of the field's core textbook material.
2. See, for example, BBC (2015a), which begins: 'Alton Towers owner Merlin Entertainments says the rollercoaster accident in June at the theme park has significantly reduced visitor numbers. Since the beginning of the year, it has reported a 11.4% drop in revenue compared with last year at its Resort Theme Parks.' So the BBC chose to highlight the anticipated £30 million drop in profits before discussing the sixteen people

who were injured, several of them seriously, including two young women who each had a leg amputated.
3. There is so much research in these areas that we can provide only a token sample here as examples.
4. The outline of Bourdieu's ideas presented here is based on our reading of a number of his works, including Bourdieu (1984, 1992, 2005) and Bourdieu and Wacquant (1992). We have not cited them in the text as doing so would have made it too cumbersome and difficult to follow.
5. In Benjamin Jowett's translation: 'I am that gadfly which God has attached to the state, and all day and in all places I am always fastened to you, arousing and persuading and reproaching you' (Plato, 1988: 47).

10 Events and misrule

Introduction

Bakhtin (1984) famously writes about the 'carnivalesque' – the riotous, counter-hegemonic, transgressive mood that overturns normal life in the liminal spaces of festivals. His work begins with, and uses for its main argument, the medieval festivals known as carnivals, associated with Roman Catholic holy days. But he follows the traces of the carnivalesque into modernity and the industrial age when he was writing.

In the home town of one of the authors of this book, Skipton, a well-established puppet festival now attracts performers from across Europe. At the heart of the festival is a parade through the town centre, during which the professionals mix with local community groups and schools. It is an aesthetic and political reproduction of the carnivalesque. It is aesthetically carnivalesque because the puppets are monstrous, vibrant and surrounded by flag-waving children, samba musicians and cheering spectators. In 2015, for example, the puppet parade was led by enormous Swaledale sheep, with a similar-scale sheepdog chasing them into line. It is politically carnivalesque because the roads are closed when it winds through the centre of town, and it promotes diversity and acceptance of the other and the unknown (Badiou, 2005). The drivers who have parked on the High Street without knowing that the parade is scheduled have to sit and wait in their cars as local people cheer multi-ethnic marching bands and puppets carried by people with learning disabilities. Although the festival includes some shows where people have to pay to get in, a significant number of the performances are free to view, including presentations of the traditional British seaside puppet show Punch and Judy (see Crone, 2012), in which a number of transgressions and carnivalesque subversions are played out, even if the subject matter remains contentiously and aggressively heteronormative and hegemonically masculine (Connell, 1995).

The traditional Punch and Judy narrative includes wife-beating, hitting a baby until it dies, and killing the policeman who arrives to investigate the crime. In the Punch and Judy performance Spracklen observed in Skipton in 2015, Punch and Judy beat each other equally, undermining the traditional misogyny, but the anarchistic, anti-authoritarian message of the show remained intact: the British flag was mocked as 'rubbish'; and the policeman was attacked and humiliated

– mocked by both Punch and the audience – before being killed. Violence was again the dominant theme in another puppet performance at the festival, which featured a joke about the victim having to wait six months for treatment because of cuts to the National Health Service. It was then suggested that things would improve when the newly installed Labour leader Jeremy Corbyn became Prime Minister.

Historically, events were spaces for the maintenance of social order through the release of energy and the playfulness of the carnival. In the Middle Ages of Western Europe, holy days and religious feasts brought communities together to worship God and honour the feudal system that bound the peasants to their lords, and their lords to their kings (Eliade, 2013). It was in the interests of the kings and the lords to provide sufficient resources for their vassals to worship correctly, and to attend to the matters of religious orthodoxy. Carnivals developed out of the parades and festivities associated with the solemn rituals of the holy days. They were integral to those holy days. But they became more than just a way to worship as they developed into important holidays and feasts, rituals that included secular leisure pursuits alongside the more obviously spiritual practices. For instance, markets were held on feast days, lords participated in sports and met with their fellows, and the lower classes got drunk in taverns. The carnivals and feasts allowed the rulers of medieval Europe to display their Christian piety as well as their secular wealth and power (Spracklen, 2011a). Only later did reforming leaders reject the debauchery and the supposed pagan aspects of carnivals (Bakhtin, 1984; Eliade, 2013; Frazer, 1922).

To some extent, this rejection was prompted by fear of the transgressions that occurred during carnivals, for these were spaces where villains could be kings for a day, and the ruling classes loosened their rigid control, albeit temporarily. In his survey of the literature that was available to him at the time, J.G. Frazer (1922) shows that all of the festivals and carnivals of medieval Europe were driven by half-remembered ideas about death and resurrection among the peasant classes. They were liminal spaces in which the people showed their collective power to shape their culture and society. People chose to reject the formal religion and morals of their rulers for a more democratic, communicative misrule. Instead of abstinence, they chose drinking and debauchery. Instead of obeying the laws of their lords and kings, they elected their own carnival king for the day, or simply ran amok. For Frazer, the king for the day is a scapegoat, a person who in earlier times would have been sacrificed to ensure the turning of the heavens and the cycle of the seasons. While this (like much of Frazer's analysis) is highly speculative and based on his partial reading of the evidence, transgressions and misrule were certainly associated with medieval carnivals. In other words, Bakhtin's (1984) account still essentially holds true for the carnivalesque in medieval Europe, and it might be similarly useful when exploring festivals in other pre-modern cultures and societies. The question is: can this idea of the transgressive and misrule also help us understand and critically analyse the role of events today?

A growing body of literature is making this case for events, tourism and leisure (Haydock, 2015; Hubbard, 2013; Matheson and Tinsley, 2016; Spracklen and

Spracklen, 2014; Weichselbaumer, 2012). We acknowledge that literature and recognize the evidence that suggests we can use the idea of misrule to understand modern-day events. However, we want to theorize further the idea of transgression, misrule and the carnivalesque in events. Hence, in this chapter we develop a critical account of the idea that events may be spaces for misrule and transgression. In the first section we introduce theories of transgression and apply them to events. In the second we develop Bakhtin's idea of the carnivalesque through a discussion of the meaning of liminality in modern events. Finally, we return to Debord (1977) and examine how events might be seen as spaces for subversion and communicative forms of spectacle.

Theories of transgression

Transgression can be an act of human agency, an act of human constraint, or both. For something to be transgressive, there needs to be a set of norms and values against which the transgression is judged. Those norms and values are shaped by the elites of any given society, and they reflect the assumptions and prejudices of those elites, as well as their fears. So transgression is something that breaks the rules, the norms and the values, the holy commandments or the law. The transgressor may not view what they are doing as transgressive, but any act can be classified as such if the elites make it illegal: for instance, smoking in bars never used to be transgressive, but it is now, in many countries. Someone might continue to smoke in bars because of ignorance of a new law, or they might do so in deliberate defiance of the law and the government that introduced it. Both of these acts are transgressive, but in the former case the transgression is dictated by the elites and the norms and values they have imposed, whereas in the latter it is wilful and forms a complex political action against the modern nation-state.

The act of transgression may be condemned as completely against society's norms and values, or it may be accommodated into those norms and values as something that is tolerated or allowed under certain circumstances. In many religious systems, for example, disobedience towards the divine authority of elites or kings has been considered a serious form of transgression that is punishable by death (Frazer, 1922). In other belief systems transgressions against sexual and gender norms have been condemned as contrary to right thinking and good society. How much transgression is allowed by any given community, culture or society depends on the needs of its rulers, and the power of its subaltern groups. In modernity political liberalism has granted individuals enormous freedom in both the private and the public spheres, but legislation still bans some things that deemed to be bad for (post)modern society. John Stuart Mill's (1998 [1859]) argument that all kinds of actions and thoughts should be permitted in private spaces is potentially undermined by the rise of digital technology and the post-industrial 'security state' (Spracklen, 2015). So transgressions remain both possible and, for many individuals, desirable as means of rejecting the norms and values of 'polite society'.

As Foucault (1973, 2005) shows, the medicalization of deviance led to catego-
rizing any transgression of social and cultural boundaries as a mental problem that
needed to be cured. Moreover, if the transgressor could not be cured, they would
be locked away for their own and society's safety. Anything that transgressed the
norms and values of the polite, Christian West was deemed 'deviant': drinking,
gambling, engaging in radical politics, socializing with different classes, races or
genders, sexual activity outside of heterosexual marriage, and breaking the law.
Legal experts and philosophers advocated tightening the law so that it fully
reflected the moral values of nations, and sometimes the politicians followed their
advice. For instance, the United States prohibited the sale and consumption
of alcohol for more than a decade, and many nations still ban the use of other
mind-altering substances.

In medical textbooks throughout the twentieth century people who engaged in
'deviant' behaviour were treated as if they were suffering from a disease. However,
in the second half of the century the rise of cultural studies as an academic discipline resulted in a transformation in thinking about transgression and deviance.
Foucault (1973, 2005) argues that madness was a cultural construction, a product
of the increasing scientization and rationalization of modern life. For him, there
was no genuine deviance, no true mental health problems. These were simply
failures of modern nation-states to recognize (or allow) the full diversity of human
thought and human behaviour. Other academics started to use Foucault's insights
to explore the construction of deviance and transgression, and the importance of
such behaviour in human development. Transgression serves important functions
in defending the Habermasian lifeworld, providing a space for counter-hegemonic, subaltern resistance, and providing community and belonging to those who
reject the instrumental mainstream of contemporary society.

Judith Butler (2006) shows that the hegemonic power of heterosexual men is
expressed through the performance of heteronormativity, but in contemporary
society women and men who play with their gender roles in a transgressive
manner threaten this heteronormativity. The normative performances of gender,
and their transgressive equivalents, are undertaken by both men and women. For
men, being heteronormative is to play a traditionally dominant role, stereo-
typically articulated through masculine sports and leisure pursuits, such as watching football, shooting and drinking beer. For women, heteronormativity involves
playing a traditionally subservient role – domestic, private, appearing attractive to
men and allowing them to have their fun. Butler differs from radical feminist
theory because she believes in the power of individual agency to undermine such
performativity. It is perfectly possible, she claims, for individuals to transgress the
heteronormative order. Butler uses drag as an example of such transgression:
homosexual men and women can and do subvert heteronormative performances
by playing grotesque caricatures of the other gender, so lesbian drag-kings, for
example, smoke pipes and wear moustaches, while drag-queens hide behind
garish make-up, feather boas and sequins. This notion of transgression as counter-
hegemonic performance can also be applied more broadly to the transgression of
other societal, cultural and political norms. So, in the medieval period, the king

for a day or the lord of misrule was deliberately chosen to represent the marginal and subaltern members of the community. He would stand up – albeit temporarily – and show society's injustices through the performance of power.

How might these theories of transgression be applied to events? As we have shown throughout this book, most events are organized, planned and controlled by the elites of contemporary society, or used by them to keep subaltern groups in check. But it could be argued that some events provide opportunities to roam freely against the norms and values of society because they are freely chosen spaces of leisure and pleasure (Haydock, 2015). In the next section we will say more about this liminality and how it relates to Bakhtin's notion of the carnivalesque. But for now we need to reflect on the idea that all events are leisure spaces where pleasure is sought and individuals can and do show signs of nascent rebellion against order.

In British association football grounds from the 1960s to the 1990s, this disorder manifested itself in hooliganism within the confines of the sports events (Frosdick and Marsh, 2013). It happened in the spaces where football spectators chanted, sang, swore at rival teams and threw missiles on to the pitch (Spaaij, 2008). Sociologists influenced by Elias have described football fans' active participation in this period as a mimetic form of violence, or a de-civilizing spurt in the civilizing process (Dunning, 2000). But clearly it was a form of communicative action that was designed to create a form of misrule. The fans effectively took over the grounds and the streets around them, banishing police and club officials from their rule and establishing their own codes of conduct, which typically rewarded violence against rival gangs and the police. This was an ugly, misogynistic and racist form of subaltern resistance and misrule, but it happened regularly in the UK until the football authorities used the power of television contracts and health-and-safety legislation to sanitize and gentrify the game (at least to some extent; see Frosdick and Marsh, 2013). In other parts of the world similar processes of gentrification and commodification have been less successful at eliminating football fans' misrule, but in general their opportunities for resisting have been reduced to chants, flags and bands.

Music festivals are also closely controlled and commodified these days, but attendees still have some opportunities to challenge the norms and values of mainstream society. In many studies the typical festival experience is presented as a reaction against the normal rules of everyday life (Dowson *et al.*, 2015). In the festival context excess is favoured over decency, so drinking alcohol, taking drugs and casual sex are all prevalent. But the music festival is moving closer to the old idea of misrule in the way that people welcome the performance of spectacle and carnival. If it is raining and the fans are covered in mud, they embrace the mud as make-up and play at being wild things. If the sun is out, they strip and draw symbols on their bodies with suntan lotion or face paint. There are opportunities to express disgust and disdain for modern life and its rules, even though such expressions are mediated by the commodification of the festival experience. In their pursuit of an authentic, boutique festival, others seek a spiritual connection with the idea of misrule. They want to find a festival or some other event that allows them to be truly liminal, truly unruly, truly spectacular. This quest for 'authentic' misrule has been met by the events industry and its *ersatz* products, but people continue to search for it because they know that such spaces are traditionally associated with it.

Bakhtin and liminality

Everybody wants to belong, and many of us are on that quest for the authentic experience of misrule that lies at the heart of liminality. Turner (1969) introduced and popularized the idea of the liminal space in his broader work on community and belonging. Liminal spaces lie at the edges of communities, at the boundaries of the rules of those communities, where individuals can find freedom from the rules that bind communities together. As they flee from the rules they construct their own rules about the relationship between the liminal space and the community centre. In practice this means that all societies and cultures have cores and peripheries, and it is possible to find both pleasure and belonging at the periphery. Old-fashioned tourist resorts, such as Blackpool in the UK, are perfect examples of the idea of liminality (Hughes and Benn, 1997; Lashley and Rowson, 2007). Blackpool was constructed by the sand and sea purely as a holiday destination. In its prime, at the height of modernity, it was filled with visitors who went on holiday collectively from their workplaces in the mills and factories of the north of England. Once in Blackpool, these visitors could drink beer, eat chips, dance and make love without worrying about the consequences, or the morals and rules of their home towns. As this relationship with heavy industry disappeared, Blackpool transformed into a centre for stag and hen nights, but this new generation of visitors behave exactly as their great-grandparents did. Tourist resorts are constructed on the notion that it is possible to purchase liminality, and people who travel to places such as Blackpool understand the rules of the game. They do not go there to be modest and virtuous; they go to be unruly and liminal.

Tourists obviously search for liminal experiences during their holidays and on their travels, and the entire modern tourist industry seems to be designed to give them a form of the authentic, liminal experience, even if that experience is mediated (Hubbard, 2013; Spracklen and Spracklen, 2014; Taylor, 1969). We all want to find that spot away from our mundane, secular and rational working world where we can be transformed and uplifted. We all want to find the adventure of the liminal space during our travels – the chance meetings with fellow travellers and locals, the fine food and the wild intoxicants. Events might be viewed simply in the same terms: that is, as liminal experiences. At any event, people attend to escape from the everyday and to find adventure, belonging and satisfaction. The very idea of an event is that it is some sort of liminal space, or at least some sort of space that allows liminal actions to take place (Badiou, 2005). In the wider subject field of leisure studies the analytical lens of liminality has been applied to subcultures and alternative music scenes, where people supposedly find fellow agents who want to use their fashions and their music choices to express resistance to the mainstream (Spracklen and Spracklen, 2012, 2014). Subcultural fashions then become suitably spectacular and carnivalesque, because they express the desire to be overtly unruly and anti-authoritarian. So the liminal space in such subcultures is symbolized through 'offensive' imagery, fashions and styles that are specifically designed to upset mainstream tastes and conventions. In this subcultural liminality one might find all manner of events aimed at those who wish to participate in these alternative scenes (Spracklen and Spracklen, 2014). But such alternative subcultures are always vulnerable to hegemonic takeover, as Hebdige (1979) and Williams (1977) both pointed out back in the 1970s. But before they are taken over by the mainstream and co-opted into mainstream culture and tastes, these subcultures can provide transient moments of true liminality. For a moment in the 1950s, for instance, respectable middle-class white people in the United States and the United Kingdom were genuinely scared of rock and roll. By the 1970s, the Teddy boys had grown up and were no longer a cause for concern, but punks then became objects of equal fear, precisely because they also came from the margins and seemed to signify misrule. Thereafter, for a time, heavy metal appeared to be a potential liminal and counter-hegemonic subculture, and it has globalized as such, although there is debate over its continued liminality (Spracklen, 2014b). Some scholars argue that the postmodern, global world in which we live makes such resistive spaces impossible to create, but we are not so pessimistic. We believe it is possible to find communicative meaning and purpose in leisure and culture, but such liminal moments are few and far between. At present, a marginal and carnivalesque youth subculture that we are unaware of (because we are middle-aged, full-time academics) is no doubt growing and offering its members a sense of satisfaction and belonging as well as resistive identity.

We can see that Bakhtin's account of the carnivalesque maps onto Turner's notion of the liminal in many ways. The carnivalesque is the spirit of misrule and resistance, and the Debordian spectacle of dissent. People participate in carnivals and festivals because they want to express anger at the system; they want to rally and protest at the injustices they see, using whatever means are available. Such anger and protest appear in overt forms as well as occult ones, where the protest is expressed through symbolism, colour, embodiment and music. But people seek the carnivalesque because they want to subvert the system through transgressing its norms and values. This is not necessarily about protesting against injustice; rather, the transgression is used to make a statement about transience. The carnivalesque makes fools of rulers, who wave and smile as the participants march past in their colourful parades, unaware that the noise and the activity are denigrating their autocracy. No matter how much the misrule is used as a way to let angry citizens and subjects 'let off steam' and direct their anger away from actual revolution, the elites are always mocked and reviled. The liminal is a physical space or a state of mind where the same motivations are at work among human agents. Turner says we seek it out because modern society is rationalized and disenchanted. By contrast, we find meaning and purpose, and ritual and misrule, in the liminal. The carnivalesque is just one form of the general rule of liminality: it is always possible to be unruly, to find common cause with others, and to find ways of living that resist the ruling elites, if only for a brief moment, in liminal spaces. The carnival's overturning of norms and values, then, and the provision of spectacle are predicated on liminal space and liminal action. So, while there are differences of purpose and construction, the carnivalesque and the liminal draw on the same notions of human agency and human freedom. Our needs and desires are fulfilled in such spaces and through such actions, even if what we do is still constrained by elites and their rules. Bakhtin argues that modern elites, such as capitalists and nation-states, co-opt and control the notion of misrule, turning it into a pale imitation of itself in sports, flag-worshipping and national day parades. Meanwhile, Turner believes that the liminal, by its very nature, is always marginalized and vulnerable to commodification by the brutal instruments of capitalism and modernity. Yet liminal spaces and actions continue to flourish because humans demand and need to find ways to express both belonging and exclusion, happiness and dissatisfaction.

Where are misrule and the carnivalesque evident in modern events? We might think that sports events and music festivals are obvious liminal spaces. At these events there is usually some kind of performance by a set of agents, watched by a crowd that cheers and shouts its appreciation or disapproval. We have been in these situations and can report that they certainly *feel* liminal. In a football stadium, in the midst of tens of thousands of people, it is quite possible to be transported by the chanting and the singing, and the highs and lows of watching a team win or lose. It feels like a shared emotional journey, one that allows us to express our feelings openly by swearing, cheering, laughing or crying. Modern sports events may be controlled and commercialized, mediatized and commodified, but they still give spectators a space where they can dress up and chant obscene songs about the quality of the match officials. They still give spectators opportunities to display their disdain for the instrumental forces that shape modern society. The owners of sports clubs and sports leagues tolerate such carnivalesque activity as long as it adds to the atmosphere and makes the spectacle more attractive. Sponsors and broadcasters pay more money for sports events that have boisterous crowds who sing and cheer. But the free expression of political opposition to the mainstream – open antipathy towards the elites of nation-states and global capitalism – is discouraged and constrained as much as possible. Sometimes fans air racist and fascist views, and the authorities receive widespread support when they clamp down against such behaviour (Spracklen, 2013). But in the process other forms of free expression and radical politics are also constrained and eliminated from sports events. At global mega-events private security guards swiftly suppress every aspect of the carnivalesque, quashing every opportunity to resist through the misrule of political chants and slogans.

There are music festivals in all shapes and sizes, for all musical genres. Those that might still be associated with the misrule of the carnival fall loosely under the category of pop music. For the sake of this argument, pop music encompasses all genres and forms of music that emerged in the West in the twentieth century. Adorno (2001) derides it as a product of high modernity and commodification, aimed at the young and the disaffected as a means of keeping them happy by giving them a sufficient level of cultural satisfaction. Pop music is the industrialized music of modern culture, or America and the West, from rock and roll onwards. Sub-genres include heavy metal and hip-hop, as well as the EDM and heart-throb music that dominate the charts.

Having defined the genre, we can say that pop music festivals still seem to give their spectators some sense of carnival and unruliness. Many members of the crowd have a good time by having a wild time. They dance with strangers, get muddy, get intoxicated. There are numerous carnivalesque diversions that overturn the polite manners and tastes, as well as the norms and values, of the ruling elites. At alternative music festivals there is also a sense of solidarity as a liminal person in opposition to the mainstream – the biggest cheers are reserved for musicians who mock the commercialized pop mainstream of reality television, or the superficiality of dance music. At punk festivals political elites and global capitalism are frequently derided (Guerra and Quintela, 2014). The bigger pop music festivals may be owned by corporations and emblazoned with sponsors' adverts, but festival-goers can still find good company in the middle of the mosh-pit, or in the beer tent, or in the corner of a field. People attend pop music festivals to experience the carnivalesque. They want to break the rules of the mainstream, do things that are out of the ordinary, and find community in the liminality of the festival spaces.

Such festivals are only ever quasi-carnivalesque, however. We do not wish to belittle the experiences and feelings of the people who attend them, but those feelings and experiences are always mediated, and invariably temporary. Attending a festival, and being unruly there, now costs a huge sum of money and involves the accumulation of a large amount of cultural capital. So the experience of the carnival, and the experience of the misrule, is limited to those who are in the hegemonic centre – the elites and the middle classes. For them, with their abundant money and their considerable cultural capital, pop festivals provide a Baudrillardian simulacra of the carnival. They are the ruling classes, and they do not need the moment of misrule to vent their frustrations about the inequalities of contemporary society. So their enjoyment and experience merely validate their hegemony and cultural capital, rather than challenge that hegemony. Authentic, counter-hegemonic misrule might occur at free or at least affordable pop festivals, or when the festival highlights a marginal form of pop music. But even these festivals are marginalized by the events industry and the eventization of leisure more generally.

Debord, the spectacle and the unruly

We have already discussed Debord's (1977) notion of the spectacle. From a Debordian perspective, the spectacle is a glamorous form of propaganda that keeps the people in their place. Or one might see the spectacular in events as a means of disrupting the elites' control, and allowing communicative rationality and communicative identity-making. When an event is a mega-event or a corporate festival there is little space or freedom to be communicatively spectacular: one has to pay to attend, and one's movement and choices are restricted even if one finds some way to be unruly. But when events are organized and controlled by their participants, the spectacle is also controlled by those participants. In such circumstances it is possible to be counter-hegemonic, because one uses one's communicative leisure to construct the Habermasian lifeworld (Habermas, 1992b, 1992c): that is, the participants use their freedom of involvement, and their democratic or anarchic organizing structures, to be as unruly and as spectacular as they can possibly be. At the ideal event where such misrule and spectacle are sustainable all participants are treated equally, there are no divisions between performers and spectators, and money is not exchanged to delineate performers from paying customers. Such events obviously take place in protest spaces, especially those that are relatively spontaneous and unrestrained by security agencies. In such instances the misrule (sometimes literally) overturns the symbols of authority, and participants have the chance to construct alternative ways of living. They also get to be spectacular through the creative licence that defines such communicative lifeworlds. All of the anti-austerity protests and actions of the early twenty-first century were striking because of their colourful, highly visual parades. This is deliberate Debordian intent.

But what about festivals that are not protests? Some events take place according to the communicative principles of anarchism, such as anti-racism football festivals in Italy (Sterchele and Saint-Blancat, 2015), which feature communicative space and Debordian misrule. These events are explicitly political, radical in their aims and in their attempt to disrupt the norms and values of mainstream society. But the spectacular and the unruly can also be seen in what might be described as mainstream, non-political events.

Let us return to the Skipton Puppet Festival. On the surface, this is the usual commodified event that is designed to bring in money for the festival itself and the town. The brochure advertises performances that cost money. The local newspaper promotes the arrival of the festival as something that is good for business. Local companies and organizations provide support and sponsorship, and their names and logos appear in the brochure. At the festival hub people and companies sell food, drink and items that are related to the puppet theme. An ice-cream van has been converted to sell finger puppets. Real ale from a local brewery is sold in the main tent. The town council's officers are out in force, helping visitors to find their way to and from the official festival sites, and around the rest of the town. Yet an air of misrule still hangs over the festival. The puppets are, by their nature, spectacles, but the festival makes them even more spectacular in the Debordian sense. The parade includes professionals with huge and scary puppets walking alongside young people with their home-made puppets. Everyone is treated equally. It is a co-production of creative artists, teachers and young people. As well as the giant sheep, there is a giant bird, shoals of fish, and insects. This is spectacular because it is a bizarre and disconcerting thing to see on Skipton's main street. The normal routine of the high street – the angry men in cars papping their horns at pedestrians who only want to cross the road, the traffic jams and the fumes – has been temporarily banished. The puppet parade has appeared as if from nowhere to transform the road into a carnival. The king of the road in his white van has been replaced – for a day – by children dancing to the samba beat of a marching band.

It is not only the parade that demonstrates the puppet festival's communicative, Debordian potential for misrule. As many of the performances are free, visitors are encouraged to think that this is not merely an instrumental contract between a performer and a paying customer. The visitors watch enthralled as the performers stage their free shows, and they modify their behaviour accordingly. At the shows that are celebrations of technical accomplishment, the audiences clap politely and watch carefully. At the shows that are comedic, such as Punch and Judy, the performers encourage the members of the audience to cheer and boo, and they oblige. These latter performances evoke the true Debordian spectacle at work in Bakhtinian misrule. The Punch and Judy audience is an equal partner in the performance, and an equal and complicit partner in the misrule. The children learn that it is morally good to question authority, to express anger and happiness, to laugh at jokes that mock kings, flags, leaders and ghosts. They learn the value of sitting with other children and participating in the singing and the shouting, even though, at home, their parents have probably told them many times to be quiet. Here they learn from each other that it is sometimes okay to be unruly and to ignore their parents, who stand at the edge of the crowd and look on nervously, seemingly fearful that the children might turn on them. The adults also find temporary release from the strictures of being parents and obedient workers in our contemporary, post-industrial society. In the alternative logic of Punch and Judy, it is right and proper to fear work, avoid work and be a bad parent.

It is the truly communicative Debordian spectacle, the truly unruly carnival, which the events industry tries to tap into and control. At events where there is no instrumental logic to control and shape the proceedings, people are truly free to express themselves, to find their belonging and identity. In such leisure spaces events can become more than things that happen. They are like the fools of medieval courts, or the slave who carries Caesar's laurel wreath: communicative events turn the world upside-down and allow the weak to speak truth to power. The fools and Caesar's slave rejected the norms and values of their societies by whispering to their lords that they are only men and their power is only transient. This is the transgression of all transgressions, more communicative than merely behaving outrageously. In the spectacle of liminality rulers are fearful of hearing the truth, so such spectacles, such unruly action, is policed and repressed, or converted into an instrumental form of itself. This can be seen in the way that modern mega-events have adopted the styles of the spectacle and the carnival (Bakhtin, 1984): there is a superficial subversion and transgression of norms and values, but this does not take place in a truly liminal or communicative space, so it becomes a way of controlling spectacle, and of selling tickets and merchandise. In the Olympics, for example, there are enormous parades and festivities. During the 2012 opening ceremony, the audience was presented with a supposedly subversive, alternative version of Britishness and British identity. Conservative commentators complained that the ceremony promoted a version of Britain that drew on radical-left political narratives: a Britain that was and is multicultural, for example; or one that celebrated the formation of the welfare state and the NHS as positive aspects of its collective imagination. But while the ceremony did make these concessions to alternative, radical politics, at the heart of the narrative and the spectacle was an assumption that Britain was great because of the Queen and our quaint traditions. Hence tradition and the monarchy were presented in an entirely positive light, not as highly problematic, egregious aspects of modern British society. The other ceremonies and spectacles in the Games reproduced all of the instrumental rationality of global capitalism and the nation-state, from the sponsors' logos, through to the teams' processions behind flags, and the inevitable flag-raising and national anthems whenever winners were awarded their medals. This version of the Debordian spectacle is not just a chimera. It is an abomination of the spirit of the idea of spectacle, and the ideology of misrule.

There is even more instrumental use of spectacle at music festivals. In the main arena of a rock festival, for example, there is much that is unruly and carnivalesque. There is transgression, and the freedom to leave the arena and see another band somewhere else. But for those who submit to the spectacle of the rock band, there is submission to instrumental logic and instrumental spectacle. The band plays music that is carefully controlled through technology to generate various emotional reactions and thoughts. The lights are manipulated to exaggerate the effects of the music. The band will often have an attractive, charismatic singer. All of this works to make the crowd easy to control, pliant, which creates opportunities for the festival owners and the band to sell records and merchandise. They like the fact that the members of the crowd are entranced or moved by the music, because this means they are happy, so they will probably return to the festival in future years or buy tickets for the band's next tour. All spectacle at a music festival is designed to turn the fans into consumers. When they enthuse about the bands that put on the most spectacular shows, they act like viruses to spread the instrumentality of the market. There is no defence against this appropriation of the spectacle. All the fans can do is buy more T-shirts, keep calm and stay happy.

Conclusion

There is something essentially communicative in the idea of misrule. When the norms and values of mainstream society are overturned, we are free to construct our own notions of right and wrong, good and bad. We are free to transgress, and to explore new ways of living. When everything is transformed by spectacle into the carnival, every space becomes liminal. Events that allow this to happen have the potential to be transformative, counter-hegemonic or radical. That is, we can construct our own lifeworlds in these unruly, liminal and transgressive spaces. But for such transformations to take place in a leisure space, the events have to be truly communicative, truly democratic and free of instrumentality. When this happens, we find a true spectacle that allows us to experience what it is like to be free of the powers and structures that constrain the world. For a moment, we are able to laugh at our superiors. We are able to find meaning and purpose, belonging and identity. True spectacles make the world a better place. However, when this does not happen – when the event is part of instrumentality – the spectacle becomes a narcotic, a way of making consumers forget the horrors of modern society, a hallucinogen that makes us believe that the world of consumption and inequality is fine. In such circumstances we have to make a choice about whether we want to remain at the event or leave. And we have to critique it, because otherwise instrumentality will colonize the lifeworld a little bit further.

11 Can there be an emancipatory event studies?

Introduction

John Humphrys, the BBC journalist who is renowned for his dogged pursuit of a direct answer to a direct question, might be satisfied with one answer to the question that is posed in the title of this chapter: 'Yes!' However, as anyone with a passion for, and fascination with, intellectual exploration will understand, a much richer and more nuanced web of thinking lies behind such a straight-forward response. Yes, event studies can be emancipatory; the work, discussions and examples in the preceding ten chapters are, to some extent, a testament to that. For a truly *critical* event studies there would seem to be a requirement that research should seek to critique domination and exploitation, but such a response is not immediately obvious if we are to consider the field's lineage in events management. A concentration on operational and managerialist concerns within events management, and a framing of 'event' that owes more to a paradigm tethered to the hegemony of a dominant cultural political economy of neo-liberalism, means that most of the research associated with events management omits a consideration of power, domination and, consequently, emancipation. However, as we have seen elsewhere in this book, CES does not have such a simple parentage.

In this chapter we look at the roots of CES as an emancipatory event studies by showing that it shares a common inheritance with other critical fields and approaches. Using an overview of a range of areas of academic activity as a step-ping stone, we consider the theoretical framework that constitutes the foundation and structures that form the building blocks of CES as a critical and emancipatory event studies.

Is event studies emancipatory?

CES is connected to events management via event studies. Now, while event studies attempts to give some deeper credibility to a consideration of power and domination, it falls short of being an emancipatory field itself. Before we investigate other critical fields, and CES's resonances with and linkages to them, it is worth spending a little time reflecting on why event studies does not quite fit that bill. Among the numerous scholars who are doing fascinating and pioneering work within the field of event studies, here we highlight three as exemplars of some of its central developments. Those developments are: a recognition that event studies research is, to varying degrees, a cross-disciplinary project; an acknowledgement that studying events places them in a wider socio-cultural frame of reference; and a recognition that events occur in a discursive context, at least to some extent. The three people who are working across each of those developments are, in loose chronological order of their published engagement, Maurice Roche, Donald Getz and Chris Rojek.

In *Mega-events and Modernity*, Roche (2000) explores the links between the Olympic Games (since 1896) and the World Expo movement (since the Great Exhibition of 1851) and the emergence and growth of global culture. His central argument is that mega-events 'are important substantively and more formally in understanding structure, change and agency in modern society' (ibid.: 7). Yet, while he suggests a central role for a sociology of events, he also acknowledges that mega-events can be understood only if they are perceived as multi-dimensional, in terms of scale *and* in respect of the disciplinary areas that are required to interrogate them fully as phenomena within late modernity (Roche, 1992). This point is most clearly echoed by Getz (2007) in *Event Studies: Theory, Research and Policy for Planned Events* – an early attempt to define the field – where he sets out the three principal domains across which event studies operates: event tourism, events management and 'disciplinary perspectives'. Judging by the sheer number of disciplines and fields that appear on the contents page of the second edition of that book (Getz, 2012), his notion of what constitutes event studies is very wide: as well as management and related areas, he includes anthropology, religious studies, environmental psychology, law, history and future studies. Similarly, although less explicitly, Rojek (2013, 2014) draws on a broad spectrum of the social sciences as well as political philosophy and ethics.

As well as recognizing the importance of multidisciplinarity for event studies, Roche acknowledged the significance of studying events by placing them in a wider socio-cultural context. In his paper 'Mega-events and micro-modernization' he asserts that a purely sociological study of events is too narrow (Roche, 1992). Rather than focusing on economic impacts and functions, an understanding of events should be concerned with the problem of contextualization. This, he argues, 'is better done in broad rather than narrow terms and in terms which take account of contexts of structural change and discontinuity and reorganization of local economies' (ibid.: 565). While Getz is particularly strong on connecting event studies to a wider context of disciplines and fields, and explaining how the latter can illuminate the wider impacts of an event, he seems less interested in how that socio-cultural context might impact on an event itself. The disciplinary perspectives he identifies act in a somewhat subordinate role to the fields of events management and event tourism. Rojek (2013, 2014), alternatively, argues explicitly for the need to understand events in the context of relationships, both socio-cultural and those of its place within a functioning political economy. For him, it is through interrogating an event in that richer context that we are able to see how it is used to manage and manipulate people. In his discussion of the appropriation and transformation of such events as the Rio Carnival and Sydney's Mardi Gras into global, multi-million-dollar businesses, he suggests:

> The seizure of folk traditions or gatherings involves the commercialisation of time-honoured practice and the imposition of bureaucracy and policing. The commercial logic is that the economic value of traditional events is underdeveloped if the dominant organisational principle is the preservation and accumulation of cultural capital without the attachment of a monetary value. Folk traditions are therefore monetised . . . Event appropriation involves the co-option of history, the obliteration of identity and the redefinition of space.
>
> (Rojek, 2013: 153)

In this line of reasoning the context reveals how events are used to manage participants/attendees. By contrast, Getz's approach uses a broader understanding of that context to help us gain greater insight into how better to manage an event.

Of the three identified developers of event studies, Getz most clearly recognizes that events take place within a range of discursive practices. That said, he has a more limited sense of discursive practice than the one that we present in this book. His construal of discourse in its connection to event studies lies along two main tracks. The first is most closely aligned to his consideration of the three domains, which he terms the 'three predominant subdivisions (or discourses) concerning planned events' (Getz, 2012: 15) and across which his formulation of event studies operates. His second, more implicit, use of discourse is associated with the practices of those who work within the events management and events tourism sectors. Here his consideration of discourse is similar to what Wenger (2000: 82) refers to as a 'community of practice', where, over time, 'the joint pursuit of an enterprise creates resources for negotiating meaning'. This is where the Events Management Body Of Knowledge (EMBOK), developed by Bowdin *et al.* (2012) and others, sits – as a framework through which meaning can be negotiated and the body of 'event managers' can be identified as a coherent community.

Despite its recognition of its interdisciplinary status as a field, its willingness to interrogate events by placing them in a wider socio-cultural context and an understanding that events occur within a discursive space, event studies still cannot be classified as an emancipatory field. There at least two principal reasons for this. First, Roche, Getz and Rojek do not engage with the question of how to conceptualize what the 'event' part of 'event studies' signifies. In all of these cases the concept of event is seen as transparent to the reader, to the extent that it can either be overlooked as a question of no relevance or simply illustrated through the construction of some form of event typology. A consequence of this is that the events that are considered fall comfortably within a paradigm of 'event' that best suits the hegemony of the dominant cultural political economy (Sum and Jessop, 2013). This is one of the things that marks out CES as distinct from event studies, for CES construes 'event' as that which intervenes in the social field and thereby exposes discursive relationships of power.

This point about the event exposing discursive relationships also indicates the other way in which event studies struggles to be emancipatory. Although Roche recognizes the importance of examining events sociologically, Getz understands that they need to recognize the multiplicity of other disciplinary perspectives underpinning them and Rojek seeks to provoke by exposing them as master manipulators, all three see events as relatively stable entities with managed or manageable identities. But this assumption overlooks a crucial contestation that opens all events up to counter-values, alternative construal, disagreement, dissent, protest and, potentially, unrest. Importantly, 'event' understood as that which intervenes in the social means that acts of dissent, protest and so on, by forcing the exposure of discursive relationships in the social sphere, become prototypical 'events'. In excluding such instances from the repertoire of event studies, resistance becomes something that cannot be articulated in a positive way; thus, emancipatory endeavours become problematic for event studies.

The remainder of this chapter is split into two parts. In order to show the character and importance of criticality to CES we make a number of connections to sister fields. The list of example fields is not intended to be exhaustive or definitive; instead, it is intended to illuminate how the 'critical' part of 'critical event studies' fits into the work and ideas of those who attempt to engage in emancipatory scholarship. In the second part the emancipatory character of CES is broken down into a number of theoretical building blocks. As with the previous part, we acknowledge that this is only one way of constructing CES as an emancipatory event studies; others may construct it differently. Throughout both parts examples of research undertaken by CES academics and academic activists will illustrate how CES is being used to study events.

Making connections

We will discuss the connection between CES and other emancipatory fields along two tracks. First, we will look at a number of existing fields that are concerned with enquiry that has a strong axiological focus on social justice. We will then consider how a critical turn is impacting on those areas that are frequently associated with event studies and events management: studies of tourism and hospitality. Finally, the two tracks will be drawn together to reflect on the centrality of criticality, and on CES's close ties to the critical study of discourses and other – wider – theoretical perspectives.

The four emancipatory fields for which we provide brief – and consequently somewhat limited – overviews are: critical race theory (CRT); radical feminism; queer theory; and disability studies. This list is far from exhaustive, and it is not meant to highlight any strength of connection to CES. Instead, it represents, more idiosyncratically, a combination of the authors' interests and some of the areas in which we have worked.

Critical race theory

In their appraisal of the last twenty years of CRT both Trubek (2011) and Crenshaw (2011) begin by suggesting its roots were laid in resistance – at the Harvard Law School and the University of Wisconsin Law School – to a specifically black perspective within critical legal studies (CLS). As a movement and disciplinary field, the diversity of research associated with CRT is loosely connected to two dominant themes, articulated across different contexts. The first of these proposes that white domination is maintained over time at a level that goes far beyond the power of any racist individual. Societal and institutional structures play central roles in sustaining power relations that work to reproduce discriminatory and oppressive practices. Significantly, the second theme within CRT is the blurring of theory and practice (academic investigation and activist action) around the formulation of possibilities for transforming those same societal and institutional frameworks, and the pursuit of projects that confront subordination and support racial emancipation.

While CRT, as a field, emerged in response to CLS (Trubek, 2011), over the last ten to fifteen years it has extended its reach to connect with other areas where ingrained discriminatory practices can be found. In his analysis of affirmative action (a form of 'positive discrimination') within academia, Adalberto Aguirre Jr. (2000) contrasts the *stock stories* of institutional practice associated with affirmative action with the stories of those who have encountered it in operation. Drawing on the work of Delgado (1989), Aguirre argues for three stock narratives which he claims institutions employ when implementing affirmative action policies:

- that they are motivated by benevolence, suggesting a gracious extending of the hand towards previously excluded people;
- that they have little impact on the actual constitution of the institution's departments, with a sub-text that suggests that the policy will apply to only a handful of applicants; and
- they are used to frame the institution as neutral with respect to blame or responsibility in its recruitment, in that it becomes articulated as simply following a procedure, with the implied assumption that policy is, to some extent, structurally considered to be racially neutral (Mutua, 2006).

By gathering applicants' personal experiences of affirmative action policies, Aguirre found that the arguments for adopting such policies commonly supported an institutionalized majoritarian (pro-white) discriminatory position. He concludes, 'we may dream about how affirmative action can shape academia into an inclusive and multicultural institution, [but] we should not be deluded about how affirmative action in implemented' (Aguirre, 2000: 331).

More recently, the work of Kevin Hylton (2010), Jonathan Long (Long *et al.*, 2011) and others has turned the lens of CRT onto sport and leisure. Incorporating a review of existing literature and an empirical study of new migrant communities in Leeds, Long *et al.* (ibid.) suggest that spaces might be encoded by particular ethnic groups to mark them as associated with particular arrangements of ethnicities, and that new migrants might bring with them an understanding of leisure spaces that carries an ethnic dimension which impedes their access (see also Long *et al.*, 2014; Spracklen *et al.*, 2015). Such 'internalized racism' (Pyke, 2010; Pyke and Dang, 2003) resonates with a Gramscian construal of 'whiteness' as hegemonic oppression.

Radical feminism

Just as CRT recognizes the societal and institutional othering of non-whiteness, so radical feminism asserts that patriarchy is so ingrained within the structures of society that women are still systematically oppressed and marginalized. Similar to CRT, much of the research done within this field explores one of two familiar themes: whether the location of oppression is much broader and deeper than its expression at an individual level; and an active approach to reordering society to end patriarchy. In the introduction to her anthology on radical feminism, Koedt (1973) argues for a breaking down of the barriers between activism and academic scholarship. She asserts that the anthology is a forum where analysis and activity, within the radical feminist movement, are to be used for transformational ends.

Rowland and Klein (1996) locate the emergence of radical feminist theories and approaches in the late 1960s. Growing consciousness that incremental legislative changes were either too slow or implicitly maintained hegemonic – in this case patriarchal – power (as Aguirre similarly found in his work on race and the implementation of affirmative action policies), and that class-based action was too fragmented to effect change, resulted in a more positive stance on direct action and campaign-orientated research. As Bunch and Pollack (1983: 248; emphasis added) assert, radical feminism is not simply an academic practice but 'a process based on *understanding* and *advancing the activist movement*'. The commitment of a field to scholarship that confronts real oppression and seeks transformational change to patriarchal hegemony has resulted in the application of its lens to areas as diverse as criminology (Chesney-Lind and Morash, 2013) and tourism studies (Aitchison, 2005)

Queer theory

It is thought that the film theorist Teresa de Lauretis (1991) was the first academic to use 'queer theory' in an intellectual project. In *Queer Theory: Lesbian and Gay Sexualities* she argues that there needs to be a critical rethinking of sexuality and gender in order to confront the societal norms that lie at the heart of a male/female binary, which, in turn, construct identities of 'gay' and 'lesbian' that are defined by the dominant hegemony. Alternatively, she suggests, gender and sexuality should be seen as multiple and, importantly, unstable. In 'Popular culture, public and private fantasies' (de Lauretis, 1999) she goes further, arguing that queer theory should not encompass the study of a category called 'queerness'. Instead, it should try to understand the socio-historical context that constructs sexual acts and identities into any form of categorization, while recognizing that those acts and identities are always already contested.

While the associated fields of gender studies and queer studies have developed numerous analytical tools to interrogate the construction of gender and sexual identity across a broad spectrum of human activity and interaction, neither has confronted oppression in the same way as CRT and radical feminism have in their domains. In this regard queer theory, which blurs the distinction between theoretical conceptualization and direct action for social justice, is more closely aligned with those earlier fields. In Gamson's (1996) work on lesbian and gay film festivals in New York, for example, the festivals' role is explored as a means of maintaining and legitimating a distinct lesbian and gay identity within the wider social milieu in which it participates. It does not question, or seek to challenge, the dominant hegemony's role in constructing those identities. More recently, Adrienne Shaw's (2012) work on the *gaymer* community of gay online gamers, and Lamond's ongoing autoethnographic work on participation in Pride, has suggested that sexual identity in those contexts tends to be divided between those who buy into stock frameworks for identity construction, which connect most strongly to a prevailing hegemonic binary, and those who celebrate its essential contestedness.

Disability studies

According to Grue (2015), there is considerable regional variation in how disability is conceptualized within disability studies as a disciplinary field. For the purposes of this chapter, the frame of reference will be the one that is most commonly found in research activity in Britain and the United States (although there is considerable variation in the latter). Both draw heavily on a social construction of disability: dominant in the UK is a model of disability that construes the disabled person as a member of an oppressed class; meanwhile, in the United States, the disabled community is usually conceptualized as an ethnic-cultural minority. These are generally referred to as the social model and the minority model, respectively, and both are commonly set against what has become known as the medical model. However, Grue (ibid.) claims that it is unclear whether the medical model is an actual model of disability. To him, it seems more like an amalgam of discourses associated with a broader medicalization of the individual (see Illich, 1976), established as contra-distinctive to the social and minority models.

Common to disability studies from both of these perspectives are its roots in advocating a necessary connection between activism and research. As one of the pioneers of disability studies in the UK wrote in 1992:

> The very idea that small groups of 'experts' can get together and set a research agenda for disability is . . . fundamentally flawed . . . Agenda setting, whether it be in politics, policy-making or service provision, is part of a

process of struggle and this is equally true of agenda setting in disability research.

(Oliver, 1992: 102)

Oliver has frequently returned to this point (see Oliver, 1998, 2009; Oliver and Barnes, 2010), and it sits at the heart of both the social and the minority models. However, he does acknowledge Germon's (1998) point that, in practice, the connections between activist and academic agenda are frequently left to chance. Yet, even if we accept that, we can still see a common thread that links the emancipatory fields we have selected. Emancipatory research carries two basic requirements: the capacity to expose power relations and social injustice by locating the object of analysis (race, gender, sexuality or disability) in a socio-cultural and socio-economic context that is much larger than individual instances; and dismantling of barriers between the academic and the activist to facilitate research that can confront oppression and subjugation head on.

Critical tourism and critical hospitality

As we mentioned at the beginning of this section, a turn towards a critical approach has also had an impact on fields that are frequently thought to be close to event studies. We suggested this in our discussion of tourism at the end of the subsection on radical feminism, and it is also being felt within hospitality studies. Here we briefly consider those impacts.

Of the two, critical *tourism* studies (CTS) has the longer history and a more substantial body of work to support it. It was in the late 1980s and early 1990s that John Urry first advocated a sociology of travel (Urry, 1988, 1990a). In 'The Consumption of Tourism' (Urry, 1990a: 23) he argues that a fuller understanding of how tourist services are consumed is possible only if those services and their consumption are inseparable 'from the social relations within which they are embedded'. This refocusing of theorization around the study of tourism away from a construal of place that resonates most closely with trying to interpret it as some sort of thing in itself (and a weighting towards vendor- or supplier-like relationships between 'guest' and 'host') to others that locate guest/host/place in complex networks of interaction, power and the interrelational dependencies around agents, social structures and the environment allows CTS to be open to a broad range of theorizations, methodologies and critical perspectives that can facilitate locating tourism in a wider socio-cultural, political and economic context. Significantly, CTS, through tourism practice, teaching and scholarship, seeks to effect real social change. This makes it a truly emancipatory field (Platenkamp and Botterill, 2013; Xin *et al.*, 2013).

Of the many people who are active in CTS, the work of John Tribe and his colleagues at the University of Surrey stands out most strongly (Tribe, 2008; Xin, *et al.*, 2013). From some of his earliest work, such as 'The indiscipline of tourism' (Tribe, 1997), Tribe has challenged preconceptions of what constitutes the study of tourism and the values it should adopt. In the last paragraph of that paper he notes that 'the search for tourism as a discipline should be abandoned', before adding, 'tourism studies seems likely to remain in a pre-paradigmatic phase . . . this should not be seen as a problem. Rather tourism studies should recognize and celebrate its diversity' (ibid.: 656). That celebration of its diversity, as a field, which lies at the core of CTS was reiterated sixteen years later in a paper that Tribe co-authored, 'Conceptual research in tourism' (Xin, *et al.*, 2013). This concludes that the power of conceptual research in CTS is that it bridges the worlds of thought and of practice. Its criticality, its emancipatory credentials, rest on its drive to effect real social change.

Critical *hospitality* studies (CHS) has a far shorter pedigree, though interest in it seems to be increasing. One of the first references to CHS within the hospitality literature is Scarpato's (2002) paper 'Gastronomy studies in search of hospitality'. In it he argues that hospitality's theoretical framework is restricted by its definition as an economic activity; instead, it should see itself as 'both a community and cultural industry that cannot escape social commitments' (ibid.: 152). More recently, the breadth of research within CHS has widened considerably to include such topics as: aesthetic and emotional labour (Duncan, *et al.*, 2013), guest/host relationships and the theme of the 'stranger' (Lynch *et al.*, 2011; Molz, 2012), and the regimes of power in the connections between family, culture and hospitality (Russo, 2012). Currently the relationship between dissent/social movements and hospitality seems under-explored, such as community hospitality during the miners' strike and hospitality arrangements within protest camps. We feel this would be a natural development within the field.

Interim summary

The emancipatory fields we have considered above, from the well established (radical feminism, queer theory, CRT and disability studies) to those that have emerged more recently (CTS and CHS), all share a number of characteristics that help inform our consideration of how CES can be understood as an emancipatory event studies. A shared starting point for all of them is a problematizing of the ontological character of their object(s) of investigation, using that central critique as a driver to enable the field to generate new theorizations and research approaches. In so doing, those core ideas are shown to be contested and contestable; they are opened up and made accessible to wider discussions in a broader range of the social sciences and the humanities, which also increases their influence within those discussions.

Themes addressed within those emancipatory fields, through developing an interrogation of how their central concepts operate in wider societal contexts, show a greater interest in developing critiques of the existing social order. This challenges dominant paradigms by blurring the region that tends to separate academic theory from social practice, exposing the interconnections between language and power. The motivation for doing this is to liberate research and enable it to produce socially meaningful conceptualizations and frameworks that highlight relations of power. In developing tools that can confront domination, exploitation and subordination they actively seek to draw the academic and the activist into a closer working relationship, and at times dissolve any distinction between them by combining them into a hybrid activist/academic (see Tribe (2002) and his conceptualization of the 'philosophic practitioner').

This array of characteristics indicates that these fields are strongly linked to critical theory, drawing heavily on motifs originally articulated by the Frankfurt School sociologists Max Horkheimer and Theodor Adorno as well as the Italian Marxist political theorist Antonio Gramsci. In its initial articulation (Horkheimer, 2002) critical theory stood in opposition to positivistic and logico-reductivist epistemologies that attempted to confine the production of knowledge to frameworks that depoliticize and decontextualize. *Traditional* theory, Horkheimer argues, works to sustain existing repressive political ideology by maintaining and reproducing a reality that enslaves us to that dominant ideology (ibid.: 213). *Critical* theory focuses on the historical and cultural specificity of oppression, drawing upon the major social sciences and humanities in a project that seeks real change for people in their daily lives by providing them with tools that can be used to confront domination and repression (Adorno and Horkheimer, 1997). In this initial formulation the ideology to be confronted was a political economy of industrial capitalism. Later developments within critical theory, which have followed a more Gramscian hegemonic trajectory and, particularly, ideas drawn from the work of Habermas and his followers, have recognized how capitalism itself changed over the twentieth century. It has become, to use Bob Jessop's (Sum and Jessop, 2013) terminology, a cultural political economy that manipulates and oppresses through the 'imaginaries' it uses colonize our 'lifeworld' and the framing of enquiry as an apolitical act. If the study of events is to be emancipatory, it must also look to the ways in which it has been complicit in sustaining and reproducing subordination and oppression. It needs to awaken its political consciousness and apply that reorientation to its relationship to its field of study by refocusing its research philosophy, its methodological approaches and its modes of analysis.

In this section we have noted that a number of fields, both established and emergent, operate within a *critical* frame of reference. From this we have drawn a number of conclusions relating to what it is that makes them so. In the next section we consider those elements, drawn from earlier chapters of this book, which go into forming the theoretical building blocks of an emancipatory event studies, constituting it as a truly *critical* project.

Building an emancipatory event studies

To continue the metaphor of construction, we will consider the building of an emancipatory event studies through a four-phase process. First, we shall lay the foundations of the field by considering those theoretical elements upon which we are to build. Drawing on ideas and principles addressed in earlier chapters, we will establish the below-ground-level theory that forms the ontological basis of CES. Next, we shall build the structural frame. This is a set of connected structures that are put in place to give a building the strength and support it requires. However, while elements of the frame inform the final appearance of a building, the frame does not determine the building's precise external manifestation. Similarly, the structural framing of the field will indicate trajectories for empirical research. What *is* externally visible is the structure's cladding, which forms the third phase. A building's cladding usually determines how it is initially encountered. Over time the cladding may change, adapting to changes in the environment. Equally, the same structure may be clad in different ways by different occupants. This is meant to suggest that the way the field connects to its context can change diachronically but also synchronically – the same structure can present itself differently in different contexts. Here we will consider the cladding that most closely links with the authors' research agendas, although obviously others may clad the field differently. The final stage involves decorating the rooms according to the functions that they have been assigned to them. This represents the variety of topics that can be drawn into the field, and the numerous methodological approaches that it can encompass. If the foundations are understood to be the most stable, most resistant to change, aspects of the construction, the decoration and room assignment are the most flexible. This phase will be illustrated using some short examples drawn from recent research in the field.

Foundations

From the first chapter, and throughout this book, we have challenged the dominance of operationalist and instrumentalist conceptualizations of 'event'. Broadly we support the position taken by, for example, Rojek (2013) and Moufakkir and Pernecky (2015), who seek to confront the assumption that the business orientation behind much mainstream event studies/events management literature and teaching is ideologically neutral. We empathize with the latter's frustration with the current events curriculum and applaud their observation, which is echoed by others (Andrews and Leopold, 2013: Finkel *et al.*, 2013; Foley *et al.*, 2012; Merkel, 2013), that events are 'underpinned by ideologies, and are therefore political; events are necessarily a part of societies, and are therefore social; events also speak of traditions, customs and meanings, and are therefore cultural' (Moufakkir and Pernecky, 2015: xvii).

But much of what these authors articulates is either *framing* or *cladding*, rather than *foundational*. Either because their focus lies elsewhere or because they do not feel it necessary, they do not consider the ontological foundations of a critical approach to the study of 'event'. That is, they do not ask what it means to be critical and to what 'event' refers. As well as the discussion within this chapter, which illuminates the link between critical and emancipatory research, criticality was a significant element within our reflections on the connections between event and space (Chapters 2 and 5) and power (Chapters 3 and 4), and in our discussions on the commodification of events (Chapter 6) and the colonization of event discourse (Chapter 8). The ontology of 'event' has also been a recurring theme throughout the book. Initially addressed in Chapter 1, it has appeared in one guise (as contestation and dissent in Chapters 2 and 7) or another (for example, as ordered disorder in Chapter 10 and as a politicized dimension of identity in Chapters 5 and 9) in several places. The ontic status of 'event' is recognized as contested. Peculiar in that it is not an object, a thing in itself, or a process, its identity is more clearly differentiated through patterns of repetition and, importantly, difference (Deleuze, 2014 [1968], 2015 [1969]). What we frequently call events when we approach them and study them are actually complex and interconnected managed discourses, curated histories and choreographed narratives (a point we will take up in our final chapter). At a foundational level, 'event', within a critical event studies, is that which intervenes in the social field and exposes discourses that are at work within it. Here we found resonances within perspectives that construe event as 'rupture', discernible in the ideas of Derrida (2001), Badiou (2003, 2013) and Žižek (1989, 2014), who themselves can be placed in a long philosophic tradition that is associated with a Platonic conceptualization of truth as *aletheia*.

Frame

In any building the frame is usually more complex than the foundations, as it is composed of an array of load-bearing beams and joists, connected by a variety of joints. A significant part of our frame draws on social and political theory, in particular the ideas of the Frankfurt School, from its early iterations in the work of Adorno, Horkheimer (e.g. Horkheimer, 2002) and others to its more recent articulation in the work of Habermas (1992a, 1992b, 1992c). It is that part of the frame which bears much of the weight with regards to a concentration on the critique of society and an explicit interest in working to confront repression and exploitation. Associated with that solid core are Gramsci's (1973) conceptualization of hegemony and his argument that hegemonic domination can be effectively combated/ resisted only through the creation of a culture that stands in opposition to it. Another significant social theorist upon whom we draw to support the core of our frame is Pierre Bourdieu. A commitment to 'event' as that which intervenes in the social field requires a construal of what 'social field' means. In this regard Bourdieu's (1984, 1992) description of the social field, the different forms of symbolic capital, *habitus*, symbolic violence and *doxa* (as discussed in Chapters 4 and 9) all have a close affinity to how they are understood in CES. Through such a conceptual framework we also gain insight into the importance of resistance in this field.

In addition to social and political theory the frame works with the associated idea of discourse, in particular an understanding of discourse that recognizes it as a social practice, combining concerns for the relationship between language and power. When we consider the way 'event' can expose discourses that are at work, the form of 'discourse' that is employed is a melange of its formulations in the works of Foucault's middle period (e.g. Foucault, 1973), Bourdieu (1992) and Habermas (1987). Such a perspective on discourse draws on linguistic and non-linguistic usages of the term and is also connected to the significance of language as a means of repression and liberation found in Adorno, Horkheimer and Gramsci.

Foucault's later work, which develops the ideas of both biopolitics and parrhesia (2008, 2011a, 2011b), is of specific interest to the CES frame when considering issues of power and resilience.

A significant part of the CES frame is also found in the linkage between the study of 'event' and the notions of spectacle (Debord, 1977) and the carnivalesque (Bakhtin, 1984). Both of these (as considered in Chapter 10) highlight key aspects of how events are spaces of coordinated transgression and liminality, while, upon further reflection, Debord's analysis can be used as a lens through which events may be seen as spaces of subversion and communicative action.

Cladding

As we suggested earlier in this section, how a building is clad is most closely related to the style of those who dress the building's frame. In modern buildings especially very little weight is borne by the exterior shell. Between the two authors of this books there are two motifs that resonate throughout the structure we have been advocating. Both will be distinguishable to anyone who has been paying attention, though each is strongly associated with the other. One of these motifs is discourse studies, specifically that which follows a trajectory that begins with the later work of Wittgenstein (1951), travels through the work of Foucault (most notably the ideas he developed in his lectures at the Collège de France) and its expression in formulations of governmentality, such as that of Nikolas Rose (see Rose and Miller, 2008), and cultural political economy (as in Jessop, 2002; Sum and Jessop, 2013), and becomes central to the principles of critical discourse analysis (as in Fairclough, 2002) and the discourse-historical approach (see Reisigl and Wodak, 2001). The other builds on the work of Habermas, particularly his descriptions of the lifeworld, public sphere, commodification and colonization and communicative action (see Habermas, 1987, 1992a). Such an association is important in anchoring the connectivity between CES and critical leisure studies. Protest and dissent as prototypical events within CES cut across both motifs. They are interventions in the social field that deliberately set out to expose discursive connections while also exhibiting strong traits of 'serious leisure' – following Robert Stebbins's tripartite conceptualization of leisure (Stebbins, 1982, 2006, 2014) – as viewed through an interpretive lens of Habermas's description of communicative action.

Decoration

Where the foundations marked the strongest connections between a critical event studies and other emancipatory fields, how our building is decorated, what the function of the different spaces within it are and how those spaces interconnect will vary even more widely than how the structure has been clad. This is not intended to be a book that explores different methodologies that are appropriate for CES (see Lamond and Platt, 2016); nor is it intended to be a work that illustrates the variety of research questions that are currently exercising those who are interested in developing event studies as an emancipatory field. (The edited collections by Moufakkir and Pernecky (2015) and Finkel *et al.* (2013) are excellent examples of the latter.) Rather, our focus has been to ground CES robustly as a field, one that is fundamentally interested in confronting domination, exposing exploitation and challenging hegemonic power. That said, we feel it is appropriate to provide a few examples of how different decorators have begun to embellish some of the rooms within the house.

With contestation so central to 'event' within CES, it is unsurprising to find a number of academics in the field who are interested in how contestation is articulated. Rammelt (2015), for example, considers how anti-militarist groups in Romania were strengthened through their shared opposition to state support for the 2008 NATO summit in Bucharest. Meanwhile, Wise and Mulec (2015) and Dowson *et al.* (2015) have used qualitative approaches to evaluate certain celebratory events and festivals as political action. In Chapter 5 we illustrated the links between event and identity through Dominique Ying-Chih Liao's (forthcoming) analysis of the reorientation of memory following *Troy, Troy . . . Taiwan*, but there is also significant interest in gender and sexuality issues' connections to events, as examined in a case-study approach by Markwell and Waitt (2013) and auto-ethnographically by Dashper (forthcoming) and Lamond. Discourse-analytic approaches of various kinds have also been developing, from those that are overtly focused on a linguistic perspective, such as Jaworska's (forthcoming) work on global sporting events, through those that adopt a more qualitative discourse studies perspective, such as Montesano Montessori's (2009) analysis of the Zapatista movement and Occupy in Spain (see also Montesano Montessori and Morales López, 2015), to those that have a more thematic orientation, such as Lamond *et al.* (2015).

Conclusion

We began this chapter by suggesting that the answer to the question of whether there could be an emancipatory event studies was an unequivocal 'Yes!' However, it was noted that such a direct response, while correct, served only to hide what was actually quite a complex set of connections and relationships. Our first step was to consider whether research that currently fits the frames of reference set by mainstream event studies and events management could be considered emancipatory. Despite some clear efforts to address concerns of manipulation and power, it was found that even those more radical trajectories could not really be understood as making the field emancipatory.

In the second part of the chapter we reviewed a number of fields, both established and emergent, that have sought not just to expose the abuse of power but confront it, offering critique as a means of challenging the dominant hegemony. The articulate, in their own ways, something akin to the Socratic 'gadfly' defence (see Chapter 9), presenting the idea that the activist academic endeavours to deny those who abuse power a peaceful resting place. The review established a set of characteristics that marked those fields as emancipatory.

In the final section we used those characteristics to draw a distinct line of connection between them and the foundations of critical event studies, then built on those foundations to suggest how a critical approach to the study of events could be constructed to become a truly emancipatory event studies.

12 Events histories and narratives

Introduction

Running through many of the previous chapters has been what might be called a 'historical analysis of events'. We have been interested in how events have developed historically. We have explored how events are used in modernity and postmodernity. And we have touched on the idea that events are myths, that they are shaped by myths, and that they in turn shape myths. All cultures and communities create myths about themselves and their histories. These myths may or may not be based on things that have actually happened. What is important to the people who write myths is that they believe them to be true and to hold inner truths about how the world actually is. Spracklen's Ph.D. and related work (e.g. Spracklen, 2007, 2009) explore the myth-making around rugby league and rugby union in the north of England. For many people involved in rugby union in the early 1990s, when Spracklen was conducting his research, rugby league was a 'professional' but marginal version of their sport that had broken away from the official Rugby Football Union. For many people involved in rugby league in the same period, their sport had split away from the Rugby Football Union because northern players and clubs did not want to be dictated to by the posh elites who ran the game in the south of England. The split, for them, defined their game and their working-class, northern identity. It was both a reaction against the elites and a means for working-class men to earn money. Because rugby union considered rugby league to be professional – as well as a marginal and illegal form of rugby – rules were created to ban rugby union players from playing rugby league. These rules prohibited any contact with rugby league, and even since rugby union turned professional in 1995 its governing bodies in a number of countries have tried to get rugby league banned in those countries. As recently as 2015, the person who had set up a rugby league in the United Arab Emirates was arrested because the union authorities there claimed that they had sole rights to play and organize rugby in the country.

Who are right? The league fans who claim their game is a legitimate defender of working-class culture, or the union fans who claim their game is the true and official version of rugby? In truth, both are right. Both sports use history to make cases for their existence and their ideology. That is, both use history to construct a sense of an imaginary community. The only difference between the two sports' use of historical mythologizing is in their relation to wider power structures. When we look at these connections, we can see that rugby union propagates the interests of national and global elites, whereas rugby league has never been played or supported by any globally significant hegemons. The latter is a marginal sport in every country aside from Australia and Papua New Guinea. In England and France, especially, the ruling elites have *deliberately* marginalized it by depriving it of access to schools and universities, the military, state funding, the media and the wider public sphere. In Australia rugby league now boasts more supporters and greater wealth than rugby union, yet even there it is still seen as a working-class game that is supported by working-class men in the eastern states. By contrast, rugby union – in all countries aside from Wales – has been a sport of the elites, showered with money and supported in the media. So when it indulges in myth-making it does so to sideline or remove rugby league and to perpetuate the ideologies and the hegemonic power of the ruling classes.

The Rugby World Cup was taking place as we wrote this book in 2015. Note that this event is known simply as the Rugby World Cup. In fact, it is the Rugby *Union* World Cup. There is a Rugby League World Cup, too, which was established more than three decades before the union version. But rugby union does not care about that: it uses its mega-extent to change the facts of history and pretend that there is only one code of rugby, and only one rugby world cup. Only in Papua New Guinea does rugby league shape the myth-making of a nation and its ruling classes; but Papua New Guinea is not part of any global elite.

In this final chapter we explore what we call the 'hidden history' of events: that is, events as oppression; events that solidify relationships of power/domination; and events as propaganda. First, we explore theories from history and political studies that shed light on the forms and structures that hide the narrative purpose of cultural activities, such as events. Next, we use specific events, such as food and drink festivals, to show how such histories and narratives are hidden by the normalization of the everyday and the mundane. Finally, we look at how such hidden histories and narratives might be brought to light and played with by subversive, counter-hegemonic appropriations of such event spaces.

History, historiography and the politics of events

What is history? It is the discipline that helps us make sense of the present by imposing some sort of order on the past, in the hope that such order may tell us what really happened. In the example of rugby league and rugby union, some historical facts are clear. In August 1895 some rugby football clubs in the north of England met at the George Hotel in Huddersfield to announce the formation of their own Northern Football Union. Rugby union continued to be played and to prosper in the north and elsewhere, but the Northern Union thrived too, and eventually changed its rules and its name to become the Rugby Football League.

How might we explain what happened in this division of the game of rugby into two codes? In historiography, it is recognized that history is never simply the objective presentation of the facts of the past. Rather, histories are always present-centric: that is, they are partial accounts of the past that are written by historians for their own ends (Anderson, 1983; Wilson and Ashplant, 1988). There may be facts about the past that are universally accepted – such as that the Normans invaded England in 1066 – because they are predicated on primary sources and/or material evidence. But all accounts of those facts have to make decisions about which sources to use, and about the gaps in the source record. Where there is no evidence for something, historians might choose to construct their narratives from parallels and trends, or they admit that some things are simply unknowable. The Dark Ages in what is now the United Kingdom, for example, were not so named because they were less enlightened or civilized than earlier or later times; rather, historians who tried to make sense of the period were continually frustrated by gaps in the primary sources. While eminent academic historians and archaeologists are often cautious about trying to fill in these gaps, others are not. Hence, hundreds if not thousands of books have attempted to identify King Arthur as a post-Roman British warrior leader; and debates over the Saxon invasion of Britain are often coloured by authorial prejudice that is based on political and ethical beliefs about nationalism and violence, rather than objective evidence. The reliability of primary sources is supported or questioned because of those beliefs: followers of traditional Anglo-Saxon history cite Bede and the *Anglo-Saxon Chronicles* as reliable sources, whereas scholars who argue that change was slow and generally peaceful question those sources and present material evidence instead. But even when there are reliable and trusted records to help historians make sense of the facts, the presentation and interpretation of those facts is inevitably a subjective process. It is impossible to write a history that presents *everything* that happened in the past; rather, one must choose the parts that are important to one's narrative and then present them in a convincing way. Moreover, it is impossible to write a history that is not theory-laden; the language that we use is always filled with theories and concepts. History, then, is always shaped by those who use it.

How does an event shape history? Or, more specifically, how do events make their own histories, and how much of that process is hidden? The reinvention of the Olympic Games is a perfect example of the relationships between power, myth, history and eventization. When the first modern Olympic Games were held in Athens in 1896, the founders and supporters explicitly linked this event to the ancient Olympics (Guttman, 2002). They did this because nineteenth-century Western elites had earlier established classical Greece and Rome as their exemplars for a perfect society – one that valued manliness, learning, art and valour in warfare (Spracklen, 2011a). These elites believed they were the inheritors of that classical world, so they trained their children in Greek and Latin culture (ibid.). For the Greeks who supported the modern Olympics, their identification with the ancient Games gave their modern country legitimacy and continuity, and it helped to obliterate hundreds of years of Ottoman rule. Athens was chosen as the venue because it was the capital city of the new (modern) Greek kingdom; and, conveniently, it had an abandoned stadium that could be reconstructed and re-covered in white marble. The Greeks could celebrate their Greekness by purifying this stadium in the sacred rites of the ancient Olympians, just as they had purged the years of Islamic rule by destroying the houses where the Turks had lived and removing their mosques. The salvation of Christian and hence classical Greece from the Muslim Turks had been a theme of romanticism and neo-classicism throughout the century. Elites in Western Europe supported the establishment of the Greek state in this period, and its expansion into the Ottoman Empire. So, for many people at the time, the modern Olympics justified Greece's very existence and its seizure of Greek territories from the Turks. It both fostered and vindicated Greek nationalism, as well as other national movements against the Ottoman Empire, which eventually led to that empire's collapse – in a tumult of warfare and genocide – in the first quarter of the following century.

For Baron Pierre de Coubertin and his friends, the foundation of the modern Olympics also legitimized their own beliefs about the importance of sport and physical activity in shaping young men's morals. They were concerned that the West – that is, white Europe and its similarly white offshoots in 'the colonies' and North America – was in danger of losing its economic and political hegemony over dark-skinned non-Christians through poor breeding, worse morals and inter-European warfare. They wanted the Games to bring the best of European and other Western men together to compete as individuals. The Olympics were specifically designed to promote Western manliness, Western power and Western civilization's mythological roots (ibid.). So, the majority of the competitors at Athens were Greeks, because they had the most to justify and legitimize, but the remainder were from Europe and its offshoots (Guttman, 2002).

As the Olympic movement has grown into the modern commercialized Games of this century, these origin stories have been hidden or lost, or mythologized for the purposes of those who are now in charge of the Olympics. De Coubertin is celebrated for his pacifism and his internationalism, while the King of Greece's attendance at the 1896 Games is accepted as a simple matter of fact, because it has become the norm to link host cities with political leaders.

Marx's historical materialism can help us make sense of the important role of events in making history, and in hiding that making. We do not have to accept the Hegelianism of Marx's historical materialism to use his insight that all human action is constrained by the structures that we have inherited from the past (Marx, 1973; Marx and Engels, 1987). And the structures we have inherited from the past at this particular stage in our history are the class inequalities and hegemonies associated with high modernity (Gramsci, 1973; Habermas, 1992a). Our age, this postmodern, post-industrial century, has been shaped by the struggles over power that preceded it. That is, our lives and our society have been shaped by the nation-building, imperialism and high capitalism that made the world today. This historical specificity of our condition means how we think, how we make sense of the world and how we make sense of our past are all conditioned by the norms and values that were constructed in the rise of imperialism and capitalism. In that moment of high modernity the old elites were overturned or forced into sharing their power with bourgeois capitalists. But nationalism and imperialism allowed the old elites to retain as much of their power as possible, while also allowing the capitalists to increase their wealth and power. This political order shapes how we think today, and how the elites use history to shape and limit the way we think. For Marx, historical materialism is a way of revealing the truth about the normalization of power in and through history. The elites use their version of history to tell a myth of national heroism, national individualism, the overthrow of tyrants and foreigners and the God-given right of the nation to be ruled by its rulers (Hobsbawm, 1988).

This version of history is not just written in textbooks. It is performed in every ritual, celebration and commemoration in every religious and public place. Flags become sacred icons that are carried solemnly by their bearers, as if their misuse would be a crime against God (Anderson, 1983). National anthems remind their singers that their country and their rulers are blessed. Prayer-books and church services ask individuals to accept their inequality and their rulers' wealth as the will of God. Myths of victories are circulated through the public sphere and ossified in remembrance events and other formal ceremonies, normalizing yet hiding the grab for power of earlier times as well as the subsequent maintenance of that power up to the present day. In the United Kingdom the grab for power occurred when one man killed some other men to take the crown and the land for himself. Although we have a parliamentary democracy, the hegemonic power still resides within an establishment that includes the monarchy, feudal landowners, the military and the capitalist bourgeoisie (Hobsbawm, 1989). Every time we lick a stamp or spend money we are reminded that we should feel honoured to be ruled by the Queen. Ever more events celebrate moments from our recent past, with the two world wars of the last century providing numerous opportunities to remind ourselves how great we are. Every time there is a big sporting event the national anthem is sung and we thank God for placing such a wonderful person on the British throne:

> God save our gracious Queen!
> Long live our noble Queen!
> God save the Queen!
> Send her victorious,
> Happy and glorious,
> Long to reign over us,
> God save the Queen.
>
> Thy choicest gifts in store
> On her be pleased to pour,
> Long may she reign.
> May she defend our laws,
> And ever give us cause,
> To sing with heart and voice,
> God save the Queen.
> (www.royal.gov.uk/
> MonarchUK/Symbols/
> NationalAnthem.aspx,
> accessed 25 November 2015)

This anthem – which is drilled into every British child from primary school onwards and at events, churches and ceremonies – is as egregious as it is dangerous. First, it assumes that God exists, and that He is on the side of one nation – our nation – so we naturally believe that our nation is best. Second, it asks God to protect our Queen so that she may continue to rule over us and lead us to more victories over our enemies. We want her to receive even more gifts than she currently possesses. We want her to rule over us for ever. Personally, we think that if you believe in God, and you want that God to intervene in the world, you should probably ask Him to help people who are fleeing from tyranny and violence, the poor, the oppressed and others who are living in fear, rather than a multi-millionaire.

You may think that the Queen is unimportant, and the pantomime associated with her power trivial, but singing the national anthem at public events is used as a signifier of belonging and exclusion. In 2015 the newly elected Labour leader Jeremy Corbyn attended a memorial event for the Battle of Britain at which he elected not to sing the national anthem. The BBC (2015b) reported, 'Mr Corbyn's decision to remain silent attracted a lot of comment on social media … Conservative MP Sir Nicholas Soames – grandson of Sir Winston Churchill – accused the Labour leader of being "rude" to the Queen.' The comments were not restricted to social media – the right-wing press launched a blistering attack, too – and Corbyn agreed to sing the anthem in future, as members of his own party questioned his judgement or leapt to his defence by stressing his patriotism. He was castigated as a traitor to his country, an enemy of the nation. As we have seen, the spirit of Winston Churchill was even invoked to remind us what was at stake. The Conservative Party and its supporters in the press merely have to say that Corbyn is unpatriotic for the historical myths of their nationalism to spring into action. In the BBC report a *Labour* politician – Kate Green – informs her leader that singing the national anthem shows respect for the soldiers who have fought to safeguard 'our freedoms'. We believe that the complexity of the actions and motivations of the people who fought in the Battle of Britain are in fact dishonoured and forgotten if the remembrance is reduced to a public event of ritual acclamation of respect for the nation and the monarchy.

Another way of thinking about the historical narratives and myths at play in events is to return to Antonio Gramsci's (1973) hegemony theory as it is filtered through the world of Stuart Hall (1993) and the Birmingham School. Gramsci believes that hegemony is assured by the faction or class that manages to control the cultural and political sites of hegemonic production, such as schools, universities and the media. As he shows in the examples he cites from Italian history, Machiavellian tactics must be used to maintain power. When Italy was founded as a nation-state in the nineteenth century, the nationalists knew that they had to bring together all of the people of the peninsula and make them forget their local traditions and histories so that they would view the concept of Italy as normal and natural. This entailed taking control of education and the newspapers, creating a monarchy, designing a flag, writing a national anthem and publishing key stories from Italian history that stressed continuity between the Roman imperial past and the modern Italian present. Against this attempt to establish nationalist hegemony, liberals, socialists and communists all fought for control of their own spaces, their independent association and unions, their political parties and their media. But, ultimately, the Fascists came to power because they convinced the Italian people that they were the true inheritors of the past, and the vanguard of a new world where Italy would be strong and united. They adopted imperial Roman symbols for their parades, saluted the King and honoured the Pope.

For Gramsci, the success of the Fascist hegemony lay in its total monopoly on history, which was normalized in the rituals and events of Fascism. The Fascists employed their control of historical narratives to ensure that no one noticed that those narratives were partial and supportive of the Fascist hegemony. Sports, radio, newspapers, magazines and parades were all spaces where the history and society of Italy were rewritten. When people stepped out of line they were brutally crushed, but most people did not step out of line because they thought the Fascist new age marked the end of history. For Gramsci, then, hegemony is achieved when people who are without power do not realize that they have been tricked by elites who achieve and maintain their power through a combination of the boot and the flag.

Gramsci was concerned primarily with Italian nationalism and Italian Fascism, because he was a victim of both, but his theory can be applied more generally to modern society. The tools for reshaping history and hiding that shaping are easier to find in the age of television and computers (Spracklen, 2013, 2015). Stuart Hall's (1993) extension of Gramsci's hegemony theory applies it more saliently to the realm of popular culture. Hall argues that popular culture is the site of a struggle between two ideologies – the hegemonic ideology of the ruling classes and the counter-hegemonic ideology of those who can resist those elites. Every part of popular culture becomes a site of contestation, where different histories are shaped and used to try to justify or legitimize inequalities of power. In one corner of this power struggle, then, hegemony is constructed using historical myths about tradition, nation, divine approval and legitimacy. But in the other corner others are free to establish alternative histories that legitimize their own identity and belonging – as long as those histories do not threaten the established hegemonic ideologies too much.

Hall's work on hegemony helps to account for the two histories of rugby that were outlined at the start of this chapter. There is the official history of rugby union, with its Rugby World Cup mega-event, which is part of global capitalism and an effect of Western imperialism (Collins, 2015). Then there is the history of rugby league, which its supporters use to create their own counter-hegemonic identity, but which might be wiped out if it is noticed by rugby union. At work in the realm of popular culture is the materialist legitimation of the 'land grabs' of previous centuries, whether invasions and appropriations, such as those that took place in the United States, or empires and corporations, such as those of the United Kingdom and France. This power is passed on and legitimized in popular culture through every subsequent generation.

Events are important in this materialist legitimation. They bring people together to celebrate in public spaces. They bring people together to perform roles, to find belonging and identity. But they are strictly controlled by the elites. The myths that are celebrated in these events are imagined in ways that are defined by the elites, for the benefit of their hegemonic power. These myths are the normalization of nation or region; or the normalization of authority. So events fly the flags of cities and countries, and become spaces where prayers are said for acclaimed kings, queens and presidents. The events hide the controversial and problematic nature of the community-building of the nation-state, and the power concentration of local and global elites. We explore these ideas in more detail in the next section.

Food and drink tourism, food and drink festivals

There is a wealth of literature on the experiences of tourists who consume local produce at food festivals and other events (e.g. Everett, 2012; Lin *et al.*, 2011; Spracklen, 2011b). Tourists want to sample local food and drink because these products are supposedly more 'authentic'. The tourist wants to eat and drink how the locals do; or, rather, how the locals do when they are able to consume their native produce. So tourists search for events, festivals and other spaces that introduce them to authentic food and drink. Or they book excursions that allow them to sample local products in villages far away from the cities, or to visit the farms, bakeries and vineyards where local products are made (Everett, 2012). This is a growing part of the tourist industry, catering to tourists' perceptions of authenticity. To be in a different country or community, one has to eat and drink things that are not parts of the supposedly inauthentic, globalized, homogenized popular culture. This quest for the authentic food and drink of a culture assumes that this produce is a survival of a culture and tradition unchanged by time. Seeking it out is a way of confirming the assumptions the tourist has about the purity of the culture of the other, in comparison to the tourist's own culture. For the tourist, the food and drink act as symbolic markers of fixed, timeless heritage, living connections to a pre-modern, agrarian culture that valued taking time to make 'real' foodstuffs, a culture untouched by industry, modernity or globalization. This vision of the 'real', anti-modern culture is also expressed in the growth of food and drink festivals across the Global North. People want to eat street food rather than hamburgers from a global chain. They want to eat the 'real' food which they believe their parents and grandparents ate, so they bake their own bread and drink craft beers (Murray and O'Neill, 2012). And they become tourists when they attend events that give them opportunities to buy these products – farmers' markets as well as formal food and drink festivals.

Food festivals have become a popular way of reinforcing this historical narrative of purity and national or local culture. They provide quick food – what is sometimes called street food – from various tents, stalls and vans. They may be defined to reflect one particular kind of food: for instance, in the United Kingdom there are various iterations of the curry festival to promote the nation's favourite fast food. Where these specialist food festivals occur, the narrative of purity is not always at work; and, as at the curry festivals, more inclusive local or national identities might be celebrated. Various South Asian culinary traditions have been combined with British-Asian inventions, such as the balti, to create a diverse and multicultural British food with regional variations dictated by post-colonial immigration patterns. So, for example, the curry that is eaten in the fancy city-centre restaurants of Bradford and Leeds draws on the skills of chefs and owners whose ancestors migrated from Mirpur, a small region of Azad Kashmir.

But all too often food festivals serve up dishes that perpetuate exclusionary practices, with food that is not 'mainstream' construed as 'ethnic' food, as if food eaten by mainstream, white people is not ethnic (Spracklen, 2013). Middle-class white people attend such festivals to eat exotic food that is presented as 'othered' food – strange produce that is associated with essentialist, narrow views of culture, nation and 'race' (ibid.). 'Real' food fans get a chance to explore new tastes, new geographies and new cultures. The ethnic food is authentic because it is the food that others eat. Contrasted with the ethnic food is the street food that is considered normal and mainstream. This is included in the food festival because of the way in which it is produced. So British food festivals serve up pie and mash, or fish and chips, but in expensive versions that are made with organic ingredients and sprinkled with the latest foodie fetish condiment. The current obsession with such 'real' food is a product of the media and popular culture. We live in a post-industrial age where the elites use their power to keep the rest of us in chains. In this world we know something is not right, but we are easily distracted into thinking the solution is to bake cakes. Over recent years a meme has floated around the internet: a poster from the Second World War instructing people to 'Keep Calm and Carry On'. The popularity of this message is partly to do with the mythology of the war and little Britons being patriotic and obedient, but also partly to do with the faking of authenticity. You can eat anything you like so long as you can pay for it (Bauman, 2000).

Food festivals reduce food to another commodity, but they present capitalism as absent from the commodification. People attending such events usually pay for tickets, or pay a premium to taste the products. The street-food vendors are all determined to make a business out of making the food, and they are ruthless about securing the best spots for their stalls, so they make good profits. They are seduced by capitalist instrumentality while suffering from the romantic myth of authenticity (or, if not, they are using that myth just to make a profit, which is worse). Food festivals fetishize the other, construct authenticity, reify and normalize the nation or the region, and legitimate the inequalities associated with capitalism.

We can see similar processes of normalization and legitimation in festivals and tourism that focus on drinks. In wine-growing regions the wine festival or the wine trail is seen as way of selling that region, the nation of which it is a part and the historical myth of purity and agrarianism. Similarly, in Scotland whisky is associated with a particular kind of Scottishness. As Spracklen (2011b: 111) says:

> Scotland and Scottishness are seen by the tourists as being made authentic through the mediation of the global brand and its relationship to heather, Highland kilts, clan tartans, bagpipes, haggis and mountains ... There is nothing existentially authentic in the make-believe tartanicity of the whisky

trail, no moment of individual self-realisation in the shopping centres selling whisky-flavoured fudge and sheep-themed blended whiskies. From a Habermasian perspective, what is at stake is the agency of individuals seeking to make sensible, rational explorations of Scottish history and Scottish whisky and the instrumental imperative to constrain those explorations to a commodified, capitalised 'authentic experience'.

Whisky tourism and whisky festivals are big business in Scotland. And the people who attend these events are living the myth of pre-industrial, Celtic Scotland, which owes more to *Braveheart* or the novels of Walter Scott than to the lives of people who actually live in Scotland today. They want to believe that they are sampling the true taste of Scotland, its land and its history in every dram, but of course they are not.

The craft beer movement has made a deliberate attempt to break with the instrumentality of global capitalism (Murray and O'Neill, 2012; Thurnell-Read, 2014). The global beer industry is dominated by a handful of transnational corporations who own brands such as Budweiser – inoffensive but bland lagers that are brewed in factories in every regional market. By contrast, craft beers are made by individuals, or small operations, in small quantities, often just for the bar that the brewers own. Craft beer began as an exercise in rejecting the corporate, global lagers, so the first craft breweries – in North America – resurrected or recreated types of beer that were no longer found there: pale ales, stouts, old ales, English bitters, Belgian fruit beers and wheat beers. Now, craft beer itself has become a global leisure pursuit, with craft breweries appearing as far apart as Japan, the Netherlands and Finland. It is possible to sit in places modelled on US bars, British pubs or German *bierkellers* and sample the local craft beers, which is odd, because the beers are all made in the same handful of styles established as 'proper' craft beer by the Americans who started it all.

Craft beer has spread around the world along with the related hipster culture, an initially North American subcultural trend associated with young, bourgeois, urban white men. Hipsters drank craft beer between riding around on their fixed-gear bikes, eating flat bread, growing their beards and waxing their moustaches. The hipster look and its related obsessions with craft and the authentic have become the new mainstream global popular culture to such an extent that the beards are worn by professional footballers, and the most popular programme on British television is about baking cakes. The United Kingdom now has its own craft beer movement, with its own bars and the beers stocked in mainstream pubs, too. For instance, the Wetherspoon's chain now offers craft beer in all its outlets. And big brewing companies are starting to buy craft breweries (one of the big corporations has recently bought Mainstream in Greenwich, one of London's first craft breweries) or marketing their own beer – such as Greene King – as 'hand-crafted'. Craft beer festivals are popping up in every city to offer visitors a variety of beverages, along with the ubiquitous street food. There is even a craft beer movement in Leeds, including a bar that sells vegetarian Indian snacks, and another that has its own brewery behind the bar. Craft beer has become the latest thing in the search for the authentic, the quest to escape the clutches of modernity and find the purity of local stuff.

This is rather odd, because in Leeds (and every other corner of England) there is a local beer called real ale, which is more authentic than craft beer (Spracklen, Laurencic and Kenyon, 2013; Thurnell-Read, 2014). Real ale is what the Americans might call English bitter. But unlike American craft beer bitter, real ale does not undergo chemical and technological processes that kill the ongoing fermentation of the drink when it leaves the brewery. Instead, the yeast is allowed to continue fermenting, which adds flavour. This is why it was called *real* ale by those who campaigned for its preservation back in the 1960s, when many of the brewers started to abandon the method. The Campaign for Real Ale (CAMRA) was set up to argue that beer left to ferment in the barrel was the UK's true, authentic beer. It was how beer was meant to be made and served – drawn naturally from the cellar by hand-pumps, with a limited life span of just a few days before it went off. The big brewers at the time wanted to eliminate this secondary fermentation so beer would be easier to handle and would last much longer in kegs, cans and bottles. But killing the fermentation meant losing the gas, so the beer had to be artificially carbonated, just like soda drinks. Craft beer is not real ale because it does not use the traditional methods of secondary fermentation and hand-pump delivery. Instead, it is usually processed just like lager, its fermentation is stopped, and it sits still in a keg, waiting to be injected with carbon dioxide.

For many years, the real ale revival in the United Kingdom relied on the support of working-class northerners, trainspotters, football fans and other unfashionable types. Fans set up their own small breweries from the late 1970s onwards, and these grew as bigger, older regional and family brewers declined. Many of the latter were bought out by national then transnational corporations, only to be closed down shortly afterwards. Real ale fans were frequently stereotyped as obsessives, or cranks. Then came the middle-class search for authentic food and drink, and hipster culture, and real ale's stock started to rise (Thurnell-Read, 2014). Generous tax breaks have boosted the spread of micro-breweries and pubs that serve real ale, and politicians now make a point of posing in their local pub with a pint of real ale in their hand. Hipsters have set up real ale breweries and frequent real ale festivals, with the result that working-class real ale drinkers feel that their leisure spaces are being colonized by the middle classes. CAMRA newsletters feature regular complaints about being priced out of city-centre real ale pubs. More worryingly, real ale breweries are starting to produce craft beer, because that is what many of their customers now demand, as they don't know the difference between real and fake. Moreover, some (recent) members of CAMRA want the organization to include craft beers in the portfolio of drinks it supports.

It is argued that real ale is only as authentic as the Victorian science and technology that facilitated the growth of the brewing industry. That is true. Real ale *is* a product of modernity, the factory system and capitalism. It is associated with working-class white men in regional towns and cities, which of course is problematic (Spracklen, Laurencic and Kenyon, 2013). We do not want a return to the twentieth-century world of men-only pubs, in which the crude jokes scrawled on the toilet walls were often as racist as they were sexist. And we recognize that not every working-class man spent his leisure time in the pub drinking bitter. But real ale does represent authentic working-class, English culture for those who are used to making it, and those who are used to drinking it. So its appropriation by the middle classes and its confusion with craft beer are troubling.

Subverting narratives and histories

As we have shown in earlier chapters of this book, there are processes and actions through which it is possible to subvert the mainstream. These might only ever be temporary actions, rather than the catalysts for permanent change, but they are worth considering again here. One of the actions that might disrupt the dominant mythologies at work in events is the writing of a book like this one. We want to reveal the normative morality and ideology at work in events spaces, so that other academics and students can think more critically about the purpose of events in contemporary society. We are explicitly political in our intent. But it is questionable whether academics like us have any power to shape the things we critique, or even teach. A more appropriate subject to explore in this final section is how the hidden histories and narratives that play out in events might be brought to light and played with by subversive, counter-hegemonic appropriations of event spaces.

CAMRA has positioned itself as counter-hegemonic. In its original form the organization set out to challenge the brewing industry's attempts to limit choice, close breweries and sell global brands in British pubs. CAMRA's activists were not just romantic conservatives bemoaning the end of a particularly English tradition. They argued that local diversity should be protected, that smaller forms of capitalism were preferable to global ones, and even that real ale pubs were spaces where working-class culture needed to be protected. In addition to campaigning for real ale, they railed against the instrumentality of the modern 'hospitality' industry. They organized letter-writing campaigns and lobbied the government and both Houses of Parliament. They published information about where real ale could be bought, and which breweries made it, in the form of local pamphlets and the now famous national *Beer Guide*. Finally, they organized a national real ale festival, and encouraged branches to create their own smaller, local versions. The campaign continued through the 1980s and 1990s, fighting against modern drinking trends and the power of the transnational capitalists. Successful lobbying led to successive Conservative and Labour governments passing a number of acts in support of the real ale movement and the smaller, local breweries. More recently, there has been an exponential growth in the number of local real ale festivals, as ever more people have become active volunteers within CAMRA. The organization even offers training for people who want to join its branch committees, as well as for those who wish to volunteer at the festivals. In addition to introducing new people to real ale the festivals generate profits that CAMRA invests in bigger events and in its campaigns against the worst effects of neo-liberalism.

CAMRA is now campaigning to protect pub manager–tenants from some of the rapacious companies that own their pubs. These companies have bought up huge amounts of real estate, which they see as just another resource. In this neo-liberal, capitalist age, the pub companies seem more concerned with squeezing as much short-term profit as they can from their tenants, rather than helping those tenants build sustainable local businesses. So they force the tenants to buy their beer as well as other drinks and goods directly from them at high wholesale prices, and force them out of business if they do not meet their profit targets. Many of the pubs owned by these companies have been closed down and sold on to developers, who have turned them into small supermarkets, restaurants or housing. Consequently, many villages and communities across the country have lost their local pubs. In light of this, CAMRA worked with progressive and radical community organizations and movements to change the law, and recent legislation means that buildings with value for a local community, such as pubs, can now be protected. CAMRA, then, has become a counter-hegemonic, activist-led campaign, fighting against neo-liberalism and its egregious effects, as well as for a smaller, more diverse drinks industry. Its events have become spaces to cheer on this fight, as well as to raise a drink to the good health of the activists.

Rugby league fans also took counter-hegemonic action in the 1990s, when Rupert Murdoch's corporation essentially bought the Rugby Football League (creating the European Super League) and launched the Super League in Australia to rival the Australian Rugby League. In England, when the Super League plans were announced, including controversial proposals for mergers of several clubs, the Rugby League Supporters Association developed its fanzine and its website as spaces for free debate (Spracklen, 1996). The merger issue was particularly upsetting for many rugby league fans, who had seen the industries in their towns collapse over the previous fifteen years. Fired by their anger, these fans launched a campaign group called Rugby League Fans United, which organized protests and petitions at all of the major rugby league events in 1995. Both of these fans' organizations protested against selling every aspect of their game to a trans-national corporation, even though some supporters were more worried about the professionalization of rugby union and the potential future of league without sponsors' money. English rugby league fans' radical activism had been exempli-fied earlier by their mass rejection of the British Coal logo on the jerseys of the Great Britain team in 1992: hundreds of fans attended a match against Australia with the words of the mine-closing company obliterated with masking tape. In 1995 these same fans were determined to show their disgust at the secret negotia-tions with Murdoch's agents, and the proposal to give the corporate sponsors everything they demanded. They found allies in the (non-Murdoch) media and in Parliament, and then among the club owners who still had to approve the deal. In the end the merger plans were withdrawn, along with several other proposals.

Other professional sports have also felt the impact of well-organized fan activism. Sports events are not just ways for the organizers and sponsors to make money. They rely on the passion and identity-work of the fans who support specific clubs or simply the sport itself.[1] And those fans can and do resist and reject dominant narratives and instrumentality. Some of them show their displeasure merely by refusing to buy a season ticket, but others go further – creating their own clubs or struggling to gain control of their event spaces by founding co-operatives and other social clubs.

Conclusion

Narratives and myths associated with hegemonic ideologies are built into events. But it is always possible to resist them. For all the jingoism associated with the singing of national anthems and the honouring of flags and rulers, such things can be rejected. For all the myth-making associated with food, drink and sports events, the people involved in them can find ways to subvert them.

Note

1. By 'identity-work', we mean social actors' performativity of identity; see Spracklen and Spracklen, 2014.

13 Conclusion

It is an academic stereotype that we spend too long writing books, blogs, papers and letters that express our concerns about the state of academia. In leisure studies, for example, there is a long tradition of people bemoaning the decline of the discipline, the rise and fall of postmodern leisure, and the loss of leisure's status in sociology and the wider social sciences. We do not want this research monograph to be another of those cries from the wilderness. Rather, we want our colleagues in events management, and related fields, to realize that CES is essential if they are to continue to teach and research events. This book does not provide a set of rules to follow. But this conclusion rehearses the key critical themes that have emerged from the earlier chapters and sketches out a way forward for radical reformation in the teaching of events.

First, the narrow focus on management, industry and professional practice is indicative of failure among the academics who teach and research events. By discussing only these issues, event studies fails to get beyond the superficial appearance of events. We need to understand why events are important in contemporary society, and in all of our lives. We need to understand that they are more than just instrumental things that make money.

Second, we need to adopt social and cultural theory that can help us make sense of the importance of events in people's lives, the importance of events in the maintenance of power and hegemony, and the limits of our freedom to do certain things in these event spaces and practices. That means we have to develop a CES that draws from the theoretical source of Marxism and its structural, post-structural, existential, feminist and intersectional developments. We are aware of the many inconsistencies and weaknesses in Marxist theories of labour value, but we have yet to find a theoretical framework that captures the power relations and inequalities of modern society. And although the world may be postmodern in many ways, it remains bound to the hegemonic struggles that continue to constrain agency and leisure (Spracklen 2009, 2015). A radical, critical study of the place of events, then, cannot happen without Marxism and all iterations of Marx's thought.

Finally, post-structuralism provides a critical framework through which we may find fruitful challenges and explorations of the role of events in our lives, and the human agency that may yet be saved. Events may be viewed as spaces of spontaneous creativity and artwork, places of identity-work and spectacle and protest. Events do not necessarily have to be understood as mega-events, constructed by capitalism and the state. We suggest that they can be the smallest moments of leisure and communicative rationality. Meeting a friend for a coffee is an event in resisting the disciplines of the workplace. Reading a book is a solitary event that provides edification as well as entertainment.

For researchers of events we have a rallying cry. We need to come together to construct the new field of CES. There are hundreds like us across the world. Those already doing CES are situated in leisure studies, events management, political studies, philosophy, cultural studies, geography and sociology. For those researchers of events who have not yet joined us, we say the time is right for you to take that step across the great divide that separates the communicative from the instrumental. You should feel comfort in joining the CES network and subject field as they grow. But if you want to remain in the subject field of events management, we respect that choice. We do not reject that subject field or its work. But we say there needs to be more to it. Too much of the work that is published on events management is weak in its use of theory, weak in its criticality and epistemology, and weak ethically. If you wish to remain in events management, we urge you to do justice to your subject.

To do justice to events management, its teaching must be reformed and restructured. We believe that undergraduate degrees should be rebranded as event studies or, even better, as *critical* event studies. Such a rebranding would signify a radical overhaul of the content of those degrees. We want curricula to reflect the topics and themes raised in this book, alongside – or in place of – the traditional stuff of events management. Not teaching students this marvellous complexity and criticality does those students a disservice. Universities should construct critical thinkers, better human beings. We should help individuals and society to flourish. None of that can happen if events management pedagogy and practice remain as they are now. So we urge all of our teaching colleagues to include this critical content in their courses and degree programmes. We appreciate that this will not be easy, given the increasing marketization of higher education. But we believe that students want this content. They want to learn how to be critical in order to flourish. When all we give them is a checklist of things to do when running an event, we fail in our moral duty as teachers. So we have an imperative to act to change our courses' content, whether we are part-time lecturers, course leaders or heads of schools. We hope that this monograph has helped explain how this might be achieved.

References

All website URLs accessed on 29 January 2016.

Adorno, T. (1967) *Prisms*, London: Neville Spearman.

Adorno, T. (2001) *The Culture Industries*, London: Routledge.

Adorno, T. and Horkheimer, M. (1997) *Dialectic of Enlightenment*, London: Verso.

Aguirre, A., Jr. (2000) 'Academic storytelling: A critical race theory story of affirmative action', *Sociological Perspectives*, 43: 319–39.

Aitchison, C.C. (2005) 'Feminist and gender perspectives in tourism studies: The social–cultural nexus of critical and cultural theories', *Tourist Studies*, 5: 207–24.

Aitchison, C.C. (2006) 'The critical and the cultural: Explaining the divergent paths of leisure studies and tourism studies', *Leisure Studies*, 25: 417–22.

Aldrich, D.P. (2010) 'Fixing recovery: Social capital in post-crisis resilience', *Journal of Homeland Security and Emergency Management*. Online at: http://docs.lib.purdue.edu/cgi/viewcontent.cgi?article=1002&context=pspubs.

Aldrich, D.P. (2011) 'Ties that bind, ties that build: Social capital and governments in post-disaster recovery', *Studies in Emergent Order*, 4: 58–68.

Aldrich, D.P. and Smith, R.E. (2015) *Social Capital and Resilience*, New York: World Humanitarian Summit (WHS) Policy Brief.

Aldwin, C.M., Levenson, M.R. and Spiro, A. (1994) 'Vulnerability and resilience to combat exposure: Can stress have a lifelong effect?', *Psychology of Aging*, 9: 34–44.

Alekseyeva, A. (2014) 'Sochi 2014 and the rhetoric of a new Russia: Image construction through mega-events', *East European Politics*, 30: 158–74.

Ali-Knight, J., Robertson, M., Fyall, A. and Ladkin, A. (eds) (2009) *International Perspectives of Festivals and Events*, London: Routledge.

Anderson, B. (1983) *Imagined Communities*, London: Verso.

Andrews, H. and Leopold, T. (2013) *Events and the Social Sciences*, London: Routledge.

Ang, I., Isar, Y.R. and Mar, P. (2015) 'Cultural diplomacy: Beyond the national interest?', *International Journal of Cultural Policy*, 21: 365–81.

Arnold, M. (1999) 'Culture and anarchy', in S. Collini (ed.), *Arnold: Culture and Anarchy and Other Writings*, Cambridge: Cambridge University Press, 55–211.

Assmann, A. (1996) 'Texts, traces, trash: The changing media of cultural memory', *Representations*, 56: 123–34.

Assmann, A. (2008) 'Transformations between history and memory', *Social Research*, 75: 49–72.

Assmann, A. and Shortt, L. (2012) *Memory and Political Change*, Basingstoke: Palgrave Macmillan.

Assmann, J. (2010) 'Globalization, universalism, and the erosion of cultural memory', in A. Assmann and S. Conrad (eds), *Memory in a Global Age: Discourses, Practices and Trajectories*, Basingstoke: Palgrave Macmillan, 121–37.

Assmann, J. and Czaplicka, J. (1995) 'Collective memory and cultural identity', *New German Critique*, 65: 125–33.

Bachelard, G. (1964) *The Poetics of Space*, Boston, MA: Beacon Books.

Baddeley, A.D. (1966) 'The influence of acoustic and semantic similarity on long-term memory for word sequences', *Quarterly Journal of Experimental Psychology*, 18: 302–9.

Baddeley, A.D. (2012) 'Working memory: Theories, models and controversies', *Annual Review of Psychology*, 63: 1–29.

Baddeley, A.D. and Dale, H.C.A. (1966) 'The effect of semantic similarity on retroactive interference in land and short-term memory', *Journal of Verbal Behavior*, 5: 417–20.

Badiou, A. (2003) *Saint Paul: The Foundations of Universalism*, Stanford, CA: Stanford University Press.

Badiou, A. (2005) *Being and Event*, London: Continuum.

Badiou, A. (2013) *Philosophy and the Event*, Cambridge: Polity Press.

Bahadur, A.V., Ibrahim, M. and Tanner, T. (2010) 'The resilience renaissance? Unpacking of resilience for tackling climate change and disasters', Strengthening Climate Change Discussion Paper 1. Online at: http://dev.opendocs.ids.ac.uk/opendocs/handle/123456789/2368#.Vl1qquIseYM.

Baker, C. (2008) 'Wild dances and dying wolves: Simulation, essentialization, and national identity at the Eurovision Song Contest', *Popular Communication*, 6: 173–89.

Bakhtin, M. (1984) *Rabelais and His World*, Chichester: John Wiley & Sons.

Bang-Shin, H. (2012) 'Unequal cities of spectacle and mega-events in China', *City*, 16: 728–44.

Baudrillard, J. (1986) *America*, London: Verso.

Baudrillard, J. (1988) *Selected Writings*, Cambridge: Polity Press.

Baudrillard, J. (1994) *Simulacra and Simulation*, Ann Arbor: University of Michigan Press.

Baudrillard, J. (1995) *The Gulf War Did Not Take Place*, Sydney: Power Publications.

Baudrillard, J. (2002) *Screened Out*, London: Verso.

Bauman, Z. (2000) *Liquid Modernity*, Cambridge: Polity Press.

Bauman, Z. (2007) *Liquid Times: Living in an Age of Uncertainty*, Cambridge: Polity Press.

BBC (2009) 'Smell of meat offends Morrissey'. Online at: http://news.bbc.co.uk/1/hi/entertainment/8008602.stm.

BBC (2015a) 'Alton Towers owner Merlin rues accident effect'. Online at: www.bbc.co.uk/news/business-34276413.

BBC (2015b) 'Jeremy Corbyn "will sing national anthem in future"'. Online at: www.bbc.co.uk/news/uk-politics-34263447.

BBC (2015c) 'Lord Coe: IAAF president ends association with Nike'. Online at: www.bbc.co.uk/sport/athletics/34938953.

Beck, U. (1992) *Risk Society: Towards a New Modernity*, London: Sage.

Becker, G.S. (1964) *Human Capital: A Theoretical and Empirical Analysis with Special Reference to Education*, Chicago: University of Chicago Press.

Belfiore, E. (2004) 'Auditing culture: The subsidised cultural sector in the New Public Management', *International Journal of Cultural Policy*, 10: 183–202.

Belfiore, E. (2009) 'On bullshit in cultural policy practice and research: Notes from the British case', *International Journal of Cultural Policy*, 15: 343–59.

Belfiore, E. (2012) 'Defensive instrumentalism and the legacy of New Labour's cultural policies', *Cultural Trends*, 21: 103–11.

Bennett, W.L. (2012) 'The personalization of politics: Political identity, social media, and changing patterns of participation', *Annals of the American Academy of Political and Social Science*, 644: 20–39.

Berridge, G. (2012) 'Designing event experiences', in S.J. Page and J. Connell (eds), *The Routledge Handbook of Events*, London: Routledge, 273–88.

Bhabha, H.K. (1994) *The Location of Culture*, London: Routledge.

BIE (2015) 'Intellectual legacy'. Online at: www.bie-paris.org/site/en/publications/intellectual-legacy.

Bietti, L.M. (2009) 'Cultural memory and communicative memory'. Online at: www.collectivememory.net/2009/12/cultural-memory-and-communicative.html.

Blackledge, P. (2006) *Reflections on the Marxist Theory of History*, Manchester: Manchester University Press.

Blackledge, P. (2009) 'Alasdair MacIntyre: Social practices, Marxism and ethical anti-capitalism', *Political Studies*, 57: 866–84.

Blackmore, S. (1988) 'A theory of lucid dreams and OBEs', in J. Gackenbach and S. LaBerge (eds), *Conscious Mind, Sleeping Brain*, London: Springer International, 373–87.

Blackshaw, T. (2010) *Leisure*, London: Routledge.

Bladen, C. and Kennell, J. (2012) *Events Management: An Introduction*, London: Routledge.

Boal, A. (1998) *Legislative Theatre: Using Performance to Make Politics*, London: Routledge.

Boeder, P. (2005) 'Habermas' heritage: The future of the public sphere in the network society', *First Monday*, 10. Online at: http://firstmonday.org/ojs/index.php/fm/article/viewArticle/1280.

Bonanno, G.A. (2004) 'Loss, trauma, and human resilience: Have we underestimated the human capacity to thrive after extremely aversive events?', *American Psychologist*, 59: 20–8.

Bonanno, G.A. (2005) 'Resilience in the face of potential trauma', *Current Directions in Psychological Science*, 14: 135–38.

Bonanno, G.A., Galea, S., Bucciarelli, A. and Vlahov, D. (2006) 'Psychological resilience after disaster: New York City in the aftermath of the September 11th terrorist attack', *Psychological Science*, 17: 181–6.

Bourbeau, P. (2013) 'Resilience: Premises and promises in securitisation research', *Resilience*, 1: 3–17.

Bourdieu, P. (1984) *Distinction*, London: Routledge.

Bourdieu, P. (1992) *Language and Symbolic Power*, Cambridge: Polity Press.

Bourdieu, P. (2005) *The Social Structures of the Economy*, Cambridge: Polity Press.

Bourdieu, P. (2011 [1986]) 'The forms of capital', in I. Szeman and T. Kaposy (eds), *Cultural Theory: An Anthology*, Oxford: Wiley-Blackwell, 81–93.

Bourdieu, P. and Wacquant, L. (1992) *An Invitation to Reflexive Sociology*, Cambridge: Polity Press.

Bowdin, G., Allen, J., O'Toole, W., Harris, R. and McDonnell, I. (2012) *Events Management*, 3rd edition, London: Routledge.

Bowditch, R. (2013) 'Phoenix rising: The culture of fire at the Burning Man Festival', *Performance Research*, 18: 113–22.

Boykoff, J. and Fussey, P. (2014) 'London's shadow legacies: Security and activism at the 2012 Olympics', *Contemporary Social Sciences*, 9: 253–70.

Bramham, P. (2006) 'Hard and disappearing work: Making sense of the leisure project', *Leisure Studies*, 25: 379–90.

Brawley, S. (2009) 'Your shire, your Sharks: The Cronulla–Sutherland Sharks and delocalization v. glocalization in Australian rugby league', *International Journal of the History of Sport*, 26: 1697–715.

Brockmeier, J. (2010) 'After the archive: Remapping memory', *Culture and Psychology*, 16: 5–35.

Brown, S. and Hutton, A. (2015) 'Why crowds are bad for events and why trying to control them is even worse, in B. Majda and S. Brown (eds), *Colloquium: Papers from Global Events Congress VI*, Adelaide: The Global Events Congress VI, 72–3.

Bunch, C. and Pollack, S. (1983) *Learning Our Way: Essays in Feminist Education*, Berkeley, CA: Crossing Press.

Butler, J. (2006) *Gender Trouble: Feminism and the Subversion of Identity*, London: Routledge.

Calvo-Soraluze, J. and Blanco, A.V. (2014) 'Stimulating attendees' leisure experience at music festivals', *Global Journal of Management and Business Research*, 14. Online at: www.journalofbusiness.org/index.php/GJMBR/article/view/1588.

Campbell, F.C. (2008) *Elements of Metallurgy and Engineering Alloys*, Novelty: ASM International.

Capell, L. (2013) *Event Management for Dummies*, Chichester: John Wiley & Sons.

Carter, A. (2014) *Peace Movements: International Protest and World Politics since 1945*, London: Routledge.

Castells, M. (2012) *Networks of Outrage and Hope: Social Movements in the Internet Age*, Cambridge: Polity Press.

Causevic, S. and Lynch, P. (2011) 'Phoenix tourism: Post-conflict tourism role', *Annals of Tourism Research*, 38: 780–800.

Chandler, D. (2015) 'Resilience and the everyday: Beyond the paradox of liberal peace', *Review of International Studies*, 41: 27–48.

Charron, N. (2013) 'Impartiality, friendship-networks and voting behavior: Evidence from voting patterns in the Eurovision Song Contest', *Social Networks*, 35: 484–97.

Chen, K.K. (2011) 'Lessons for creative cities from Burning Man: How organizations can sustain and disseminate a creative context', *City, Culture and Society*, 2: 93–100.

Chen, K.K. (2012) 'Charismatizing the routine: Storytelling for meaning and agency in the Burning Man organization', *Qualitative Sociology*, 35: 311–34.

Chesney-Lind, M. and Morash, M. (2013) 'Transformative feminist criminology: A critical re-thinking of a discipline', *Critical Criminology*, 21: 287–304.

Collins, T. (2015) *The Oval World: A Global History of Rugby*, London: Bloomsbury.

Connell, R. (1987) *Gender and Power*, Stanford, CA: Stanford University Press.

Connell, R. (1995) *Masculinities*, Cambridge: Polity Press.

Conniff, R. (2011) 'What the Luddites really fought against', *Smithsonian Magazine*, March: 227–42.

Conrad, R. (1964) 'Acoustic confusions in immediate memory', *British Journal of Psychology*, 55: 75–84.

Conrad, R. and Rush, M.L. (1965) 'On the nature of short-term memory', *Journal of Speech and Hearing Disorders*, 30: 336–43.

Conrad, R., Freeman, P.R. and Hull, A.J. (1965) 'Acoustic factors versus language factors in short-term memory', *Psychonomic Science*, 3: 57–8.

Conway, D. (2009) *The Event Manager's Bible*, London: How To Books.

Corry, O. (2014) 'From defense to resilience: Environmental security beyond neo-liberalism', *International Political Sociology*, 8: 256–74.

Costanza-Chock, S. (2012) 'Mic check! Media cultures and the Occupy movement', *Social Movement Studies*, 11: 375–85.

Crenshaw, K.W. (2011) 'Twenty years of critical race theory: Looking back to move forward', *Connecticut Law Review*, 43: 1253–352.

Crone, R. (2012) *Violent Victorians: Popular Entertainment in Nineteenth-Century London*, Manchester: Manchester University Press.

Cunliffe, R.D. (n.d.) *Blackie's Compact Etymological Dictionary*, London: Blackie & Sons.

Dashper, K. (forthcoming) 'Researching from the inside: Autoethnography and critical event studies', in I.R. Lamond and L. Platt (eds), *Critical Event Studies: Approaches to Research*, London: Palgrave Macmillan.

DCMS (2015) *Creative Industries: 2015 Focus for Department for Culture, Media and Sport*. Online at: www.gov.uk/government/statistics/creative-industries-2015-focus-on.

de Certeau, M. (1988) *The Practice of Everyday Life*, Berkeley: University of California Press.

de Groote, P. (2005) 'A multidisciplinary analysis of world fairs (= expos) and their effects', *Tourism Review*, 60: 12–19.

de Lauretis, T. (1991) 'Queer theory: Lesbian and gay sexualities', *Differences: A Journal of Feminist Cultural Studies*, 3: 3–18.

de Lauretis, T. (1999) 'Popular culture, public and private fantasies: Femininity and fetishism in David Cronenberg's *M. Butterfly*', *Signs*, 24: 303–34.

Debord, G. (1977) *Society of the Spectacle*, Detroit, MI: Black & Red.

Deleuze, G. (2014 [1968]) *Difference and Repetition*, London: Bloomsbury.

Deleuze, G. (2015 [1969]) *The Logic of Sense*, London: Bloomsbury.

Delgado, R. (1989) 'Storytelling for oppositionists and others: A plea for narrative', *Michigan Law Review*, 87: 2411–41.

della Porta, D. (2015) *Social Movements in Times of Austerity: Bringing Capitalism back into Protest Analysis*, Cambridge: Polity Press.

Derrett, R. (2009) 'How festivals nurture resilience in regional communities', in J. Ali-Knight, M. Robertson, A. Fyall and A. Ladkin (eds), *International Perspectives of Festivals and Events*, London: Routledge, 107–24.

Derrida, J. (2001) *Writing and Difference*, London: Routledge.

Ding, X., Zhao, Y., Wu, F., Lu, X. and Shen, M. (2015) 'Binding biological motion and visual features in working memory', *American Psychological Association*, 41: 860–5.

Dowson, Rev. R., Lomax, D. and Theodore-Saltibus, B. (2015) 'Rave culture', in I.R. Lamond and K. Spracklen (eds), *Protests as Events: Politics, Activism and Leisure*, London: Rowman & Littlefield International, 191–210.

Duncan, T., Scott, D.G. and Baum, T. (2013) 'The mobilities of hospitality work: An exploration of issues and debates', *Annals of Tourism Research*, 41: 1–19.

Dunning, E. (2000) 'Towards a sociological understanding of football hooliganism as a world phenomenon', *European Journal on Criminal Policy and Research*, 8: 141–62.

Dwyer, L. and Jago, L. (2014) 'The economic evaluation of special events: Challenges for the future', in I. Yeoman, M. Robertson, B. McMahon, E. Backer and K.A. Smith (eds), *The Future of Events and Festivals*, London: Routledge, 99–114.

Economist, The (2011) 'The Blackberry Riots'. Online at: www.economist.com/node/21525976.

Eliade, M. (2013) *The Quest: History and Meaning in Religion*, Chicago: University of Chicago Press.

Everett, S. (2012) 'Production places or consumption spaces? The place-making agency of food tourism in Ireland and Scotland', *Tourism Geographies*, 14: 535–54.

Expo 2012 (2012) *Yeosu Korea*. Online at: http://eng.expo2012.kr/main.html.

Fairbank, J.A., DeGood, D.E. and Jenkins, C.W. (1981) 'Behavioral treatment of a persistent post-traumatic startle response', *Journal of Behavioral Therapy and Experimental Psychiatry*, 12: 321–4.

Fairclough, N. (2002) *Discourse and Social Change*, Cambridge: Polity Press.

Feignbaum, H.B. (2001) *Globalization and Cultural Diplomacy*, Washington, DC: Centre for Arts and Culture, George Washington University.

Feindt, G., Krawatzek, F., Mehler, D., Pestel, F. and Trimcev, R. (2014) 'Entangled memory: A third wave in memory studies', *History and Theory*, 53: 24–44.

Ferdinand, N. and Kitchin, P.J. (2012) *Events Management: An International Perspective*, London: Sage.

Finding, J.E. and Pelle, K.D. (eds) (2008) *Encyclopaedia of World's Fairs and Expositions*, Jefferson, NC: McFarland & Co.

Finkel, R., McGillivray, D., McPherson, G. and Robinson, P. (eds) (2013) *Research Themes for Events*, Wallingford: CABI Publishing.

Finley, M.I. and Pleket, H.W. (1976) *The Olympic Games: The First Thousand Years*, London: Chatto & Windus.

Fiori, G. (1990) *Antonio Gramsci: Life of a Revolutionary*, trans. T. Nairn, London: Verso.

Flinn, J. and Frew, M. (2014) 'Glastonbury: Managing the mystification of festivity', *Leisure Studies*, 33: 418–33.

Florida, R. (2002) *The Rise of the Creative Class*, New York: Basic Books.

Florida, R. (2003) 'Cities and the creative class', *City and Community*, 2: 3–19.

Florida, R. (2005) *Cities and the Creative Class*, London: Routledge.

Florida, R. (2012) *The Rise of the Creative Class: Revisited*, New York: Basic Books.

Flusty, S. (2005) *De-Coca-colonization: Making the Globe from the Inside out*, London: Routledge.

Foley, M., McGillivray, D. and McPherson, G. (2012) *Event Policy: From Theory to Strategy*, London: Routledge.

Foucault, M. (1973) *The Birth of the Clinic*, London: Tavistock.

Foucault, M. (1976) *The History of Sexuality*, Volume 1: *The Will to Knowledge*, Harmondsworth: Penguin Books.

Foucault, M. (1984) *The History of Sexuality*, Volume 2: *The Use of Pleasure*, Harmondsworth: Penguin Books.

Foucault, M. (1986a) 'Of other spaces', *Diacritics*, 16: 22–7.

Foucault, M. (1986b) *The History of Sexuality*, Volume 3: *The Case of the Self*, Harmondsworth: Penguin Books.

Foucault, M. (1991) *Discipline and Punish: The Birth of the Prison*, Harmondsworth: Penguin Books.

Foucault, M. (2002) *The Archaeology of Knowledge*, London: Routledge.

Foucault, M. (2005) *Madness and Civilisation*, London: Routledge.

Foucault, M. (2008) *The Birth of Biopolitics*, Basingstoke: Palgrave Macmillan

Foucault, M. (2009) *Security, Territory, Population*, Basingstoke: Palgrave Macmillan.

Foucault, M. (2011a) *The Courage of Truth*, Basingstoke: Palgrave Macmillan.

Foucault, M. (2011b) *The Government of Self and Others*, Basingstoke: Palgrave Macmillan.

Foucault, M. (2014) *On the Government of the Living*, Basingstoke: Palgrave Macmillan.

Franks, S. (2014) *Reporting Disasters: Famine, Aid, Politics and the Media*, London: Hurst & Company.

Frazer, J.G. (1922) *The Golden Bough: A Study in Magic and Religion*, London: Macmillan.

Freire, P. (1970) *Pedagogy of the Oppressed*, London: Penguin Books.

Frenzel, F., Feigenbaum, A. and McCurdy, P. (2014) 'Protest camps: An emerging field of social movement research', *Sociological Review*, 62: 454–74.

Friedman, S. (2012) 'Cultural omnivores or culturally homeless? Exploring the shifting cultural identities of the upwardly mobile', *Poetics*, 40: 467–89.

Friedman, S. (2015) '*Habitus clivé* and the emotional imprint of social mobility', *Sociological Review*, DOI: 10.1111/1467-954X.12280.

Frosdick, S. and Marsh, P. (2013) *Football Hooliganism*, London: Routledge.

Fukuyama, F. (2006) *The End of History and the Last Man*, London: Simon & Schuster.

Gaffney, C. (2010) 'Mega-events and socio-spatial dynamics in Rio de Janeiro, 1919–2016', *Journal of Latin American Geography*, 9: 7–29.

Gamson, J. (1996) 'The organizational shaping of collective identity: The case of lesbian and gay film festivals in New York', *Sociological Forum*, 11: 231–61.

Gamson, W.A. and Sifry, M.L. (2013) 'The Occupy movement: An introduction', *Sociological Quarterly*, 54: 159–63.

Garnham, N. (2005) 'From cultural to creative industries: An analysis of the implications of the creative industries approach to arts and media policy making in the United Kingdom', *International Journal of Cultural Policy*, 11: 15–29.

Gavin, N.T. (2010) 'Pressure group direct action on climate change: The role of the media and the web in Britain – a case study', *British Journal of Politics and International Relations*, 12: 459–75.

Gerbaudo, P. (2012) *Tweets and the Streets: Social Media and Contemporary Activism*, London: Pluto Press.

Germon, P. (1998) 'Activists and academics: Part of the same or a world apart', in T. Shakespeare (ed.), *The Disability Reader: Social Science Perspectives*, London: Continuum, 245–55.

Getz, D. (2005) *Event Management and Event Tourism*, New York: Cognizant Communication Corporation.

Getz, D. (2007) *Event Studies: Theory, Research and Policy for Planned Events*, London: Routledge.

Getz, D. (2009) 'Policy for sustainable and responsible festivals and events: Institutionalization of a new paradigm', *Journal of Policy Research in Tourism, Leisure and Events*, 1: 61–78.

Getz, D. (2012) *Event Studies: Theory, Research and Policy for Planned Events*, 2nd edition, London: Routledge.

Gibson, O. (2015) 'BBC dealt another blow after losing control of TV rights for the Olympics', *Guardian*. Online at: www.theguardian.com/sport/2015/jun/29/bbc-loses-control-olympic-tv-rights-discovery-eurosport.

Giulianotti, R. and Klauser, F. (2010) 'Security governance and sport mega-events: Toward an interdisciplinary research agenda', *Journal of Sport and Social Issues*, 34: 49–61.

Giulianotti, R., Armstrong, G., Hales, G. and Hobbs, D. (2015a) 'Global sport mega-events and the politics of mobility: The case of the London 2012 Olympics', *British Journal of Sociology*, 66: 118–40.

Giulianotti, R., Armstrong, G., Hales, G. and Hobbs, D. (2015b) 'Sport mega-events and public opposition: A sociological study of the London 2012 Olympics', *Journal of Sport and Social Issues*, 39: 99–119.

Golombok, S. (2015) *Modern Families: Parenting and Child Development in New Family Forms*, Cambridge: Cambridge University Press.

Graham, S. (2012) 'Olympics 2012 security: Welcome to lockdown London', *City*, 16: 446–51.

Gramsci, A. (1973) *Selections from the Prison Notebooks*, London: Lawrence and Wishart.

Greenhalgh, P. (2011) *Fair World: A History of World's Fairs and Expositions*, London: Papadakis.

Griggio, C. (2015) 'Looking for experience at Vittangi Moose Park in Swedish Lapland', *Scandinavian Journal of Hospitality and Tourism*, 15: 244–65.

Grix, J. (2012) 'Image leveraging and sports mega-events: Germany and the 2006 FIFA World Cup', *Journal of Sport and Tourism*, 17: 289–312.

Grix, J. and Houlihan, B. (2014) 'Sports mega-events as part of a nation's soft power strategy: The cases of Germany (2006) and the UK (2012)', *British Journal of Politics and International Relations*, 16: 572–96.

Grix, J. and Lee, D. (2013) 'Soft power, sports mega-events and emerging states: The lure of the politics of attraction', *Global Society*, 27: 521–36.

Grix, J., Brannagan, P.M. and Houlihan, B. (2015) 'Interrogating states' soft power strategies: A case study of sports mega-events in Brazil and the UK', *Global Society*, 29: 463–79.

Gross, R. (2015) *Psychology: The Science of Mind and Behaviour*, London: Hodder Education.

Grue, J. (2015) *Disability and Discourse Analysis*, Farnham: Ashgate.

Guardian (2011) 'Egypt blocks social media websites in attempt to clampdown on unrest'. Online at: www.theguardian.com/world/2011/jan/26/egypt-blocks-social-media-websites.

Guerra, P. and Quintela, P. (2014) 'Spreading the message! Fanzines and the punk scene in Portugal', *Punk and Post Punk*, 3: 203–24.

Guex, D. and Crevoisier, O. (2014) 'A comprehensive socio-economic model of the experience economy: The territorial stage', in A. Lorentzen, L. Schroder and K. Topso Larsen (eds), *Spatial Dynamics in the Experience Economy*, London: Routledge, 119–38.

Guttman, A. (2002) *The Olympics: A History of the Modern Games*, Champaign: University of Illinois Press.

Habermas, J. (1987) *Towards a Rational Society: Student Protest, Science and Politics*, Cambridge: Polity Press.

Habermas, J. (1992a) *The Structural Transformation of the Public Sphere: Inquiry into a Category of Bourgeois Society*, Cambridge: Polity Press.

Habermas, J. (1992b) *The Theory of Communicative Action*, Volume 1: *Reason and the Rationalization of Society*, Boston, MA: Beacon Press.

Habermas, J. (1992c) *The Theory of Communicative Action*, Volume 2: *The Critique of Functionalist Reason*, Cambridge: Polity Press.

Habermas, J. (1997) *Between Facts and Norms*, Cambridge: Polity Press.

Hall, C.M. (1997) 'Mega-events and their legacies', in P.E. Murphy (ed.), *Quality Management in Urban Tourism*, New York: John Wiley & Sons, 77–89.

Hall, S. (1993) 'Encoding, decoding', in S. During (ed.), *The Cultural Studies Reader*, London: Routledge, 90–103.

Hallegatte, S. (2014) 'Economic resilience: Definition and measurement', World Bank Policy Research Working Paper No. 6852. Online at: http://documents.worldbank.org/curated/en/docsearch/document-type/620265.

Hallmann, K. and Zehrer, A. (2014) 'Limits of modelling memorable experiences: How authentic shall events be?', in H. Pechlaner (ed.), *Tourism and Leisure: Current Issues and Perspectives of Development*, Wiesbaden: Springer Gabler, 269–86.

Halvorsen, S. (2015) 'Taking space: Moments of rupture and everyday life in Occupy London', *Antipode*, 47: 401–17.

Hannam, K. and Knox, D. (2011) *Understanding Tourism: A Critical Introduction*, London: Sage.

Hardy, K. (2015) 'Resilience in UK counter-terrorism', *Theoretical Criminology*, 19: 77–94.

Haydock, W. (2015) 'The consumption, production and regulation of alcohol in the UK: The relevance of the ambivalence of the carnivalesque', *Sociology*, DOI: 003803851 5588460.

Hebdige, D. (1979) *Subcultures: The Meaning of Style*, London: Routledge.

Hegel, G. (1976) *Phenomenology of Spirit*, New York: Galaxy.

Henderson, S. (2011) 'The development of competitive advantage through sustainable event management', *Worldwide Hospitality and Tourism Themes*, 3: 245–57.

Hill, S. (2013) *Digital Revolutions: Activism in the Internet Age*, Oxford: New Internationalist Publications.

Hobfoll, S.E. (2002) 'Social psychological resources and adaptation', *Review of General Psychology*, 6: 307–24.

Hobsbawm, E. (1988) *The Age of Capital*, London: Abacus.

Hobsbawm, E. (1989) *The Age of Empire*, London: Abacus.

Horkheimer, M. (2002) *Critical Theory: Selected Essays*, New York: Continuum.

Horne, J. (2015) 'Assessing the sociology of sport: On sports mega-events and capitalist modernity', *International Review for the Sociology of Sport*, 50: 466–71.

Houlgate, S. (2012) *Hegel's 'Phenomenology of Spirit': A Reader's Guide*, London: Bloomsbury.

Hubbard, P. (2013) 'Carnage! Coming to a town near you? Nightlife, uncivilised behaviour and the carnivalesque body', *Leisure Studies*, 32: 265–82.

Hughes, H.L. and Benn, D. (1997) 'Entertainment in tourism: A study of visitors to Blackpool', *Managing Leisure*, 2: 110–26.

Husserl, E. (1999) *The Essential Husserl: Basic Writings in Transcendental Phenomenology*, Bloomington: Indiana University Press.

Huyssen, A. (2003) *Present Pasts: Urban Palimpsests and the Politics of Memory*, Stanford, CA: Stanford University Press.

Hylton, K. (2010) 'How a turn to critical race theory can contribute to our understanding of "race", racism and anti-racism in sport', *International Review for the Sociology of Sport*, 45: 335–54.

Ijzerman, H. and Lindenberg, S.M. (2014) 'The self in its social context: Why resilience needs company'. Online at: http://papers.ssrn.com/sol3/papers.cfm?abstract_id=2526389.

Illich, I. (1976) *Limits of Medicine. Medical Nemesis: The Expropriation of Health*, London: Marion Boyars.

IOC (2014) *IOC Marketing Report: Sochi 2014*. Online at: www.olympic.org/Documents/ IOC_Marketing/Sochi_2014/LR_MktReport2014_all_Spreads.pdf.

IOC (2015) *Olympic Charter*. Online at: www.olympic.org/Documents/olympic_charter_ en.pdf.

Jamal, T. and Robinson, M. (2011) *The Sage Handbook of Tourism Studies*, London: Sage.

Jaworska, S. (forthcoming) 'Using a corpus-assisted discourse studies (CADS) approach to investigate constructions of identities in media reporting surrounding mega sport events: The case of the London Olympics 2012', in I.R. Lamond and L. Platt (eds), *Critical Event Studies: Approaches to Research*, London: Palgrave Macmillan.

Jenkins, A. (2011) 'Becoming resilient: Overturning common sense – Part 1', *Australian and New Zealand Journal of Family Therapy*, 32: 33–42

Jennings, A. (2015) *The Dirty Game: Uncovering the Scandal at FIFA*, London: Century.

Jessop, B. (2002) *The Future of the Capitalist State*, Cambridge: Polity Press.

Johnson, M.K., Doll, D.T, Bransford, J.D. and Lapinski, R.H. (1974) 'Context effects in sentence memory', *Journal of Experimental Psychology*, 103: 358–60.

Joseph, J. (2013) 'Resilience as embedded neoliberalism: A governmental approach', *Resilience*, 1: 38–52.

Juntunen, T. and Hyvönen, A.E. (2014) 'Resilience, security and the politics of process', *Resilience*, 2: 195–209.

Kaiser, W., Krakenhagen, S. and Poehls, K. (2014) *Exhibiting Europe in Museums*, New York: Berghahn Books.

Kårhus, M.L. (2012) 'Sponsorship as experiential marketing: A natural experiment on how event experiences transfer to brand', unpublished master's thesis. Online at: http://brage.bibsys.no/xmlui/handle/11250/169573.

Kavaratzis, M., Warnby, G. and Ashworth, G. (eds) (2014) *Rethinking Place Branding: Comprehensive Brand Development for Cities and Regions*, London: Springer International.

Kendra, J.M. and Wachtendorf, T. (2003) 'Elements of resilience after the World Trade Center disaster: Reconstituting New York City's emergency operations centre', *Disasters*, 27: 37–53.

Kim, H. (2011) 'Neural activity that predicts subsequent memory and forgetting: A meta-analysis of 74 fMRI studies', *Neuroimage*, 54: 2446–61.

King, A. (2000) 'Thinking with Bourdieu against Bourdieu: A "practical" critique of the *habitus*', *Sociological Theory*, 18: 417–33.

King, L.A., King, D.W., Fairbank, J.A., Keane, T.W. and Adams, G.A. (1998) 'Resilience-recovery factors in post-traumatic stress disorder amongst female and male Vietnam veterans', *Journal of Personality and Social Psychology*, 74: 420–34.

Kinsey, K., Anderson, S.J., Hadjipapas, A. and Holliday, I.E. (2011) 'The role of oscillatory brain activity in object processing and figure-ground segmentation in human vision', *International Journal of Psychophysiology*, 79: 392–400.

Klein, N. (2007) *The Shock Doctrine: The Rise of Disaster Capitalism*, London: Penguin Books.

Koedt, A. (1973) *Radical Feminism*, London: Times Books.

Kohe, G.Z. and Bowen-Jones, W. (2015) 'Rhetoric and realities of London 2012 Olympic education and participation legacies: Voices from the core and periphery', *Sport, Education and Society*, DOI: 10.1080/13573322.2014.997693.

Kostov, P. and Lingard, J. (2003) 'Risk management: A general framework for rural development', *Journal of Rural Studies*, 19: 463–76.

Lamond, I.R. and Platt, L. (eds) (2016) *Critical Event Studies: Approaches to Research*, London: Palgrave Macmillan.

Lamond, I.R. and Spracklen, K. (eds) (2015) *Protests as Events: Politics, Activism and Leisure*, London: Rowman & Littlefield International.

Lamond, I.R., Kilbride, C. and Spracklen, K. (2015) 'The construction of contested public spheres', in I.R. Lamond and K. Spracklen (eds), *Protests as Events: Politics, Activism and Leisure*, London: Rowman & Littlefield International, 21–40.

Lashley, C. and Rowson, B. (2007) 'Trials and tribulations of hotel ownership in Blackpool: Highlighting the skills gaps of owner-managers', *Tourism and Hospitality Research*, 7: 122–30.

Lefebvre, H. (1976 [1973]) *The Survival of Capitalism*, London: Allison & Busby.

Lefebvre, H. (1992) *The Production of Space*, Oxford: Blackwell.

Lefebvre, H. (1996) *Writings on Cities*, Oxford: Blackwell.

Lenskyj, H. (2015) 'Sport mega-events and leisure studies', *Leisure Studies*, 34: 501–7.

Lewin, K. (1966) *Principles of Topological Psychology*, New York: McGraw-Hill.

Liao, D.Y. (forthcoming) 'Space and memory in the Huashan event', in I.R. Lamond and L. Platt (eds), *Critical Event Studies: Approaches to Research*, London: Palgrave Macmillan.

Lim, M. (2012) 'Clicks, cabs, and coffee houses: Social media and oppositional movements in Egypt, 2004–2011', *Journal of Communication*, 62: 231–48.

Lin, Y.C., Pearson, T.E., and Cai, L.A. (2011) 'Food as a form of destination identity: A tourism destination brand perspective', *Tourism and Hospitality Research*, 11: 30–48.

Long, J., Hylton, K. and Spracklen, K. (2014) 'Whiteness, blackness and settlement: Leisure and the integration of new migrants', *Journal of Ethnic and Migration Studies*, 40: 1779–97.

Long, J., Hylton, K., Lewis, H., Ratna, A. and Spracklen, K. (2011) 'Spaces of inclusion? The construction of sport and leisure spaces as places for migrant communities', in A. Ratna and B. Lashua (eds), *Community and Inclusion in Leisure Research and Sport Development*, Eastbourne: Leisure Studies Association, 33–53.

Lotan, G., Graeff, E., Ananny, M., Gaffney, D. and Pearce, I. (2011) 'The revolutions were tweeted: Information flows during the 2011 Tunisian and Egyptian revolutions', *International Journal of Communication*, 5: 1375–405.

Luxford, A. and Dickinson, J.E. (2015) 'The role of mobile applications in the consumer experience of music festivals', *Event Management*, 19: 33–46.

Lynch, P., Molz, J.G., Mcintosh, A., Lugosi, P. and Lashley, C. (2011) 'Theorizing hospitality', *Hospitality and Society*, 1: 3–24.

McGuigan, J. (2006) 'The politics of cultural studies and cool capitalism', *Cultural Politics*, 2: 137–58.

McGuigan, J. (2009a) *Cool Capitalism*, London: Pluto Press.

McGuigan, J. (2009b) *Cultural Analysis*, London: Sage.

McKay, G. (2003) 'Just a closer walk with thee: New Orleans-style jazz and the Campaign for Nuclear Disarmament in 1950s Britain', *Popular Music*, 22: 261–81.

MacMullen, R. (1999) *Christianity and Paganism in the Fourth to Eighth Centuries*, New Haven, CT: Yale University Press.

Maiello, A. and Pasquinelli, C. (2015) 'Destruction or construction? A (counter) branding analysis of sport mega-events in Rio de Janeiro', *Cities*, 48: 116–24.

Manthiou, A., Lee, S., Tang, L. and Chiang, L. (2014) 'The experience economy approach to festival marketing: Vivid memory and attendee loyalty', *Journal of Services Marketing*, 28: 22–35.

Markwell, K. and Waitt, G. (2013) 'Events and sexualities', in R. Finkel, D. McGillivray, G. McPherson and P. Robinson (eds), *Research Themes for Events*, Wallingford: CABI Publishing, 57–67.

Martin, G. (2002) 'New age travellers: Uproarious or uprooted?', *Sociology*, 36: 723–35.

Martinez, D.P. (ed.) (2010) *Documenting the Beijing Olympics*, London: Routledge.

Marx, K. (1973) *Grundrisse: Foundations of the Critique of Political Economy*, Harmondsworth: Penguin Books.

Marx, K. and Engels, F. (1987) *The German Ideology: Introduction to a Critique of Political Economy*, London: Lawrence and Wishart.

Matheson, C.M. and Tinsley, R. (2016) 'The carnivalesque and event evolution: A study of the Beltane Fire Festival', *Leisure Studies*, 35: 1–27.

Merkel, U. (ed.) (2013) *Power, Politics and International Events: Socio-cultural Analyses of Festivals and Spectacles*, London: Routledge.

Merkel, U. and Ok, G. (2015) 'Identity discourses and narratives in North Korean events, festivals and celebrations, in U. Merkel (ed.), *Identity Discourses and Communities in International Events, Festivals and Spectacles*, Basingstoke: Palgrave Macmillan, 135–52.

Messner, M. and Sabo, D. (1990) *Sport, Men and the Gender Order*, Champaign, IL: Human Kinetics.

Mill, J.S. (1998 [1859]) *On Liberty*, Oxford: Oxford University Press.

Minihan, J. (1977) *The Nationalization of Culture: The Development of State Subsidies to the Arts in Great Britain*, New York: New York University Press.

Miriam, K. (2012) 'Feminism, neoliberalism, and SlutWalk', *Feminist Studies*, 38: 262–6.

Misener, L. and Mason, D.S. (2009) 'Fostering community development through sporting events strategies: An examination of urban regime perceptions', *Journal of Sport Management*, 23: 770–94.

Molz, J.G. (2012) 'CouchSurfing and network hospitality: It's not just about the furniture', *Hospitality and Society*, 1: 215–25.

Montesano Montessori, N. (2009) *An Analysis of a Struggle for Hegemony in Mexico: The Zapatista Movement versus President Salinas de Gortari*, Saarbrücken: VDM Verlag.

Montesano Montessori, N. and Morales López, E. (2015) 'Multimodal narrative as an instrument for social change: Reinventing democracy in Spain: The case of 15 M', *CADAAD*, 7: 200–21.

Moran, D. (2000) *Introduction to Phenomenology*, London: Routledge.

Morgan, M. (2008) 'What makes a good festival? Understanding the event experience', *Event Management*, 12: 81–93.

Moufakkir, O. and Pernecky, T. (2015) *Ideological, Social and Cultural Aspects of Events*, Wallingford: CABI Publishing.

Muller, M. (2015) 'What makes an event a mega-event? Definitions and sizes', *Leisure Studies*, 34: 627–42.

Murray, D.W. and O'Neill, M.A. (2012) 'Craft beer: Penetrating a niche market', *British Food Journal*, 114: 899–909.

Mutua, A.D. (2006) 'The rise, development, and future directions of critical race theory and related scholarship', *Denver University Law Review*, 82: 329–94.

Nichols, G. and Ralston, R. (2012) 'Lessons from the volunteering legacy of the 2002 Commonwealth Games', *Urban Studies*, 49: 169–84.

Nolen-Hoeksema, S., Fredrickson, B.L., Loftus, G.R. and Lutz, C. (2014) *Atkinson and Hilgard's Introduction to Psychology*, Andover: Cengage.

Nora, P. (1996) *Realms of Memory: Conflicts and Divisions*, New York: Columbia University Press.

Norris, F.H., Stevens, S.P. and Pfefferbaum, B. (2008) 'Community resilience as a metaphor, theory, set of capacities, and strategy for disaster readiness', *American Journal of Community Psychology*, 41: 127–50.

Nye, J.S., Jr. (2008) 'Public diplomacy and soft power', *Annals of the American Academy of Political and Social Science*, 616: 94–109.

Oliver, M. (1992) 'Changing the social relations of research production?', *Disability, Handicap and Society*, 7: 101–14.

Oliver, M. (1998) 'Theories in health care and research: Theories of disability in health practice and research', *British Medical Journal*, 7170: 1446–9.

Oliver, M. (2009) *Understanding Disability: From Theory to Practice*, 2nd edition, Basingstoke: Palgrave Macmillan.

Oliver, M. and Barnes, C. (2010) 'Disability studies, disabled people and the struggle for inclusion', *British Journal of Sociology of Education*, 31: 547–60.

Ong, A.D., Bergman, C.S., Biscotti, T.L. and Kimberly, A. (2006) 'Psychological resilience, positive emotions, and successful adaptation to stress in later life', *Journal of Personality and Social Psychology*, 91: 730–49.

Osto, D. (2011) 'Theater in a crowded fire: Ritual and spirituality at Burning Man', *Religion*, 41: 499–503.

O'Sullivan, D. and Jackson, M.J. (2002) 'Festival tourism: A contributor to sustainable local economic development?', *Journal of Sustainable Tourism*, 10: 325–42.

Painter, J. (2010) 'Rethinking territory', *Antipode*, 42: 1090–118.

Pala, M (2015) 'Introduction to the 2013 Gramsci Summer School', *International Gramsci Journal*, 1: 7–17.

Pavoni, A. and Sebastiano, S. (forthcoming) 'An ethnographic approach to the taking place of the event', in I.R. Lamond and L. Platt (eds), *Critical Event Studies: Approaches to Research*, London: Palgrave Macmillan.

Pelling, M. and High. C. (2005) 'Understanding adaptation: What can social capital offer assessments of adaptive capacity?', *Global Environment Change*, 15: 308–19.

Peters, J., Suchan, B., Koster, O. and Duam, I. (2007) 'Domain-specific retrieval of source information in the medial temporal lobe', *European Journal of Neuroscience*, 26: 1333–43.

Pine, B.J., II and Gilmore, J.H. (1999) *The Experience Economy: Work is Theatre and Everyday Business a Stage*, Cambridge, MA: Harvard Business School Press.

Platenkamp, V. and Botterill, D. (2013) 'Critical realism, rationality and tourism knowledge', *Annals of Tourism Research*, 41: 110–29.

Plato (1888) *The Republic*, trans. B. Jowett, New York: Macmillan. Online at: http://classics.mit.edu/Plato/republic.html.

Plato (1973) *Phaedrus*, trans. W. Hamilton, Harmondsworth: Penguin Books.

Plato (1988) *Euthyphro, Apology, Crito, Phaedo*, trans. B. Jowett, New York: Prometheus Books.

Putnam, R.D. (2001a) *Bowling Alone: The Collapse and Revival of American Community*, New York: Simon & Schuster.

Putnam, R.D. (2001b) 'Social capital: Measurement and consequences', *Canadian Journal of Policy Research*, 2: 41–51.

Putnam, R.D., Feldstein, L. and Cohen, D.J. (2005) *Better Together: Restoring the American Community*, New York: Simon & Schuster.

Pyke, K.D. (2010) 'What is internalized racial oppression and why don't we study it? Acknowledging racism's hidden injuries', *Sociological Perspectives*, 53: 551–72.

Pyke, K.D. and Dang, T. (2003) 'FOB and whitewash: Identity and internalized racism among second generation Asian Americans', *Qualitative Sociology*, 26: 147–72.

Rabinow, P. and Rose, N. (2006) 'Biopower today', *Biosocieties*, 1: 195–217.

Rainio, K. (n.d.) 'Kurt Lewin's dynamical psychology revisited and revised'. Online at: http://goertzel.org/dynapsyc/LewinRaino.htm.

Raj, R. and Walters, P. (2013) *Events Management: Principles and Practice*, London: Sage.

Raj, R., Walters, P. and Rashid, T. (2009) *Events Management: An Integrated and Practical Approach*, London: Sage.

Rammelt, H. (2015) 'Paving the way for anti-militarism in Romania', in I.R. Lamond and K. Spracklen (eds), *Protests as Events: Politics, Activism and Leisure*, London: Rowman & Littlefield International, 75–95.

Razsa, M. and Kurnik, A. (2012) 'The Occupy movement in Žižek's hometown: Direct democracy and a politics of becoming', *American Ethnologist*, 39: 238–58.

Reisigl, M. and Wodak, R. (2001) *Discourse and Discrimination: Rhetorics of Racism and Anti-Semitism*, London: Routledge.

Reuters (2015) 'Soccer: One billion watched 2014 World Cup final on TV'. Online at: www.reuters.com/article/soccer-world-television-idUSL3N1454HP20151216.

Ricoeur, P. (2004) *Memory, History, Forgetting*, Chicago: University of Chicago Press.

Robert, L., Gibbon, M., Skodol, A.E., Williams, J.B.W. and Fi, S. (1987) *The Diagnostic and Statistical Manual of Mental Disorders*, Arlington, VA: American Psychiatric Press.

Roche, M. (1992) 'Mega-events and micro-modernization: On the sociology of the new urban tourism', *British Journal of Sociology*, 43: 563–600.

Roche, M. (1994) 'Mega-events and urban policy', *Annals of Tourism Research*, 21: 1–19.

Roche, M. (2000) *Mega-events and Modernity: Olympics and Expos in the Growth of Global Culture*, London: Routledge.

Rojek, C. (2010) *The Labour of Leisure*, London: Sage.

Rojek, C. (2013) *Event Power: How Global Events Manage and Manipulate*, London: Sage.

Rojek, C. (2014) 'Global event management: A critique', *Leisure Studies*, 33: 32–47.

Rose, N. and Miller, P. (1992) 'Political power beyond the state: Problematics of government', *British Journal of Sociology*, 43: 173–205.

Rose, N. and Miller, P. (2008) *Governing the Present: Administering Economic, Social and Personal Life*, Cambridge: Polity Press.

Rowe, D. (2012) 'The bid, the lead-up, the event and the legacy: Global cultural politics and hosting the Olympics', *British Journal of Sociology*, 63: 285–305.

Rowland, R. and Klein, R.D. (1996) 'Radical feminism: History, politics, action', in D. Bell and R.D. Klein (eds), *Radically Speaking: Feminism Reclaimed*, London: Zed Books.

Russell, B. (1967) *The Problems of Philosophy*, Oxford: Oxford University Press.

Russo, M.T. (2012) 'Home, domesticity and hospitality: A theoretical reflection', *Hospitality and Society*, 2: 309–20.

Saad, G. (2011) *Evolutionary Psychology in the Business Sciences*, London: Springer-Verlag.

Samatas, M. (2011) 'Surveillance in Athens 2004 and Beijing 2008: A comparison of the Olympic surveillance modalities and legacies in two different Olympic host regimes', *Urban Studies*, 48: 347–66.

Santos, A.D. (2015) 'War and nation in Angola: Reading Mayombe from the perspective of memory studies', *Portuguese Journal of Social Science*, 14: 9–23.

Sassen, S. (2011) *Cities in a World Economy*, London: Sage.

Scarpato, R. (2002) 'Gastronomy studies in search of hospitality', conference paper presented at CAUTHE 2002: Tourism and Hospitality on the Edge, Lismore, Australia.

Schulz, K. and Siriwardane, R. (2015) 'Depoliticised and technocratic? Normativity and the politics of transformative adaptation'. Online at: www.earthsystemgovernance.org/sites/default/files/publications/files/ESG-WorkingPaper-33_Schulz-and-Siriwardane.pdf.

Shaw, A. (2012) 'Do you identify as a gamer? Gender, race, sexuality and gamer identity', *New Media and Society*, 14: 28–44.

Shields, R. (1999) *Lefebvre, Love and Struggle: Spatial Dialectics*, London: Routledge.

Shone, A. and Parry, B. (2010) *Successful Event Management*, Andover: Cengage Learning.

Signitzer, B.H. and Coombs, T. (1992) 'Public relations and public diplomacy: Conceptual convergences', *Public Relations Review*, 18: 137–47.

Singh, S. and Bookless, T. (1997) 'Analysing spontaneous speech in dysphasic adults', *International Journal of Applied Linguistics*, 7: 165–81.

Sitrin, M. and Azzellini, D. (2012) *Occupying Language: The Secret Rendezvous with History and the Present*, New York: Zuccotti Park Press.

Smith, A. (2014) 'Leveraging sport mega-events: New model or convenient justification?', *Journal of Policy Research in Tourism, Leisure and Events*, 6: 15–30.

Smith, M.K. (2003) *Issues in Cultural Tourism Studies*, London: Routledge.

Soja, E.W. (1996) *Thirdspace: Journeys to Los Angeles and Other Real-and-Imagined Places*, Oxford: Blackwell.

Soja, E.W. (2011 [1989]) *Postmodern Geographies: The Reassertion of Space in Critical Social Theory*, London: Verso.

Spaaij, R. (2008) 'Men like us, boys like them: Violence, masculinity, and collective identity in football hooliganism', *Journal of Sport and Social Issues*, 32: 369–92.

Sperling, G. (1963) 'A model for visual memory tasks', *Human Factors: The Journal of the Human Factors and Ergonomics*, 5: 19–31.

Spracklen, K. (1996) 'Playing the ball: Constructing community and masculine identity in rugby', unpublished Ph.D. thesis, Leeds Metropolitan University.

Spracklen, K. (2007) 'Negotiations of belonging: Habermasian stories of minority ethnic rugby league players in London and the south of England', *World Leisure Journal*, 49: 216–26.

Spracklen, K. (2009) *The Meaning and Purpose of Leisure: Habermas and Leisure at the End of Modernity*, Basingstoke: Palgrave Macmillan.

Spracklen, K. (2011a) *Constructing Leisure: Historical and Philosophical Debates*, Basingstoke: Palgrave Macmillan.

Spracklen, K. (2011b) 'Dreaming of drams: Authenticity in Scottish whisky tourism as an expression of unresolved Habermasian rationalities', *Leisure Studies*, 30: 99–116.

Spracklen, K. (2012) 'Introduction', *Journal for Policy Research in Tourism, Leisure and Events*, 5: 121–2.

Spracklen, K. (2013) *Whiteness and Leisure*, Basingstoke: Palgrave Macmillan.

Spracklen, K. (2014a) 'Leisure studies education: Historical trends and pedagogical futures in the United Kingdom and beyond', *Journal of Hospitality, Leisure, Sport and Tourism Education*, 15: 20–3.

Spracklen, K. (2014b) 'There is (almost) no alternative: The slow "heat death" of music subcultures and the instrumentalization of contemporary leisure', *Annals of Leisure Research*, 17: 252–66.

Spracklen, K. (2015) *Digital Leisure, the Internet and Popular Culture: Communities and Identities in a Digital Age*, London: Palgrave Macmillan.

Spracklen, K. and Spracklen, B. (2012) 'Pagans and Satan and goths, oh my: Dark leisure as communicative agency and communal identity on the fringes of the modern goth scene', *World Leisure Journal*, 54: 350–62.

Spracklen, K. and Spracklen, B. (2014) 'The strange and spooky battle over bats and black dresses: The commodification of Whitby Goth Weekend and the loss of a subculture', *Tourist Studies*, 14: 86–102.

Spracklen, K. and Spracklen, C. (2008) 'Negotiations of being and becoming: Minority ethnic rugby league players in the Cathar Country of France', *International Review for the Sociology of Sport*, 43: 201–18.

Spracklen, K., Laurencic, J. and Kenyon, A. (2013) '"Mine's a pint of bitter": Performativity, gender, class and representations of authenticity in real-ale tourism', *Tourist Studies*, 13: 304–21.

Spracklen, K. Long, J. and Hylton, K. (2015) 'Leisure opportunities and new migrant communities: Challenging the contribution of sport', *Leisure Studies*, 34: 114–29.

Spracklen, K., Richter, A. and Spracklen, B. (2013) 'The eventization of leisure and the strange death of alternative Leeds', *City*, 17: 164–78.

Spracklen, K., Timmins, S. and Long, J. (2010) 'Ethnographies of the imagined, the imaginary, and the critically real: Blackness, whiteness, the north of England and rugby league', *Leisure Studies*, 29: 397–414.

Stanković, I. (2014) 'Spaces of memory – the presence of absence: Cultural memory and oblivion machines', *Culture*, 8: 87–94.

Statista (2012) 'Global TV audience Olympic Summer Games 2008–2012'. Online at: www.statista.com/statistics/280502/total-number-of-tv-viewers-of-olympic-summer-games-worldwide/.

Stebbins, R. (1982) 'Serious leisure: A conceptual statement', *Pacific Sociological Review*, 25: 251–72.

Stebbins, R. (1997) 'Casual leisure: A conceptual statement', *Leisure Studies*, 16: 17–25.

Stebbins, R. (2006) *Serious Leisure: A Perspective for Our Times*, Piscataway, NJ: Transaction.

Stebbins, R. (2009) *Leisure and Consumption*, Basingstoke: Palgrave Macmillan.

Stebbins, R. (2014) *Careers in Serious Leisure: From Dabbler to Devotee in Search of Fulfilment*, Basingstoke: Palgrave Macmillan.

Sterchele, D. and Saint-Blancat, C. (2015) 'Keeping it liminal: The Mondiali Antirazzisti (Anti-racist World Cup) as a multifocal interaction ritual', *Leisure Studies*, 34: 182–96.

Stone, P.R. (2012) 'Dark tourism and significant other death: Towards a model on mortality mediation', *Annals of Tourism Research*, 39: 1565–87.

Sugden, J. (2012) 'Watched by the Games: Surveillance and security at the Olympics', *International Review for the Sociology of Sport*, 47: 414–29.

Sum, N. and Jessop, B. (2013) *Towards a Cultural Political Economy: Putting Culture in its Place in Political Economy*, Cheltenham: Edward Elgar.

Sutker, P.B., Davis, J.M. and Uddo, M. (1995) 'War zone stress, personal resources and PTSD in Persian Gulf returnees', *Journal of Abnormal Psychology*, 104: 444–52.

Thornley, A. (2012) 'The 2012 London Olympics: What legacy?', *Journal of Policy Research in Tourism, Leisure and Events*, 4: 206–10.

Thrift, N. (2006) 'Re-inventing invention: New tendencies in capitalist commodification', *Economy and Society*, 35: 279–306.

Thurnell-Read, T. (2012) 'Tourism place and space: British stag tourism in Poland', *Annals of Tourism Research*, 39: 801–19.

Thurnell-Read, T. (2014) 'Craft, tangibility and affect at work in the microbrewery', *Emotion, Space and Society*, 13: 46–54.

Tomlinson, A. (2014) *FIFA: The Men, the Myths and the Money*, London: Routledge.

Total Rugby League (2015) 'Blues level Origin series'. Online at: www.totalrl.com/blues-level-origin-series.

Tribe, J. (1997) 'The indiscipline of tourism', *Annals of Tourism Research*, 24: 638–57.

Tribe, J. (2002) 'The philosophic practitioner', *Annals of Tourism Research*, 28: 338–57.

Tribe, J. (2008) 'Tourism: A critical business', *Journal of Travel Research*, 46: 245–55.

Trubek, D.M. (2011) 'Foundational events, foundational myths, and the creation of critical race theory, or how to get along with a little help from your friends', *Connecticut Law Review*, 43: 1503–12.

Trubina, E. (2015) 'Mega-events in the context of capitalist modernity: The case of the 2014 Sochi Winter Olympics', *Eurasian Geography and Economics*, 55: 610–27.

Tuan, Y.-F. (1974) *Topophilia: A Study of Environmental Perception, Attitudes and Values*, New York: Columbia University Press.

Tuan, Y.-F. (1977) *Space and Place: The Perspective of Experience*, Minneapolis: University of Minnesota Press.

Tulving, E. (1985) 'How many memory systems are there?', *American Psychologist*, 40: 385–98.

Turner, V. (1969) *The Ritual Process: Structure and Anti-structure*, Ithaca, NY: Cornell University Press.

Urry, J. (1988) 'Cultural change and contemporary holiday-making', *Theory, Culture and Society*, 5: 35–55.

Urry, J. (1990a) 'The consumption of tourism', *Sociology*, 24: 23–35.

Urry, J. (1990b) *Tourist Gaze: Leisure and Travel in Contemporary Societies*, London: Sage.

Urry, J. (2002) 'Mobility and proximity', *Sociology*, 36: 255–74.

Urry, J. (2012) *Sociology beyond Societies: Mobilities for the Twenty-first Century*, London: Routledge.

Usher, M. and Donnelly, N. (1998) 'Visual synchrony affects binding and segmentation in perception', *Nature*, 394: 179–82.

Wacquant, L. (2011) '*Habitus* as topic and tool: Reflections on becoming a prizefighter', *Qualitative Research in Psychology*, 8: 81–92.

Waddington, I. (2000) *Sport, Health and Drugs: A Critical Sociological Perspective*, London: Routledge.

Wagner, U., Kashyap, N., Diekelmann, S. and Born, J. (2007) 'The impact of post-learning sleep vs. wakefulness on recognition memory for faces with different facial expressions', *Neurobiology of Learning and Memory*, 87: 679–87.

Washington Post (2013) 'Edward Snowden comes forward as the source of NSA leaks'. Online at: www.washingtonpost.com/politics/intelligence-leaders-push-back-on-leakers-media/2013/06/09/fff80160-d122-11e2-a73e-826d299ff459_story.html.

Weichselbaumer, D. (2012) 'Sex, romance and the carnivalesque between female tourists and Caribbean men', *Tourism Management*, 33: 1220–29.

Welsh, M. (2014) 'Resilience and responsibility: Governing uncertainty in a complex world', *Geographical Journal*, 180: 15–26.

Wenger, E. (2000) *Communities of Practice*, Cambridge: Cambridge University Press.

Werner, E.E. (1987) 'Vulnerability and resiliency in children at risk of delinquency', in J.D. Burchard and S.N. Burchard (eds), *Prevention of Delinquent Behaviour*, Thousand Oaks, CA: Sage, 16–43.

Werner, E.E. (1989) 'High risk children in adulthood', *American Journal of Orthopsychiatry*, 59: 72–81.

Wikipedia. 'Burning Man'. Online at: http://en.wikipedia.org/wiki/Burning_Man.

Williams, R. (1977) *Culture and Society: 1780–1950*, Harmondsworth: Penguin Books.

Willis, M. (2014) *Politics and Power in the Maghreb: Algeria, Tunisia and Morocco from Independence to the Arab Spring*, Oxford: Oxford University Press.

Wilson, A. and Ashplant, T. (1988) 'Whig history and present-centred history', *Historical Journal*, 31: 1–16.

Winsemius, P. and Guntram, U. (2013) *A Thousand Shades of Green: Sustainable Strategies for Competitive Advantage*, London: Earthscan.

Wise, N. and Mulec, I. (2015) 'Aesthetic awareness and spectacle: Communicated images of Novi Sad (Serbia), the Exit Festival, and the Petrovaradin Fortress', *Tourism Review International*, 19: 193–205.

Wittgenstein, L. (1951) *Philosophical Investigations*, Oxford: Blackwell.

Wittgenstein, L. (1973) *Tractatus Logico-Philosophicus*, Oxford: Blackwell.

Xin, S., Tribe, J. and Chamber, D. (2013) 'Conceptual research in tourism', *Annals of Tourism Research*, 41: 66–88.

Žižek, S. (1989) *The Sublime Object of Ideology*, London: Verso.

Žižek, S. (2008 [1992]) *Enjoy Your Symptom!*, London: Routledge.

Žižek, S. (2010) *Living in the End Times*, London: Verso.

Žižek, S. (2014) *Event: Philosophy in Transit*, London: Penguin Books.

Index

Printed in the United States
by Baker & Taylor Publisher Services